UNDERCURRENTS OF DIVORCE

For

Poppy and Nico

and

in memory of

Kathleen and Frederick Farnsworth

Undercurrents of Divorce

Edited by
SHELLEY DAY SCLATER
University of East London
and
CHRISTINE PIPER
Brunel University

Routledge
Taylor & Francis Group
LONDON AND NEW YORK

First published 1999 by Ashgate Publishing

Reissued 2019 by Routledge
2 Park Square, Milton Park, Abingdon, Oxon, OXl 4 4RN
52 Vanderbilt Avenue, New York, NY 10017

Routledge is an imprint of the Taylor & Francis Group, an informa business

Publisher's Note
The publisher has gone to great lengths to ensure the quality of this reprint but points out that some imperfections in the original copies may be apparent.

A Library of Congress record exists under LC control number:

ISBN 13: 978-0-367-19708-7 (hbk)
ISBN 13: 978-0-429-24275-5 (ebk)

Contents

PART IV: CONCLUSIONS

List of Contributors

Joanne Brown is a Lecturer in Psychosocial Studies at the University of East London. She is currently working on a PhD, 'Love in the Depressive Position'. She is currently co-editing a book (with Barry Richards), *Studies in Modern Feeling: The Psychoanalytic Sociology of the Emotions* (Routledge, forthcoming).

Richard Collier is Reader in Law at the University of Newcastle upon Tyne. He has published extensively in the area of law and gender, and is author of *Masculinity, Law and the Family* (Routledge, 1995) and *Masculinities, Crime and Criminology: Men, Heterosexuality and the Criminal(ised) Other* (Sage, 1998). Richard is a consultant to the Lord Chancellor's Department research project on Evaluation of Information Meetings under section 8 of the Family Law Act 1996 and is presently writing a book on family, law and heterosexuality.

Shelley Day Sclater is a Senior Lecturer in Psychosocial Studies at the University of East London, and an Affiliated Lecturer in the Department of Social and Political Sciences, University of Cambridge. Shelley spent seven years as a divorce lawyer before embarking on research into the psychosocial aspects of divorce. She has recently completed an ESRC funded project on the Psychology of Divorce and has published articles on her work in Britain and Australia. She is author of *The Psychology of Divorce* (Ashgate, forthcoming) and co-editor of *What is a Parent?* (Hart Publishing, forthcoming).

Alison Diduck is Co-Director of the Centre for the Study of Law, the Child and the Family based in the Law Department at Brunel University. She has practised and taught law in Manitoba, Canada and now researches and teaches family law and feminism and law. She has published articles in Canadian and British journals and is the author (with Felicity Kaganas) of a critical family law text (Dartmouth, forthcoming).

Felicity Kaganas is a lecturer and convenor of the MA/LLM in Child Law and Policy at Brunel University. She has published in Britain and abroad on feminist issues in child and family law, is co-editor of *Legislating for Harmony* (JKP, 1995) and is co-author of *Critical Perspectives on Family Law* (Dartmouth, forthcoming).

Bren Neale is a Senior Research Fellow in the Centre for Research on Family, Kinship and Childhood, Department of Sociology and Social Policy, University of Leeds. Bren worked with Carol Smart on a three year ESRC funded study of parenthood after divorce and is currently extending this work on a Nuffield funded study of post divorce family life from the children's perspective.

Christine Piper is a Senior Lecturer in the Law Department at Brunel University where she was lead researcher for the study of divorce solicitors conducted by the Centre for the Study of Law, the Child and the Family. Her publications include *The Responsible Parent* (Harvester Wheatsheaf, 1993) and (with Michael King) *How the Law Thinks About Children* (Gower/Arena, 1991/1995).

Jeremy Roche is based in the School of Health and Social Welfare at the Open University. He has written extensively in the field of children's rights and the law and is co-editor of *Youth in Society* (Sage, 1997) and *Changing Experiences of Youth* (Sage, 1997) and co-author of *Children's Welfare, Children's Rights* (Hodder and Stoughton, 1994).

Carol Smart is Professor of Sociology and Director of the Centre for Research on Family, Kinship and Childhood at the University of Leeds. In addition to her recent work on divorce (Smart and Neale, *Family Fragments*, Polity Press, forthcoming), Carol has published extensively in the field of women and the law and has recently published in the subjects of sexuality and socio-legal theory (*Law, Crime and Sexuality*, Sage, 1995).

Foreword

This book quite deliberately goes against the grain of official policy or the 'new orthodoxy' on divorce and reconstituted families. It is likely to irritate, and provoke those judges, politicians, and civil servants who tell themselves and one another that now, at last, we have just about 'got it right'. The familiar images of children, mothers, fathers and families on which their policies, judgements and decisions are based, and which they expect to be reflected back to them through research and expert observations, appear in the various contributions to this book as simplifications or distortions of a highly complex reality. Instead of the comforting reassurance that they seek, they are likely to experience serious misgivings, not only about the detailed provisions of recent legislation or interpretations of that legislation in the court, but much more generally, over their current beliefs and ways of thinking about divorce. The book, for example, dares to question even that secular canon concerning the relationship between children's welfare and the reduction of conflict between their parents!

The editors of *Undercurrents of Divorce* should be congratulated for bringing the undercurrents of the title to the surface, or, to use a different metaphor, amplifying those off-stage murmurs, which have up until now largely been ignored in the courtroom or parliamentary debating chambers. Indeed, one of the questions that the book may well raise in the minds of readers is how could such important data concerning people's feelings about, and their reactions to, the break-down of marriage and the splitting of families have been quietly put to one side in order to give the impression of consensus and, what is more, a consensus supported by scientific research. Part of the answer may lie in the high level of anxiety that high divorce rates cause and the determination to protect children from the deleterious effects of family break-down. Thirty years ago, the conflict between the restrictive divorce law that Parliament had enacted and the hypocritical practices of the courts designed to overcome these statutory restrictions left some space for arguments over blame and responsibility for these moral issues to be addressed in the public arena. Today, however, the overriding issue of child welfare virtually precludes any public consideration of morality. Virtue has become 'doing the right thing for the children' and vice is 'ignoring the children's interests'; and the debates and court arguments proceed as if we all know what is good and bad for children and where their interests lie. There is no public moral debate any more on which people may take sides. Yet, as several of the contributors to this book demonstrate, not only does this debate carry on in private in the fierce conflicts that consume and obsess husbands and wives often for many years after their marriage has ended, but also in the ways that the terms 'children's welfare' and the 'best interests of the children', interpreted by judges, lawyers, mediators and welfare officers, conceal a powerful moral agenda, which is never explicitly acknowledged.

The marginalizing of those whose knowledge, experience and opinions were seen to be irrelevant or unhelpful to the government's political agenda was a characteristic of a long political era in the United Kingdom, which now, hopefully, has ended. Its legacy, however, remains in the political influence over academic research in the social sciences, which finds expression in pre-selection of topics meriting research funding and the continuing domination of the criteria of short-term utility and economic expediency in the distribution of research funds. Yet the dangers of pre-judging what issues are important and of too much agreement concerning the overriding objectives of social policy are only too clear from the undercurrents of disquiet that this book has uncovered. Once politicians, administrators, lawyers and the mass media are all in agreement over what the problems are and what needs to be done, confining the role of university researchers to devising and testing solutions to these pre-defined problems, who will be left to observe and, where appropriate, question and criticise those taken-for-granted beliefs and understandings which allowed the policy issue to be constructed in the first place? This book is a timely reminder that undercurrents cannot simply be ignored out of existence. Its editors have performed a valuable service in bringing together contributions by academic commentators who are not afraid to step out of line and raise difficult questions about the current law, practices and policies in divorce and who are careful to avoid offering the kind of glib solutions that have in the past proved so short-sighted. One can only hope that their collective challenge to the prevailing wisdom receives the attention that it deserves.

Professor Michael King
Centre for the Study of Law, the Child and the Family, Brunel University

PART I
INTRODUCTION

1 The Family Law Act 1996 in Context

SHELLEY DAY SCLATER AND CHRISTINE PIPER

Divorce has been talked about *ad nauseam* by politicians, the media, a wide range of professionals and religious leaders. What else is there to say? Within the terms of the public debate, it seems, nothing, except more of the same. The preliminaries to the implementation of the Family Law Act 1996 are well underway. It crystallises a vision of the post-divorce family as harmonious and enduring, a vision which first found legislative expression in the Children Act 1989, a vision which emerges from a particular discursive framework that takes as axiomatic the need to reduce divorce-related 'conflict' and to encourage both parents to remain involved with their children. Talk about divorce within the public arena has, therefore, been constrained by a set of 'gate-keeping' principles of this nature; the ideas which have entered the public domain have been those which fit the dominant discursive framework. The result is that much has been left unsaid. It is the purpose of this book to address those silences and to give voice to a range of ideas which challenge the dominant discourses and provide new ways of thinking about divorce as both a social phenomenon and an individual life-event.

To achieve this aim, the authors of the essays in this book each address a different aspect of the divorce process; the hitherto unacknowledged politics and psychology of divorce emerge as the 'undercurrents' of the process, and as crucial at a number of levels, from policy-making, through day-to-day professional practices, to the everyday experiences of those involved. Together, the essays explain how and why these undercurrents have been marginalised in professional and political discourse, and seek to make visible the effects (practical, legal and emotional) of their exclusion from the public arena.

There are good policy reasons for exploring these undercurrents. Policy that is based on an incomplete understanding of how family law is implemented by professionals 'on the ground', or of how individual adults and children experience divorce runs the risk, at best, of failing to alleviate people's problems or, at worst, of compounding them. If divorce policy is confined to the issues currently raised in public debate (a debate which has been constrained by financial and ideological imperatives), such that the undercurrents are neither known nor heeded, there is a real possibility that the reforms will be swept away by the undercurrents for which no provision has been made. This book attempts to broaden the sweep of the divorce debate; it is about divorce as a political and a personal as well as a legal issue. The contributors to this volume all work within an interdisciplinary framework, drawing on recent research and insights from law, sociology and psychology to address a range of crucial, though neglected, issues.

The contributors to this book, each in their own way, address four themes which characterise the dominant discourses with which we are concerned. First, there is a rhetoric of 'harmony' which provides the *raison d'être* of the Family Law Act and which underlies the conceptual shifts and provides the rationale for the new procedures. Here, matrimonial 'fault' appears as a damaging and unnecessary fiction; it is seen as creating undesirable 'conflict' and our legislators appear to assume that removing 'fault' by changing the divorce process will eliminate acrimony and blame.

Secondly, our legislators have declared explicitly that marriage is to be supported, and this is embodied in the 'principles' in section 1 of the Family Law Act. The underlying assumption is that marriage remains the preferred forum for the raising of children and the basis for family life. Divorce, on this view, is undesirable and potentially damaging; the Act provides for a damage-limitation exercise in cases where divorce is, unfortunately, inevitable. In so doing, however, the Act facilitates the continuance of 'the family', albeit in a different form.

Thirdly, particular interpretations of children's welfare, which have been invoked to justify the removal of fault, participate in the construction of the child as the vulnerable victim of divorce. The new law has been carried along on a tide of concern about the welfare of children, but there are very particular interpretations of 'risk' and 'harm' being made. Children's welfare has become synonymous with freedom from exposure to parental conflict, and their interests are seen as best served by continuing contact with both parents, regardless of circumstances.

Finally, there is a fourth theme implicit in the Act and in the discourses that inform it: that of gender. The provisions of family law are explicitly gender-neutral, a development which has been regarded by many as a wholly positive one. But, as the contributors to this volume show, the realities of gender differences which are manifested structurally, materially and psychologically, continue to provide powerful undercurrents in the divorce process. Importantly, the gender-neutrality of the formal law renders the complex issue of gender marginal in the public debate. In what follows, we discuss these strands of the dominant discourses in more detail.

'Harmony' in Divorce and the Emergence of the New Post-divorce Family

The Family Law Act received the Royal Assent in July 1996 after a turbulent passage through Parliament. At the time of writing a number of pilot studies are underway; the divorce related parts of the Act are due to be implemented in 1999 at the earliest, when the results from the pilot studies are available and their implications have been discussed. The Act provides for two fundamental changes to the old scheme; first, the removal of fault from divorce and, secondly, the introduction of state-funded mediation (through the Legal Aid scheme) as the preferred dispute resolution procedure. Both of these provisions are part of a wider, and longer standing, dissatisfaction with adversarial premises and processes in family proceedings, as well as a move from formal to more informal and administrative modes of justice in divorce. At an ideological level, the Act is testimony to the dominance of the welfare discourse; it makes its ultimate appeal to 'the best interests of the child' (Lord Chancellor's Department, 1993, 1995), but its provisions apply to all divorcing people, regardless of whether they have children or not.

The removal of fault from divorce has not been and will not be, we suspect, easy to achieve. One of the central aims of the Divorce Reform Act of 1969 was the removal of matrimonial fault. That Act introduced 'irretrievable breakdown' as the sole ground for divorce but, such was the heated and ideological nature of the debates as the Bill passed through Parliament, that fault, in fact, lived on in the guise of the 'facts' required to prove the irretrievable breakdown. Similarly, the passage of the 1996 Act was troubled by a vocal lobby who argued that removal of fault represented an undermining of marriage and 'the family'. This lobby was undoubtedly placated by the introduction of the 'principles' at the Report stage, which include a provision that 'the institution of marriage is to be supported' (now in section 1 of the Act), but this principle, coupled with the removal of fault, conveys powerful messages in which many tensions are manifest. The removal of fault from the legal process represents a legislative expression of the primacy of a discourse of harmony and one that prioritises a particular interpretation of children's interests. The principle that marriage is to be supported connotes a concern that marriage should remain the preferred basis for 'the family' and the best forum for raising children. But the passionate nature of the divorce debates, in 1969 and in 1996, indicate that in the popular mind at least, fault remains important and significant in divorce. As in 1969, we may find that we are not able to legislate it away.

At an individual level, studies show that divorcing people are deeply concerned about issues of blame, which colour their perceptions of fairness and their ideas about justice (see, for example, Davis, Cretney and Collins, 1994). For many, the notion of fault, of attributing blame to one party and exonerating the other, is what the legal system should be about, it is what ensures that justice is not only done but also is seen to be done. Brown and Day Sclater, in their chapter on the psychodynamics of divorce, argue that there are good psychological reasons why many divorcing people feel this way; faced with the loss that divorce inevitably entails, as well as the need to build a new life, the imputation of blame can feature prominently on the psychological agendas of divorcing people. These psychological 'roots' provide a bedrock for a culture in which divorce is pathologised and where fault goes hand-in-hand with divorce. There is clearly a tension between the kind of harmonious divorce that is envisaged for us, and the needs and expectations of divorcing people.

But it is important to bear in mind that the reform of the divorce law has come at a time of widespread concern about a 'crisis in the family'; the pro-family agendas of the main political parties, all seeking to claim to be *the* party of the family, have exerted a powerful influence. There can be no doubt that we, as individuals and as a culture, have a deep investment in 'family' as the guarantor of a stable society. Our so-called divorcing society has been held to be responsible for a whole range of social ills, and many feel 'the family' to be under threat. Anxieties about a whole range of broader social changes commonly touch base at the level of 'family', which provides a convenient ideological location to address those wider concerns. In this context, it is perhaps unsurprising that a reform of the divorce law should seek to provide support for marriage. Arguably, however, the new law goes further than that; there is a sense in which it addresses concerns about the 'decline of the family' by providing for the emergence of a new post-divorce family.

Reconstructing 'the Family'?

Carol Smart (1997) argues that recent changes in family policy, (she is referring to the Children Act 1989, the Child Support Act 1991 and the Family Law Act 1996), have become out of step with current understandings of social and ideological changes such as those discussed by sociologists Giddens (1992) and Beck (1992). She argues that, far from facilitating any adaptation to social change, family law is now taking the lead to promote further change of a particular sort, namely a return to the so-called traditional family of the 1950s. Smart sees family law as 'engineering policies to change the very nature of post-divorce family life' and she regards these as 'harmful tinkerings' which are likely to result, ironically, not in any return to the golden age of the nuclear family, but rather to preside over its demise.

Fears about the 'decline of the family' and its supposed adverse social consequences featured prominently in the Family Law Act debates. The high divorce rate was seen by many as threatening social stability and cohesion through its effects on 'the family'. For example, during the Bill's first reading in the House of Lords, the Lord Bishop of Chelmsford said:

> For the avoidance of doubt, I must preface what I have to say on the Family Law Bill with a statement that the House of Bishops of the Church of England is second to none in its belief that marriage is part of the order of God's creation, designed to be a joyful and enriching partnership, bringing comfort and mutual help to those who commit themselves to it. The Bishops also believe that the family is essential to the health and well-being of our society and that no effort should be spared to prepare people for marriage and to assist them in understanding what it takes to maintain faithful marriage relationships and to provide a stable family life (Hansard, HL col 152, 20 November 1995).

This view was closely echoed by the then Lord Chancellor, Lord Mackay of Clashfern, during the Bill's second reading:

> I personally believe that marriage should be for life. This is the ideal I believe most couples who marry strive for. It is this ideal which provides the most stable and secure background for the birth and development of children (Hansard, HL col 704, 30 November 1995).

These contributions to the divorce reform debates evidence a commitment to marriage, and are premised on the idea that 'the family' is central to both personal fulfilment and social stability. However, this powerful ideology exists alongside a recognition that our society has undergone a range of profound social and demographic developments which herald fundamental change in the meanings of 'family'. Coote *et al* (1994), for example, discuss recent evidence of demographic patterns which show a number of distinct trends: a rising divorce rate, a declining marriage rate, increasing cohabitation, increases in the numbers of children born outside marriage, a separation of sex and marriage, and of marriage and parenthood, and so on. They point out that changes in family patterns are part and parcel of broader social, political and economic trends, as they have been throughout history. Seen in this light, it would appear that a family law which seeks to address, or even reverse, changes in 'the family', simply by means of legislation is attempting an impossible task.

But demographic changes are only one part of the story. According to sociologist Anthony Giddens (1992), our culture is currently characterised by changing mentalities, particularly in the sphere of intimacy; people are beginning to think quite differently than they did fifty years ago about the meanings of intimacy and marriage, as the ideology of romantic love is progressively eroded. Giddens sees an increasing tendency towards emotional investments in what he calls 'confluent love', a love which is pragmatic and contingent and which lacks the 'for ever' quality of romanticism. The search becomes that for the perfect relationship, rather than for Mr or Mrs Right. Giddens sees this 'transformation of intimacy' as closely tied to an ascendant individualism; the individual is seen as having rights to personal autonomy and fulfilment; where one relationship fails to satisfy, the individual must be free to move on to try another. Late modernity, he argues, is characterised by our preoccupation with what he calls 'a reflexive project of the self', as people become less bound by ideas of duty and obligation and more prone to reflect upon whether certain courses of action are in their own interests or not. Thus he sees changing beliefs and expectations associated with intimacy as not reducible to structural or economic change, but as representing new mentalities which are driving the contemporary separation of marriage, sex and parenthood.

Giddens also considers two further aspects of this transformation of intimacy which are relevant to our discussion on the undercurrents of divorce. First, he argues that the transformation is gendered; women have been at the forefront of redefining their place in both the public and the private spheres, whilst men, he says, are 'lagging behind'. This is evidenced in the fact that almost three quarters of divorce petitions are currently presented by wives. Secondly, Giddens discusses the psychological correlates which accompany the transformation of intimacy he describes. Drawing on psychoanalytic theory, he considers the psychic configurations which predispose, respond to and result from changing gender relations and patterns of intimacy. What is important in his argument for our purposes is the notion of there being a close linkage among individual psychologies and broader social and discursive frameworks; social change both depends upon and impacts upon us at a material and a psychological level. In divorce, the law may provide us with new discursive frameworks (or it may reflect older, dominant ones), and it may provide us with the opportunities for new dispute resolution practices but, at the end of the day, it will be living, passionate people (Plummer, 1995) who must negotiate the power of law, and on whom the successful functioning of the new procedures depend.

Remarkably little is known about how adults experience separation and divorce. As Day Sclater argues in her chapter, the policy makers should not assume that implementation of the divorce reforms will proceed unproblematically. At the very least, the emotional investments which divorcing people have in engaging in conflict, and in dwelling on the past is something which should be taken into account by the professionals whose task it is to manage dispute resolution. Further, we cannot assume that divorcing people will uncritically accept or follow the prescriptions of the dominant discourses. Research shows that the exhortation to remain amicably involved with the other parent after divorce 'for the sake of the children' can clash quite dramatically with the need for a final separation, such that the desired independence and autonomy can be pursued. This is particularly crucial for mothers, with whom most children remain after divorce; many find the children's contact times particularly difficult and painful. In these cases, one finds concrete examples of the tension between the prescriptions of the welfare discourse, and the contemporary ideals of autonomy and individualism Giddens talks about. These tensions are not easy to resolve at an individual level, or to address at the level of social policy.

Smart (1997) argues that recent family law attempts to stem the tide of confluent love by forging links between a child's parents when the adults involved have no desire other than to end their relationship. Crucial in these developments has been an emphasis on 'the welfare of the child', interpreted to mean that children's interests are best served by continued relationships with two parents who are able to remain amicably involved with each other after the divorce. We will be discussing this emphasis on the welfare of the child in more detail in the next section but suffice to say at this stage that, during the Family Law Act debates, both proponents and opponents of the Bill mobilised ideas about the centrality of children, and of 'the family' for children. The paradox is, as both Piper and Roche, in different ways, argue in their contributions to this book, there are few provisions in family law which, in fact, promote children's welfare, and the opportunities for hearing the 'wishes and feelings' of children are bedevilled by adult-centred practices and structural and financial constraints.

The positioning of children as victims of divorce - the incompetent objects of welfare discourse - is, of course, not new, but it now permits those who wish to re-assert the primacy of 'traditional family values' to utilise a powerful discourse in support of their case for arresting 'the decline of the family' and for the restoration of the old nuclear arrangement. At the same time, this positioning of children provides a basis for those who see 'the family', not as in decline, but as a social institution in a gradual process of transformation, to envisage new, non-threatening family formations which are consistent with broader historical changes. Arguably, the Family Law Act represents a site of tension between the kinds of regressive 'social engineering' aspirations that Smart (1997) discusses, and a more progressive (in some sense) attempt to keep up with and respond to, as well as manage, social change.

Divorce Law as the Solution to the 'Crisis in the Family'?

'Family' is a very powerful signifier, and the strength of feeling in relation to it should not be underestimated. As Lord Ashbourne said during the Family Law Act debates:

> The decline of the traditional family and family values is disturbing, to say the least. The illegitimacy rate has escalated from being a little over 8% in 1971 to now well over 30% ... If the Government are really concerned about the problems of law and order and child abuse they must end the policies that encourage the one-parent family and introduce others that build up and support the traditional nuclear family ... Unless the Government are prepared to confront the threat which the collapse of the traditional family presents to the nation the problems will continue to escalate (Lord Ashbourne, HL col 170, 20 November 1995).

This quotation illustrates the kind of tension we have been talking about. On the one hand, the speaker recognises the reality of the demographic change (here, in relation to the increasing numbers of children born outside of marriage) but, on the other hand, is calling for some action to restore stability to family life, as traditionally conceived. There is some evidence from the Family Law Act debates, and from the Government papers that preceded them, to suggest that divorce, once pathologised as chaos and disaster, is in the process of being normalised as merely a transition in the family life cycle. In this way, the social anxieties generated by the fears about family breakdown can be addressed; if divorce is simply an event in the family life cycle, then it no longer unequivocally signifies either the breakdown of families or the decline of 'the family'.

In the USA, there has long been a lobby which views divorce as a normative family transition. For example, Furstenberg and Spanier (1984) state, (in words which prefigure Giddens' argument) that:

> The high rates of divorce... are not just an indication that marriage as an institution is being devalued; in fact, just the opposite. But as the cultural importance placed on the personal gratifications of marriage grows, the commitment any given couple makes to the marriage becomes more conditional as either partner must be able to exit from the relationship in the event that it is not living up to her or his expectations ... Divorce is not so much an escape hatch from married life but a recycling mechanism (p.53).

Similarly, McIsaacs (1995) sees the shift from the adversarial process of dispute resolution to mediation as consistent with the emergence of a 'new family system' in our post-industrial age. This new family system is to be brought into being by a discourse which represents divorce as a 'reorganisation of the family, not an end of the family', and it is dependent upon a 'concept of not being "divorced from" someone but being "divorced to" them' (McIsaacs, 1995, p.ix). Constance Ahrons and her co-workers (Ahrons, 1983; Ahrons and Rodgers, 1987; Ahrons, 1995) argue that divorce is best seen, not as the destruction of the nuclear family, but as productive of the 'bi-nuclear family'. For Kaslow and Hyatt (1981) divorce is a potential 'growth experience' for the 'extended family'. Coleman and Ganong (1990) talk about step families in terms of extended families. In the UK, Robinson (1991) talks about divorce as 'family transformation' and includes the 'post-divorce family' in her family life cycle scheme. Divorce is thereby presented as an opportunity to restructure families and to preserve 'the family' in the face of the demographic evidence of the diversity and multiplicity of family forms. In this sense, the Family Law Act paves the way for a new post-divorce family to emerge, one which is constituted within the discourses and practices of welfare, and which coheres around a child positioned as incompetent, vulnerable, innocent and victimised by divorce.

However, there is a powerful gendered dimension to these discourses and, perhaps, the fundamental object of concern is not any change in 'the family' *per se*, but the progressive erosion of traditional paternal authority accompanied, as it has been, by increasing formal legal rights for women in the public sphere, and developments in the economy which have impacted most adversely on men. As Richard Collier argues in his chapter, a further undercurrent here is the reinforcement of the values of heterosexuality in relation to family life.

If we are prepared to follow Giddens' train of thought, we might think about the enormous box-office success and world wide acclaim recently accorded to *The Full Monty*; here are the changed mentalities Giddens talks about, and here are masculinities forging new cultural positions for themselves in positive ways, and ways which express the emotional vulnerabilities of men. These are men who have taken up where Giddens left off, and who are facing the hardships of economic restructuring as well as the absence of any psychological space in our culture for vulnerable (or 'feminine') masculinities. Importantly too, for our purposes, this film says something new about divorce; it carries a new cultural script which suggests to us the inevitability of divorce in some circumstances. The pain is there, but so are positive images; the family is not altogether broken by divorce, but survives in a different form, conveyed in an appealing portrayal of the relationship between a divorced father and his son.

What is going on here? It seems that there is, at one level, a denial that there is any 'crisis' or 'decline' in 'the family'; instead, the concept of 'family' is being altered, and its boundaries shifted. But, it is noteworthy that these changes depend too upon older ideas, which are themselves being rejuvenated and transformed. The new family involves people who are tied to each other by blood, kinship, marriage or divorce. As Bren Neale and Carol Smart argue in their chapter, as marriage recedes as the basis for family life, it is being replaced by a new emphasis on (biological) parenthood. And, as Richard Collier argues in his chapter, the 'new' family continues to be structured by an ideology of heterosexuality.

The provisions of the Family Law Act may be seen in the light of these ideas; there is a sense in which the Act legislates this 'new' family into being, building upon the foundations laid down in the Children Act, denying 'family breakdown' and reconstructing divorce as a normative transition. Importantly, the new discourse is capable of addressing the anxieties which accompany demographic change and talk about 'the decline of the family', as well as those which arise from the erosion of the old patriarchal authority.

The Welfare of the Child

Child as Victim

Crucially, this new family depends on the close linkage of divorce with the dominant welfare discourse. The new family coheres around a vulnerable child, who is the object of that discourse. Importantly, however, children's vulnerabilities are themselves constructed, as Felicity Kaganas argues in her chapter, around particular notions of 'risk' and 'harm'; their primary need is constructed as one for a relationship with the father. As Irving and Benjamin (1995) state: 'There is a strong association between negative consequences of parental divorce and ongoing dysfunction in the relations between these children and their biological parents, stepparents, or both' (p.85). These authors are opening the way for new formulations of 'dysfunction' to emerge; a dysfunctional post divorce family is one in which relations between children and their parents are disrupted in some way. What we might call the traditional divorce, in which the parents each claim rights and individually pursue entitlements, where the children stay with the mother, and may or may not maintain a relationship with the father, has become the thing to avoid at all costs.

It might seem that this emphasis on the needs of children is right and proper and that we, as adults, have a duty to protect the interests of those weaker members of our community. It is certainly true that recent family law has focused on children, but as several of the contributors to this volume note, it is certainly not the case that family law can adequately ensure that children's needs are, in fact, met or their interests ascertained and protected. On the contrary, there is an argument to be made that family law actually perpetuates the social exclusion of children, another undercurrent that we would wish to bring to the surface.

The 'best interests of the child' is a pervasive notion in law, and the welfare discourse in which it acquires meaning is increasingly entering into our culture's stock of common sense. But, the best interests principle has no fixed meaning, although it informs (or perhaps justifies, retrospectively) legal decision-making. The positioning of children as innocent, dependent, vulnerable, incompetent, and as requiring the protection of adults and of the state has the effect of perpetuating the structural powerlessness of children as a group, as Kitzinger (1988) has argued in relation to child abuse. The images of children as the 'victims' of divorce (Piper, 1996)[1] are powerful and seductive; they pervade the research which addresses the issue of the 'effects' of divorce on children, as well as legal practice.[2] The result, as Piper argues in this volume, is that children's voices are effectively ignored. Rodgers and Pryor (1998), concluding their recent extensive review of the vast literature on children and divorce, express a concern that echoes those of Roche and Piper in this volume:

> The Family Law Act (1996) pays lip-service to its concern for children's well-being, but fails to provide concrete mechanisms to enable children to have a say in decision-making. Rather, parents are exhorted to take their children's views into consideration (p.45).

Potentially, the research could provide a scientific underpinning for the welfare discourse and for the meanings to be attributed to the concept of 'best interests', although it has long been recognised that the relations between law and social scientific discourse are far from straightforward (see, for example, Dingwall and Eekelaar, 1986; King, 1991; Sales *et al*, 1992; King and Piper, 1995). What is important for our argument here, however, is the point that the scientific research is often pervaded by the very same ideologies and images of children as are problematic in law. Furthermore, the findings from research studies remain equivocal, and general conclusions are difficult to draw, as there are undoubtedly many factors involved. For example, Rodgers and Pryor state that:

> The relationship between the amount of access to the non-residential parent and child adjustment is not straightforward. Some studies find that frequent contact is associated with better adjustment for children; however, others find

> no relationship. A few find a negative relationship between frequent levels of contact and child well-being. These diverse findings suggest that the relationship between contact and well-being is moderated by other factors (p.42).

Nevertheless, the dominant message of the research is taken to be that divorce is damaging to children. Invoking social scientific research, as did the Lord Chancellor in the Consultation and White Papers which preceded the Family Law Act, lends a degree of certainty, of scientific validity, authority and convincingness to arguments which would otherwise appear to be merely rhetorical or ideological in tone. For divorce discourses do not merely reflect particular visions of childhood and children, they help to construct them too and, in doing so, contribute to the social exclusion of children.[3]

Visions of Childhood

Trinder (1997), for example, explores the paradoxical situation whereby a range of adult professionals (court welfare officers) construct the very children whose voices they seek to represent. Importantly, she includes in her discussion some attempt to understand what children themselves make of the situation, although she points out that research here is extremely thin on the ground (most recently, see Smart and Neale, 1998). For our purposes, two important points emerge from her analysis. First, adult perceptions are based on idealised and stabilised conceptions of childhoods, with no distinction between 'children' as living beings and 'childhood' as a historically and culturally shifting set of ideas. Secondly, children see themselves, and their role in decision-making, in ways which do not coincide with adults' perspectives. She argues that children's interests would be better served if there were ways of appreciating their individuality, and the complexities and ambiguities of their individual lives. In the various constructions of childhood that Trinder discusses, however, the image of the child as vulnerable is present.

McWhinney (1997) talks about the 'moral imperatives' inherent in the notion of the child's best interests, and he raises the important, though neglected question, of why it is that the state assumes any responsibility for children at all. His answer to this question is framed in terms of the ways in which we, as a society, choose to conceptualise childhood. He talks, idealistically, of childhood 'innocence'; he says that human sensitivities are 'easily coarsened', especially by violence, including the 'violence of knowing too soon' and of being 'disillusioned prematurely'. Adults he sees as disillusioned, as 'separated from the sacred', as 'evicted from the garden'. He says that children remind us of what we were, what we have lost, although what we might still retrieve or become.

It is difficult, however, to challenge the dominant discourses which see children as vulnerable and as the privileged possessors of our lost innocence; these discourses are rooted in a construction of childhood subjectivity in wholly rational terms, and they have immense emotional appeal, and we have come to think that this emotional appeal has deep psychological roots. It is perhaps precisely because children are structurally powerless *vis a vis* adults, and precisely because the discourse ignores the irrational and the unconscious, that it has its emotional appeal. By this we mean that we, as adults, have an emotional investment in seeing children in this way - perhaps it is serving some psychological purpose for us.

But our own emotional investments in particular visions of childhood are not the only reasons why the discourses are so difficult to challenge. Bell (1993a), for example, looks at the politics of images of childhood. Using a Foucauldian framework, she considers the ways in which 'childhood' is deployed in governance. Children have become the objects of a range of 'psy-discourses', and the need to protect them and to ensure that they follow proper and desirable developmental pathways (themselves the province of science and psychology) is the route by which the state regulates the behaviours of individuals *through* 'the family'. There are thus, as Bell and others argue (see, Bell, 1993a; Burman, 1994; Morss, 1995), political imperatives embedded in particular social constructions of what children are. All this is now fairly commonplace but perhaps needs to be re-stated, since insights of this type are notable for their absence when it comes to thinking about children and divorce. The point is that we have both a political and an emotional investment in continuing to construct childhood in the ways that we do. Let us think a bit more about the psychological investments that are made at a social level.

In *The Good Society and the Inner World*, Rustin (1991) argues that the Kleinian psychoanalytic tradition has much to offer in understanding politics and culture, as well as individuals. Such an enterprise is not intended to reduce social, cultural and political formations to the level of individual psychology (such a psychologisation of society would be morally and politically insupportable), but it is intended to give us new tools with which to think about the many levels on which politics and power operate. In a similar vein, sociologist and group psychotherapist Ian Craib (1994) uses a Kleinian framework to understand, amongst other things, the way we, as a society, organise grief. He argues that the human inability to reflect on or even to tolerate overwhelming emotions is reflected at a social level in institutional mechanisms that facilitate the denial of our deepest vulnerabilities. In the case of grief, it is our deep-set inability truly to accept the uncomfortable fact of our own mortality that underlies the production of theories about bereavement and the practices around death and grief. These insights are important when we think about children and divorce too.

The dominant image of childhood in our society today is one that is informed by developmentalism (Burman, 1994; Morss, 1995) which renders childhood as a predictable series of stages, knowable to the psychological experts. This idea of developmental progress is also reflected in the work on children and divorce, much of which seeks to document a predictable process of adjustment, and to inform us of the variety of factors which predispose one outcome or another. Ambiguities in adjustment and ambivalences in feelings are left out of account in the traditional model. Further, knowledge of these factors and processes has been claimed by psychological experts as their own province. What we have here is an underlying idea that things are controllable, that the disruptive emotions thrown up by family break-ups can be fashioned and contained by appropriate legal and psychological procedures. In relation to the massive social anxieties which are repeatedly generated by social changes which seem to threaten the centrality of 'family values', it is perhaps not surprising that we, as a society, seek to manage those anxieties by encouraging our experts to create theories and practices which put those anxieties at one step removed. As Walker (1991) puts it: 'We probably all have a vision of a society composed of "happy families". Pain and conflict, particularly for children, are a serious threat to that vision' (p.371). It is perhaps for this reason that social policy has seemed to ignore the equivocal nature of divorce research.[4] What we are arguing here is that our social policies are in the business of managing emotions; there is a psychological subtext to the laws and practices of divorce, and that our images of childhood are intimately linked to desires to contain the anxieties caused by apparent threats to 'the family'.

So, where does this take us? In summary, we have statutory provisions for children's voices to be heard, but, in practice, they fail children miserably and, as Jeremy Roche points out in this volume, our present system actually militates against the achievement of rights for children. In other words, we must ask ourselves whether we are excluding children by the very means we seek to use to protect their interests. We think that we are, and we would now like to move on to explore some possible explanations for this paradoxical undercurrent.

Mason and Steadman (1997), discussing the Australian child protection system, argue that the barriers against children's voices being heard lie in the powerlessness of children as a social group, a powerlessness which is reflected and perpetuated by psychological notions of the child as dependent. However, we would like to go beyond this political argument, and look at the psychological constellations which underpin this state of affairs. We have argued that the welfare discourse positions children as vulnerable: what children say is heard *through* this welfare discourse, where children speak from a position of vulnerability, dependence and of being in need of protection. We think that the welfare discourse, in this way, may act as a repository for the vulnerable feelings of adults. Where feelings of vulnerability threaten to overwhelm us, we can disown them unconsciously, push them outside of ourselves, and locate them elsewhere. This is a process known in psychoanalysis as projection; its function is to protect the person who projects from experiencing an overwhelming anxiety, as it puts intolerable feelings at one step removed. So, in divorce, we adults can experience our own vulnerability in a tolerable way because we project it onto children, and it is the welfare discourse that facilitates this complex psychological manoeuvre.

We talked earlier about how we, as a society, deal with the anxieties generated by the prospect of family breakdown by taking refuge in discourses in which unruly emotions seem to be manageable. We are now talking about a similar phenomenon at an individual level. As Day Sclater has argued elsewhere (Day Sclater, 1998a), adults' vulnerabilities around separation can be acute, but there is little room for their expression within the way divorce is currently organised. Men may suffer particular difficulties in this regard, since they have traditionally been under strong social pressures to hide their dependent and vulnerable feelings (Chodorow, 1978; Giddens, 1991, 1992; Maguire, 1995, Minsky, 1998). There are well-documented gender differences in the ways in which women and men negotiate threat and psychological vulnerability, and the varied meanings these have for each of us. In relation to divorce, these issues provide another undercurrent which is not often brought into the open (Day Sclater, 1998b).

The Question of Gender

Parenthood is a gender-neutral concept in law but, in practice, it remains the case that men and women do different things as fathers and mothers, both before and after divorce. Divorce discourses intersect in complex ways with broader social discourses about masculinities and femininities and the practices of motherhood and fatherhood. As Maguire (1995) argues, male dominated social structures provide men with opportunities to deny their own dependency needs whilst permitting women to carry the practical and psychological burdens of caring and emotionality in the family. In so far as the dominant discourse makes available a new position for men as involved fathers, it could help to facilitate the construction of new masculinities. However, in the face of the substantive inequalities which continue to constrain women, the 'new' fatherhood has been perceived by many as another manifestation of the assertion of the old paternal authority (see, for example, Fineman, 1995). Thus, as Richard Collier argues in his chapter, divorce seems to provide a forum for the expression and strengthening of traditional (heterosexual) masculinities and gender differences, a far cry from the gender-neutrality of parental responsibility in family law.

Empirical research would seem to support such a contention. For example, Arditti and Allen (1993) examined distressed fathers' perceptions of inequities in divorce. They found that the fathers expressed strong negative feelings about the legal system, the emotional hardships they had suffered, and they spoke of a range of injustices. These men rarely saw divorce in neutral terms, but they saw things in clear black and white, being likely to blame others (lawyers, the ex-wife) for their negative feelings. They did not accept responsibility for their own negative and destructive impulses, which resulted in an enduring sense of injustice, a preoccupation with the unfairness of it all, and a prevailing hostility towards the perceived sources of the inequities.

Similarly, in a study of 91 divorced fathers (Simpson *et al*, 1995; Walker, 1997), interviewed 6 years after the divorce, none were content with the contact arrangements. 25% reported that they had been able to maintain a parenting role in the face of considerable opposition, and these fathers were the most angry and unhappy. They reported feelings of powerlessness, an inability to forgive past actions, were bitter and unwilling to readjust to their new circumstances. Arendell (1995) too shows how the divorcing men in her study were primarily intent on preserving a sense of masculine identity on divorce, with all the implicit ideas about male privilege.

What we are seeing here, we think, is an acute vulnerability which some men find difficult to express in ways other than anger and hostility, and where their relationships with their children are infused with an emotional investment which derives, not only from parental love, but also from the need to rid themselves of their own painful feelings. The welfare discourse enables us to fight for the perceived needs of our vulnerable children, it acts as a repository for our own overwhelming feelings; in a word, we have an emotional investment in seeing things in the way that we do and in acting in the way that we do. This, perhaps, is why achieving true autonomy rights for children is proving to be such a difficult thing to do.

It is probably significant that particular interpretations of the best interests principle have gone hand in hand with what amounts to an extension of fathers' rights (Brophy, 1985, 1989; Smart, 1989a, 1989b; Harne and Radford, 1994; Hooper, 1994), and that this is happening at a time when traditional masculinities are under threat (Giddens, 1992; Collier, 1995; Connell, 1995; Frosh, 1996). As Deech (1993) points out, men's vulnerabilities may be particularly acute in relation to fatherhood, as the availability of new reproductive technologies have at least the potential for autonomous motherhood. In a climate where women have made quite considerable advances in their quest for autonomy, it perhaps should come as no surprise that we are currently seeing attempts to define a new role for men, a role which includes participation in the family sphere which was previously the province of women. We are beginning to hear quite loud calls for extending the 'rights' of unmarried fathers (see, for example, Lowe, 1997) and the Government has recently indicated an intention to extend parental responsibility to all those unmarried fathers who jointly register their children.

The chapters by Kaganas and by Neale and Smart in this book both support the idea that the deployment of the welfare discourse in divorce is linked as much to adult moral, emotional and political agendas as to the welfare of children. This is an undercurrent which underlies the continuing social exclusion of children and militates against their achievement of citizenship rights. As Smith (1997) puts it:

> [E]ven the most convincing evidence about children's competence to decide and even the most thorough philosophical challenge to presumptions about capacity and autonomy, will not achieve fundamental changes in the way the law thinks about children. It may achieve some change ... But change will not

> go so far as to reject a legal distinction between children and adults or allow that rights will take precedence over welfare, for the law itself only reflects and confirms a particular social construction of childhood. No wonder we bump into children's best interests at every turn - *adults* simply cannot manage without them (p.136).

These best interests are also linked to gender because conflict in divorce is gendered. Perceptions of children's interests have been constructed in relation to their 'need' for parents who can co-operate with each other, and on the assumption that some form of father-presence is essential for their well being. In the prevailing socio-political climate, when femininity no longer unproblematically signifies dependence, and when women are actively resisting being positioned as vulnerable in this way, we see the dominant welfare discourse as providing, primarily, a repository for masculine vulnerability. As women increasingly refuse men's projections of dependence and vulnerability, men are being forced to confront these difficult 'feminine' aspects of themselves (Maguire, 1995; Minsky, 1998). It has perhaps been easier for women to integrate their 'masculine' parts than it is for men to accept their feminine ones, simply because the characteristics of masculinity remain more highly culturally valued than those traditionally associated with femininity. Giddens (1992) suggests that male sexual violence, which has its roots in the inherent fragilities of masculinity (Maguire, 1995), will inevitably increase as part and parcel of the transformation of intimacy he describes.

But not all men are dealing with their vulnerabilities in this way. Some are actively trying to own and express qualities which have traditionally belonged to women but, in doing so, they must surmount considerable structural as well as psychological barriers. The prescriptions of the welfare discourse not only encourage a denial of the conflictual and gendered dynamics which emerge on the breakdown of an intimate relationship, but also facilitate the displacement of vulnerabilities and encourage men to compete with women on the terrain of mothering. In short, the discourse feeds directly into masculine fantasies that women can be dominated and that men can triumph (see, for example, Maguire, 1995). In this light, it perhaps should come as no surprise that recent research indicates that, far from ensuring parental co-operation and reducing litigation, the Children Act seems to have resulted in an *increase* in both litigation and delay in children cases (Bailey-Harris *et al*, 1998).

Clearly, parenting is changing, but lasting social change can only be brought about if there are psychic changes too. In our view, our legislators have made the mistake of ignoring the important psychological undercurrents of divorce and, relatedly, the complex issues around gender. Neither parenting practices nor gender relations will change fundamentally simply because the law says they should. The welfare discourse continues to provide an institutionalised means of defence against male anxieties and, in the process, denies children both agency and competence. There will have to be political change, cultural change and psychic change before mothers and fathers can become 'equal' parents, and gender difference can become a source of richness and diversity, rather than a basis for conflict and oppression.

As Alison Diduck argues in her chapter, the discourses and dynamics of gender also influence the division of family assets on divorce. Feminists have long argued that mediation of the financial matters 'ancillary' to the divorce has the potential to be detrimental to women (see Bottomley, 1985; Fineman, 1991; Grillo, 1991); the crux of the argument is that the dominant discourses fail to take adequate account of the realities of women's lives. Similarly, Diduck shows how current and proposed means for dealing with finances and property militate against women achieving equitable outcomes, and she proposes new solutions which take account of the range of contributions which both sexes can make to the marriage. Hitherto, contributions whose value cannot be directly assessed in financial terms have been effectively bypassed in legal decision-making, because they both depend upon and support gendered readings of what is expected of women and men in a marriage. Gendered discourses are thus important undercurrents which both inform and are reproduced by family law, in relation to both children and financial matters (see Smart, 1992).

Children and Parents, Husbands and Wives

'Children and Parents' and 'Husbands and Wives' constitute the two main parts of this book. Opening the first section, Bren Neale and Carol Smart aim to shed some light on the realities of post-divorce parenting. They draw on an empirical study, recently completed, to show a range of post-divorce parenting patterns. Their findings challenge the assumptions of the dominant welfare discourse that the authors see as providing a narrowly prescriptive model for parenting which is impossible to achieve. They illustrate the limitations of the ideological model that underpins the operation of divorce law, and argue for a greater recognition by policy makers of the actualities of practices, relationships and negotiations in both marriage and divorce.

In his chapter, Jeremy Roche looks at those parts of the dominant discourses surrounding divorce which sit uneasily with the languages of the modern children's rights movement. He points to the adult consensus that children - in their own best interests - should be excluded from decision-making in the divorce process and also to the effect of particular notions of family privacy which preclude languages of democracy and citizenship in relation to children affected by parental divorce. He argues further that the family justice system currently makes it more, not less, difficult to hear the voice of the child.

In the following chapter, Christine Piper examines, in more detail, how this exclusion of children arises in practice, despite the statutory emphasis on the importance of children's wishes and feelings. Drawing on recent empirical work, she reviews the relevant legal provisions and discusses the undercurrents that militate against ascertaining children's wishes in practice. Empirical research indicates that solicitors tend to rely on parental reports or assume that the court welfare officer will ascertain the child's views in the event of a dispute. The priority currently being given to parental agreement and harmony - in its own right and in the child's best interests - militates against the voice of the child being heard.

There is, of course, an inherent tension between advocating the realisation of children's rights and conceptualising children as incompetent dependants. Furthermore, whilst we maintain a particular conception of the 'abstract' child we are less likely to be able to hear the real voices of real children. We have already given reasons why we as adults are unlikely to let go of this conception of the child. But there is another sense in which the welfare discourse, and its positioning of children, is important; it also serves political purposes. Fairclough (1992) argues that we should not underestimate the power of discourse in effecting social change. Much of family law makes its ultimate appeal to a discourse of child welfare which serves to manage the behaviour of adults. There is a sense in which the discourses and practices of children's welfare regulate and prescribe for socially desirable ways of parenting.

Here we are touching again on the sorts of issues raised by Smart and Neale in their chapter. Felicity Kaganas, too, explores the ways in which particular conceptions of 'harm' have emerged in relation to contact. She argues that children are constructed as being 'at risk' unless they have continuing relationships with two harmonious parents; in seeking to manage these 'risks', family law prescribes parenting for us all. Meanwhile, many children remain at risk from a range of other factors, such as poverty (Maclean, 1991) and violence (Hester and Radford, 1996) which family law fails adequately to address in relation to divorce.

This discursive and symbolic function of law is a powerful undercurrent which is explored in more detail by Richard Collier in his opening chapter of the section on 'Husbands and Wives'. Collier addresses changing patterns of fatherhood and masculinity in the context of transformations in intimacy and changing gender relations. He uncovers the hidden heterosexuality of recent divorce reform, and demonstrates the complexities of the mutual constitutions of heterosexuality, marriage, fatherhood and 'the family' in legal discourses and practices.

Jo Brown and Shelley Day Sclater then present a psychodynamic view of divorce. Drawing on psychoanalytic theory, they expose the powerful psychological undercurrents of divorce at both a social and an individual level. Reporting on the findings from an empirical study, the following chapter by Day Sclater illustrates a range of divorce experiences, and shows how psychoanalytic theory can be used to help understand the meanings of experience. Together, these two chapters challenge the current pathologising of divorce and suggest that 'conflict' is an inevitable outcome of ordinary coping strategies.

Issues of gender are prominent in the chapters by Felicity Kaganas and Christine Piper and by Alison Diduck. As we have seen, despite the gender neutrality, in principle, of family law, it remains highly gendered in practice (Brophy and Smart, 1985; Smart, 1989; Smart and Sevenhuijsen, 1989; Fineman, 1991; Smart, 1992; O'Donovan, 1994). As Kaganas and Piper argue in their chapter on domestic violence, the ideal of the harmonious divorce, and the informal, co-operative dispute resolution practices (mediation) which flow from it, may result in a decline in the visibility of wife abuse with the result that vulnerable spouses and children may remain unprotected. Whilst domestic violence as an issue has entered the public debate about divorce, empirical evidence reveals that there is still no clear consensus amongst professionals about the nature of domestic abuse and the need for proactive policies. This situation is perhaps all the more crucial in the light of recent findings of the linkages between spouse abuse and child abuse (Mullender and Morley, 1994; Hester and Radford, 1996). It would be a pity, however, if concern for protecting children from abuse meant a diversion away from protecting spouses in their own right.

The tensions inherent in the gender-neutrality of the formal law are also evidenced in financial settlements. As Alison Diduck argues in her chapter, with the focus on the welfare of the child, and on the perceived benefits to spouses of reaching their 'own' agreements, there has been a failure to examine the consequences of the move towards informal justice in terms of the actual content of those agreements. Potentials for systematic inequities have been ignored. The undercurrents in relation to money and property, discussed by Diduck, are crucial to policy making; unless there emerges a more integrated picture of financial provision, which incorporates currently neglected issues, new policy initiatives might increase, and not reduce, the financial risks to family members who have least access to or command of resources.

Together, the chapters of this book critique the dominant discourses which have constrained the divorce debates and begin to address the complex undercurrents which will undoubtedly exert a hidden influence as the Family Law Act is implemented. The final chapter of the book draws out the themes which recur in this project. In critiquing the talk about divorce, in exposing these undercurrents and in drawing attention to professional and policy developments, we aim to introduce new ideas and perspectives into a debate which otherwise has functioned to further political, professional and moral agendas and to facilitate, in practice, the continuance of multiple exclusions.

Notes

1. Similarly, Mason and Steadman (1997) argue that the dominant adult ideological perspective is that of children as dependent, as needing protection, and as requiring the development of state systems to ensure this protection.
2. Fricker, a British judge, reflects this dominant view when he states that 'children are particularly vulnerable during separation and divorce' and he sees the child as the 'hidden client' in divorce proceedings (Fricker, 1995).
3. A number of authors have problematised the indeterminacy of the welfare principle. Kelly (1997), for example, refers to it as a 'concept in search of a meaning'. Alston (1994) says it has yet to acquire a specific content. Parker (1994) documents the criticisms which have been made on the basis of the open-endedness, indeterminacy and vagueness of the principle. He argues that it depends too much on the value system of the decision-maker, and that it can even provide a convenient cloak for 'bias, paternalism and capricious decision-making'. Parker (1994) is trying to understand the process by which 'content' is given to the best interests concept; he is looking for factors which lead to a degree of determinacy in its application, and he cites 'local'

factors as important in its meanings. It is in this context that we might raise the question of the significance of discourses as frameworks of meaning, as knowledge/power complexes, as closed systems of signification. Kelly (1997) advocates approaching the principle with more precision, drawing on psychological expertise where appropriate. Melli (1993), on the other hand, proposes abolishing it as a guiding principle, on the grounds that it seeks a goal which the machinery of law is incapable of attaining, and that it promotes litigation because of its inherent uncertainty.

4. For example, the Family Law Act is based on the desire to minimise the 'damage' caused to children by divorce. The Consultation Paper (LCD, 1993) and the White Paper (LCD, 1995) both accept that research findings 'show' that parental conflict is what damages children, and the equivocal nature of divorce research is neither acknowledged or addressed.

References

Ahrons, C. (1983), 'Divorce: Before, During and After', in H.I. McCubbin and C.R. Figley (eds), *Stress and the Family. Volume 1: Coping with Normative Transitions*, Bruner/Mazel, New York.

Ahrons, C. (1995), *The Good Divorce: Keeping Your Family Together When Your Marriage Falls Apart*, Bloomsbury, London.

Ahrons, C. and Rodgers, R.H. (1987), *Divorced Families: A Multi-Disciplinary Developmental Perspective*, Norton, New York.

Alston, P. (1994), 'The Best Interests Principle: Towards a Reconciliation of Culture and Human Rights', *International Journal of Law and the Family*, vol 8, pp.1-25.

Arendell, T. (1995), *Fathers and Divorce*, Sage, London.

Arditti, J.A. and Allen, K.R. (1993), 'Understanding Distressed Fathers' Perceptions of Legal and Relational Inequities Post-Divorce', *Family and Conciliation Courts Review*, vol 31, pp.461-476.

Association of Lawyers for Children (1998), 'The Future of Representation for Children'. *Family Law*, vol 28, pp.403-411.

Bailey-Harris, R., Davis, G., Barron, J. and Pearce, J. (1998), *Monitoring Private Law Applications Under the Children Act: A Research Report to the Nuffield Foundation*, University of Bristol.

Beck, U. (1992), *The Risk Society: Towards a New Modernity*, Sage, London.

Bell, V. (1993a), *Interrogating Incest: Feminism, Foucault and the Law*, Routledge, London.

Bell, V. (1993b), 'Governing Childhood: Neo-Liberalism and the Law', *Economy and Society*, vol 22, pp.390-405.

Bottomley, A. (1985), 'What is Happening to Family Law? A Feminist Critique of Conciliation', in J. Brophy and C. Smart (eds), *Women in Law*, Routledge and Kegan Paul, London, pp.162-187.

Brophy, J. (1985), 'Child Care and the Growth of Power: The Status of Mothers in Child Custody Disputes, in J. Brophy and C. Smart (eds), *Women in Law*, Routledge and Kegan Paul, London, pp.97-116.

Brophy, J. (1989), 'Custody Law, Child Care and Inequality in Britain', in C. Smart and S.

Sevenhuijsen (eds), *Child Custody and the Politics of Gender*, Routledge, London, pp.217-242.

Brophy, J. and Smart, C. (eds) (1985), *Women in Law*, Routledge and Kegan Paul, London.

Burman, E. (1994), *Deconstructing Developmental Psychology*, Routledge, London.

Chodorow, N. (1978), *The Reproduction of Mothering*, University of California Press, Berkeley.

Coleman, M. and Ganong, L. (1990), 'Remarriage and Stepfamily Research in the 1980s: Increased Interest in an Old Family Form', *Journal of Marriage and the Family*, vol 52, pp.925-940.

Collier, R. (1995), *Masculinity, Law and the Family*, Routledge, London.

Connell, R.W. (1995), *Masculinities*, Polity, Cambridge.

Coote, A., Harman, H. and Hewitt, H. (1994), 'Changing Patterns of Family Life', in J. Eekelaar and M. Maclean (eds), *A Reader on Family Law*, Oxford University Press, Oxford, pp.31-98.

Craib, I. (1994), *The Importance of Disappointment*, Routledge, London.

Dasgupta, C. and Richards, M. (1997), 'Support for Children of Separating Parents: Developing Practice', *Representing Children*, vol 10, pp.106-116.

Davies, B. and Harre, R. (1990), 'Positioning: The Discursive Production of Selves', *Journal for the Theory of Social Behaviour*, vol 20, pp.46-63.

Davis, G., Cretney, S. and Collins, P. (1994), *Simple Quarrels*, Clarendon Press, Oxford.

Day Sclater, S. (1998a), 'Divorce: Coping Strategies, Conflict and Dispute Resolution', *Family Law*, pp.150-152.

Day Sclater, S. (1998b), 'Divorce: Psycho-Politics?', Paper presented at the British Psychological Society, Psychology Of Women Section Annual Conference, Birmingham, June 1998.

Deech, R. (1993), 'The Rights of Fathers: Social and Biological Concepts of Parenthood', in J. Eekelaar and P. Sarcevic (eds), *Parenthood in Modern Society: Legal and Social Issues for the Twenty-First Century*, Martinus Nijhoff, London, pp.19-34.

Dingwall, R. and Eekelaar, J. (1986), 'Judgements of Solomon: Psychology and Family Law', in M. Richards and P. Light (eds), *Children of Social Worlds*, Polity, Cambridge, pp.55-73.

Fairclough, N. (1992), *Discourse and Social Change*, Macmillan, London.

Fineman, M. (1991), *The Illusion of Equality: The Rhetoric and Reality of Divorce Reform*, University of Chicago Press, Chicago.

Fineman, M. (1995), *The Neutered Mother: The Sexual Family and Other Twentieth Century Tragedies*, Routledge, New York.

Fricker, N. (1995), 'Family Law is Different', *Family and Conciliation Courts Review*, vol 33, pp.403-414.

Frosh, S. (1994), *Sexual Difference: Masculinity and Psychoanalysis*, Routledge, London.

Furstenberg, F.F. and Spanier, G.B. (1984), *Recycling the Family: Remarriage After Divorce*, Sage, London.

Giddens, A. (1991), *Modernity and Self Identity*, Polity, Cambridge.

Giddens, A. (1992), *The Transformation of Intimacy*, Polity, Cambridge.

Grillo, T. (1991), 'The Mediation Alternative: Process Dangers for Women', *Yale Law Journal*, vol 100, pp.1545-1610.

Hall, N. (1996), 'Eliciting Children's Views: The Contribution of Psychologists', in R. Davie, G. Upton and V. Varma (eds), *The Voice of the Child: A Handbook for Professionals*,

Falmer Press, London, pp.61-77.

Harne, L. and Radford, J. (1994), 'Reinstating Patriarchy: The Politics of the Family and the New Legislation', in A. Mullender and R. Morley (eds), *Children Living with Domestic Violence*, Taylor and Francis, London, pp.68-85.

Hester, M. and Radford, L. (1996), *Domestic Violence and Child Contact Arrangements in England and Denmark*, Policy Press, Bristol.

Hooper, C.A. (1994), 'Do Families Need Fathers? The Impact of Divorce on Children', in A. Mullender and R. Morley (eds), *Children Living with Domestic Violence*, Taylor and Francis, London, pp.86-101.

Irving, H. and Benjamin, M. (1995), *Family Mediation*, Sage, London.

Jolly, S. (1995), 'Case Commentary: Implacable Hostility, Contact and the Limits of Law', *Child and Family Law Quarterly*, vol 7, pp.228-235.

Jones, S. (1992), 'The Ascertainable Wishes and Feelings of the Child', *Journal of Child Law*, vol 4, pp.181-185.

Kaslow, F. and Hyatt, R. (1981), 'Divorce: A Potential Growth Experience for the Extended Family', *Journal of Divorce*, vol 5, pp.115-126.

Kelly, J. (1997), 'The Best Interests of the Child: A Concept in Search of Meaning', *Family and Conciliation Courts Review*, vol 35, pp.377-387.

King, M. (1991), 'Child Welfare Within Law: The Emergence of a Hybrid Discourse', *Journal of Law and Society*, vol 18, pp.303-322.

King, M. and Piper, C. (1995), *How the Law Thinks About Children*, 2nd ed, Arena, Aldershot.

Kitzinger, J. (1988), 'Defending Innocence: Ideologies of Childhood', *Feminist Review* vol 28, pp.77-87.

Lord Chancellor's Department (1993), *Looking to the Future: Mediation and the Ground for Divorce: A Consultation Paper*, Cm 2424, HMSO, London.

Lord Chancellor's Department (1995), *Looking to the Future: Mediation and the Ground for Divorce: The Government's Proposals*, Cm 2799, HMSO, London.

Lowe, N. (1997), 'The Meaning and Allocation of Parental Responsibility: A Common Lawyer's Perspective', *International Journal of Law, Policy and the Family*, vol 11, pp.192-215.

Maclean, M. (1991), *Surviving Divorce: Women's Resources After Separation*, Macmillan, Basingstoke.

Maguire, M. (1995), *Men, Women, Passion and Power: Gender Issues in Psychotherapy*, Routledge, London.

Mason, J. and Steadman, B. (1997), 'The Significance of the Conceptualisation of Childhood for Child Protection Policy', *Family Matters*, vol 46, pp.31-36.

McIsaacs, H. (1995), 'Foreword', in H. Irving and M. Benjamin, *Family Mediation*, Sage, London.

McWhinney, R. (1997), '*Parentes Mundi* - In the Best Interests of our Children', *Family and Conciliation Courts Review*, vol 35, pp.388-392.

Melli, M. (1993), 'Toward a Restructuring of Custody Decision Making at Divorce: An Alternative Approach to the Best Interests of the Child', in J. Eekelaar and P. Sarcevic (eds), *Parenthood in Modern Society: Legal and Social Issues for the Twenty-First Century*, Martinus Nijhoff, London, pp.325-337.

Minsky, R. (1998), *Psychoanalysis and Culture*, Polity Press, Cambridge.

Morss, J. (1995), *Growing Critical*, Routledge, London.

Mullender, A. and Morley, R. (eds) (1994), *Children Living with Domestic Violence*, Taylor and Francis, London.

O'Donovan, K. (1993), *Family Law Matters*, Pluto, London.

Parker, S. (1994), 'The Best Interests of the Child: Principles and Problems', *International Journal of Law and the Family*, vol 8, pp.26-41.

Piper, C. (1996), 'Divorce Reform and the Image of the Child, *Journal of Law and Society*, vol 23, pp.364-382.

Piper, C. (1997), 'Ascertaining the Wishes and Feelings of the Child', *Family Law*, pp.796-800.

Plummer, K. (1995), *Telling Sexual Stories*, Routledge, London.

Robinson, M. (1991), *Family Transformation Through Divorce and Remarriage*, Routledge, London.

Rodgers, B. and Pryor, J. (1998), *Divorce and Separation: The Outcomes for Children*, The Joseph Rowntree Foundation, York.

Rustin, M. (1991), *The Good Society and the Inner World*, Verso, London.

Sales, B., Manber, R. and Rohman, L. (1992), 'Social Science Research and Child Custody Decision Making', *Applied and Preventive Psychology*, vol 1, pp.23-40.

Sherwin, M. (1996), 'The Law in Relation to the Wishes and Feelings of the Child', in R. Davie, G. Upton and V. Varma (eds), *The Voice of the Child: A Handbook for Professionals*, Falmer Press, London.

Simpson, B., McCarthy, P. and Walker, J. (1995), *Being There: Fathers After Divorce*, Relate Centre for Family Studies, Newcastle upon Tyne.

Smart, C. (1989a), 'Power and the Politics of Child Custody', in C. Smart and S. Sevenhuijsen (eds), *Child Custody and the Politics of Gender*, Routledge, London, pp.1-26.

Smart, C. (1989b), *Feminism and the Power of Law*, Routledge, London.

Smart, C. (1992), 'The Woman of Legal Discourse', *Social and Legal Studies*,vol 1, pp.29-44.

Smart, C. (1997), 'Wishful Thinking and Harmful Tinkering? Sociological Reflections on Family Policy', *Journal of Social Policy*, vol 26, pp.301-321.

Smart, C. and Neale, B. (1998), 'Struggling to Listen to Children in Family Law and Family Research', Paper presented at the International Sociological Association, World Congress of Sociology, Montreal, July 1998.

Smart, C. and Sevenhuijsen, S. (eds) (1989), *Power and the Politics of Child Custody*, Routledge, London.

Smith, C. (1997), 'Children's Rights: Judicial Ambivalence and Social Resistance', *International Journal of Law, Policy and the Family*, vol 1, pp.103-139.

Stojanowska, W. (1993), 'The Protection of the Child Against the Negative Effects of Parental Conflict', in J. Eekelaar and P. Sarcevic (eds), *Parenthood in Modern Society: Legal and Social Issues for the Twenty-First Century*, Martinus Nijhoff, London.

Trinder, L. (1997), 'Competing Constructions of Childhood: Children's Rights and Children's Wishes in Divorce', *Journal of Social Welfare and Family Law*, vol 19, pp. 291-305.

Walker, J. (1991), 'From Rights to Responsibilities for Parents: Old Dilemmas, New Solutions', *Family and Conciliation Courts Review*, vol 29, pp.361-374.

Walker, J. (1997), 'Research findings on divorced fathers: an edited report of a talk by Professor Janet Walker on 25 February 1997 at the National Council for Family Proceedings AGM', National Council For Family Proceedings Newsletter, Summer 1997, p.5.

PART II
CHILDREN AND PARENTS

2 In Whose Best Interests? Theorising Family Life Following Parental Separation or Divorce

BREN NEALE AND CAROL SMART

Introduction

> Governments are always in danger of presuming a standard model of family life for which they can legislate, by making the assumption that most families do in fact operate in particular ways. In reality it is very difficult to detect a standard model, in either a descriptive sense (what people do) or a normative sense (what they ought to do) (Finch, 1997).

Taking Janet Finch's observation as our starting point, this chapter is concerned with different ways of conceptualising post divorce family life in legal discourse and how these conceptualisations relate to the complex realities of living in such families.[1] One of the major challenges facing family law in formulating its policies in this area is that of dealing with the diversity and fluidity of family structures and the rapidity with which families change over time. As Finch (1997) observes, change, fluidity and diversity are an integral part of our kinship system and thus have a long history, yet these features have become intensified and increasingly transparent under the conditions of late modernity.

Historically, the challenge facing legislators has been that of fashioning divorce laws without undermining marriage as the institutional backbone of 'the family' and of society. In a climate where there have been successive moral panics about the alleged demise of 'traditional' family values, attempts by progressive family legislators to accommodate family change have been tempered by more conservative drives to recapture an idealised version of family', where time stands still and traditional values are re-vitalised (Smart, 1997). How these changes are to be codified in the law is therefore a highly contested issue.

In exploring these themes of change and diversity we examine two ideological models of post divorce family life: lone/reconstituted families and co-parenting/biological families (as well as looking briefly at an earlier 'marriage-for-life' model) which have, in turn, underpinned the operation of family law. We explore the rationales for these models in the ethics of justice and rights and in the scientific discourse of child welfare, and we examine them in the light of empirical evidence of interviews with parents, gathered between 1994 and 1996 as part of an ESRC funded study of post divorce family life (reported in full in Smart and Neale, 1999). We also draw on interviews with solicitors, which explore how the principles of the Children Act 1989 are being put into practice. We conclude by proposing an alternative way of conceptualising post divorce family life that is based upon an ethic of care, and we argue for the importation of this perspective into family law.

The Lone/Reconstituted Family

Over the past twenty five years there has been a significant shift in the way the post-divorce family is conceptualised within legal and political discourse. The model of the lone/reconstituted family, with its roots in the institution of marriage/remarriage, the bounded household unit and the clear gendering of parenthood, has gradually given way to the new co-parenting/biological family, with its roots in the status of biological parenthood, cross-household parenting and the blurring of gender roles. It is worth considering how these two models are constituted and why things have changed.

During the 1970s, in the wake of the Divorce Reform Act 1969, it was presumed that, after divorce, the nuclear family would be broken and, where possible, reconstituted through the remarriage of the parents (Thery, 1989). Arising out of the strongly gendered practices of parental care and economic support within conventional marriages, a father would become disengaged from the mother/child unit under a 'clean break' arrangement and both parents would (ideally) seek to form second families, the father taking on new bread-winning responsibilities relatively unencumbered by his past commitments, leaving the mother with the potential to remarry, thus securing a step father for the children

(Smart, 1984; Smart and Sevenhuijsen, 1989). Parental authority was regulated between the parents as a matter of course at the point of divorce, with sole (legal and physical) custody usually granted to the mother (as the primary carer) and reasonable access, along with negotiable financial responsibilities, to the father. The father's financial responsibilities to his first family were not always legally enforced (as they now are under the Child Support Act), but were often allowed to devolve to the state, so enabling him to remarry and support his second family (Maclean, 1994). Indeed, at this time, over half of all biological fathers drifted out of their children's lives within two years of divorce and, in the process, ceased to provide any financial support for them (Eekelaar and Clive, 1977; Mitchell, 1985). Divorce, then, was a personal step that separated the old life from the new; the original family was effectively disbanded as parents opted for a clean break and entered a tacit agreement not to interfere in each other's lives.

This model of post divorce family life was driven by a rights-based discourse that was bound up with the preservation of marriage (as an institutionalised set of rights and obligations between spouses), along with the bounded household and gendered division of labour which traditionally supported it. This discourse of rights has a long history in family law. Under an earlier model of the family (the marriage-for-life model, through which marriages could hardly be broken, let alone replaced) the discourse of rights had been articulated in terms of 'father-right' - the vesting of authority over children in the father alone. If mothers left their husbands they automatically lost their children, a device which was seen as a safeguard to preserve the institution of marriage (Smart, 1989).

As father-right lost its potency as a means of determining custody, the discourse of rights was reformulated in terms of matrimonial fault. These faults (adultery and other sexual misdemeanours, cruelty and/or desertion) had to be legally proven before divorce could be granted, and a distinction then drawn between the 'innocent' and 'guilty' spouses, by awarding the children to the 'innocent' one. Under this regime, divorce did not imply remarriage, even for the 'innocent' spouse, since it was stigmatised (Thery, 1989). The original family was diminished in size through the exclusion of the 'guilty' spouse, but retained as an entity.

The lone/reconstituted family, which eventually replaced the ethos of marriage-for-life, was a pragmatic response to the rapidly growing numbers of individuals who were leaving their marriages without divorcing and forming *de facto* non-marital unions. This model was concerned less with preserving individual marriages than with preserving the institution of marriage itself. Indeed, one of the driving forces for the promotion of 'no fault' divorce leading up to the passing of the Divorce Reform Act 1969 was the view that the increasing numbers of individuals who had separated from their spouses should be able to regularise their legal status and be freed to 'retie the knot', so that they would not be forced to live 'in sin' outside the honourable estate of matrimony and, in the process, stigmatise their existing children and produce new illegitimate ones. If divorce was less stigmatised, however, it still meant a 'broken' family and implied the automatic regulation of the legal status of the parents through the award of custody to one parent alone. A strong marriage/divorce law thus continued to create a clear division between what were regarded as legitimate (marital) relationships (both spousal and parent/child) and illegitimate (non-marital) relationships.[2] The unbreakable marriage was replaced by serial monogamy, so that unsuccessful marriages (and families) could simply be replaced by successful ones (Smart, 1984). In this way, the institutional basis for family life, along with the moral values that defined marriage and married parenthood as an essential part of the 'good' life, remained intact (Finch and Morgan, 1991).

The professional discourse of child welfare also fed into this model of the lone/reconstituted family. Under the Divorce Reform Act 1969, custody could no longer be decided on the basis of the rights and wrongs of the marriage, leaving welfare considerations as the prime determinants. The 'tender years' doctrine, which had constructed mothers as vital to their children and long supported their claims against the power of father-right, was reformulated in terms of the child's emotional needs for continuity of care with their primary carer (usually, but not inevitably, their mothers) and the stability of one home in a conflict free environment (Goldstein *et al*, 1979). The child's interests were to be served by having one home, one set of bounded family relationships and a primary caring parent who could be entrusted to act in the children's best interests (Goldstein *et al*, 1979). This construction of the child's needs therefore supported the model of the lone/reconstituted family (Goode, 1965; Brophy, 1989; Thery, 1989).

The Co-parenting, Biological Family

Since the early 1980s the model of the lone/reconstituted family has gradually been replaced by that of a co-parenting/biological family. The original family is no longer to be broken under the 'clean break' philosophy, nor is it to be replaced by a reconstituted family (although new partners, whether marital or non-marital, might attach themselves to the original unit). Mothers (or fathers) are no longer to have exclusive custodial rights of authority over a child; since the Children Act 1989 parental rights (now known as parental responsibility) are automatically retained by both parents rather than being awarded to one of them alone. The potential to care for a child without the other parent, even if this is bound up with a new marriage or partnership, has a diminished value under this new ideology and, barring exceptional circumstances, can no longer be legally sanctioned. If the family can't remain intact and under one roof (still, of course the preferred option) then, as Day Sclater and Piper argue in the Introduction to this book, it must re-invent itself as a 'bi-nuclear' family spread across two households. Divorce has thus been recast as a 'stage' (albeit a painful one) in the newly extended life course of the indelible nuclear family. As one of the solicitors in our study commented:

> I think it's important to get across to people that, OK, there's been a marital or relationship breakdown, and that will inevitably change things substantially, but they will still continue as a family. ... It's a way of working towards evolving a family in a different form. [Female solicitor, SFLA member, mediator trained]

This new model dovetails with a welfare discourse that has been radically reformulated. Children are no longer said to need one stable home, one primary carer and the restabilising influence of the stepfamily. What they are now said to need is two biological parents and the restabilising influence of the non-residential father (Wallerstein and Kelly, 1980; Richards, 1982; Cockett and Tripp, 1994). One notable feature of this reformulated welfare discourse is that the child's needs are now defined in terms of what they are lacking: the lack of proper fathering and the limitations of mothering, which has culminated in a link between the 'child of divorce' and the pervasive but largely undefined notion of harm (Lord Chancellor's Department, 1993; Dennis and Erdos, 1993; Piper, 1996; Kaganas, this volume).[3] The problems of step parenting and the greater fragility of second marriages have lent force to these arguments

(Burgoyne and Clark, 1984; Cockett and Tripp, 1994). The welfare discourse has thus fed into the new model of family life, as well as perpetuating the moral panic about the demise of 'traditional' family values.

The assumption that children are 'damaged' by divorce is accompanied by another assumption - that this damage can be mitigated if particular forms of parenting and therapeutic interventions are put in place. Parents are to ameliorate the worst effects of their actions by prioritising their children's welfare, playing a joint part in their children's day to day care and developing a co-operative and unselfish sharing of parental authority. Agreements to do this are to become a necessary part of obtaining a divorce. If parents are incapable of completing this task, then a growing number of self-help manuals and professional welfare services are available to guide them, including mediation services which, with a directive as well as supportive function, aim to resolve disputes in a way that supports the new ethos (Piper, 1993; Smart, 1997).[4] Through a radical set of legislative changes this new family has been sanctioned, promoted and, more problematically for parents and children alike, enforced within the family justice system (Smart and Neale, 1997).

While, ostensibly, the new model of family life is driven by the welfare discourse alone, it is clear that less altruistic considerations also come into play. These include the treasury-led assumption that if biological fathers continue to see their children then they will carry on paying for them. Significantly, too, the new model is underpinned by a fresh articulation of the rights of fathers who argue that, since they are just as capable as mothers of caring for their children, they should be granted equal legal rights to them. Again, this shift in thinking was clearly articulated by those solicitors in our study who supported the new ethos:

> You can now say to your client, whether it's mum or dad, they both have equal rights. [Female, SFLA member, mediator trained]

> The most important change [following the Children Act] is being able to say to a client, 'you are not being given custody as a prize'. To me, it has shifted away from this 'I am the mother, I have custody, you are a second class citizen as a father'. I think it has created a better balance. [Male, SFLA member]

It is important to recognise that what is transformed under the new model is how fatherhood is constituted within legal and policy discourse. It seems that where mothers, as the day to day carers, were once constructed as vital to their children, it is fathers, as the restabilisers and potential carers, who are now constructed as essential, at least following divorce. That fathers might want a more direct involvement in day to day care is a relatively new phenomenon, deserving of explanation. According to Beck (1992), it is linked to wider social changes under which the traditional gendering of parental care and financial support is breaking down. The simple *quid pro quo* - that women have the children, while men have the money - no longer operates (Beck, 1992). To date, there is little evidence that this is occurring in practice, particularly at the crucial point of entry into parenthood and prior to divorce (Burghes *et al*, 1997). Even so, there has been an important shift in thinking around gender roles which, in itself, is encouraging fathers to feel disadvantaged at the point of divorce.

The changed attitude can also be understood in terms of the value that is increasingly placed upon emotional fulfilment within family relationships. If marriage and, perhaps more to the point, remarriage can no longer be relied upon to provide this, then the parent/child relationship may increasingly become the focus of such fulfilment. This, in turn, is linked to the rise in a romanticised vision of children as priceless emotional assets which, in the interests of parental equality, are best divided equally than awarded to one parent alone (Beck, 1992). Where mothers were once seen to be the holders of onerous responsibilities, requiring sustained emotional commitment, hard physical work and a range of socio-economic sacrifices (and deserving, therefore, of custodial status and state support), they are now seen to be in possession of valuable commodities, and any unwillingness to share them seen as discriminatory against fathers.

On this reading, women's previous claims to their children on the basis of their caring abilities are now seen as selfish. The 'situational' power of the residential parent is fully recognised and taken into account in family law, but where it was once endorsed, it is now problematised because it is seen to involve gender inequality (Smart and Neale, 1999). This new articulation of fathers' rights may also have been sharpened by changes under the Children Act, which mean that fathers can no longer exercise parental authority for their children except when they are caring for them. Parental care (caring *for*) and parental authority (parental rights, decision-making power and the more generalised caring *about*) have been conflated so that responsibilities 'run with the child'. Financial inducements for fathers to undertake parental care have also been introduced through the Child Support Act, while fathers who retain the full time care of their children avoid having to make child support payments. The new model, then, is bound up with considerations of the relative merits of motherhood and fatherhood and a desire to blur the conventional boundaries between them.

Moreover the co-parenting ethos is not just for formerly married fathers. Other legislative changes have occurred which encourage all biological fathers, regardless of their marital or former marital status, to adopt the new ethos. This process of legitimising non-marital parenthood began with the abolition of the labelling of children as illegitimate (and their parents as morally reprehensible) under the Family Law Reform Acts (of 1969 and 1987). The process will continue with the granting of the status of parental responsibility to biological fathers who jointly register the child's birth, regardless of what (if any) kind of commitment they might have to their children's care (LCD, 1998a; 1998b). This will put some unmarried fathers on an equal legal par with married fathers and mothers and will compensate them for the enforcement (under the Child Support Act 1991) of their financial obligations to their children. Again, there are clear rights-based claims driving these legislative changes, which are not necessarily related to the actual care of children.

This new model of family life, then, goes beyond the promotion of co-parenting to the celebration and veneration of biological kin ties. It has entailed a fundamental refashioning of the legal status of biological parenthood. As a result, the new family transcends not only household boundaries but also the institution of marriage itself. Since parenthood is increasingly practised outside and beyond marriage, the significance of marriage as an institution for the regulation of parenthood has gradually diminished, along with the significance of the gendered division of labour that supported traditional marriages. What marriage now endorses is a personal commitment between the partners, rather than a wider set of socio-economic practices and relationships which are usually associated with it (cf. Thery's concept of 'demarriage': Thery, 1993; Maclean and Eekelaar, 1997). In uncoupling the legal status of parenthood from the legal status of marriage, parenthood begins to supersede marriage as the bedrock of the family and as the central mechanism for the legal regulation of family life. If marriage is no longer for life, then parenthood (at least, that of a biological variety) is (Dewar, 1992).

This elevation of biological parenthood and its codification in the law has further implications for the articulation of fathers' rights. If fathers can no longer secure their rights to their children through marriage, they can now be secured through indelible, biological parenthood instead. A father's claims can be rooted in the certainty of paternity (rather than on the basis of a proven commitment to the children). On this reading, the new biological post divorce family becomes an essentialist and naturalistic entity (Morgan, 1991), which in itself is beginning to acquire all the trappings of institutional status.[5] In what looks like a process of patriarchal reconstruction (Smart, 1989) the new model seems to be returning us to a reformulated version of 'father-right' at a time when this principle has only just been removed from the statute book.

One of the striking things about these legislative changes in family law over the past decade is that they represent a clear attempt to use the law to alter family values and practices. As we have illustrated elsewhere (Smart, 1997) the new ethos has been imported quite rapidly into legal practice. Although there is no simple causal relationships between these legal prescriptions and social trends, the legal strategies adopted under the new ethos have included draconian enforcement measures (usually against mothers as the residential parents) as well as voluntary inducements and encouragement (usually for fathers). The logic seems to be that if fathers are forced to pay for their children under the child support legislation, then mothers must be forced to share parental care and authority. A father's direct involvement with his children, however, is still at his discretion. If he opts out, there are no legal sanctions against him, but if he opts in then he will, in all but exceptional cases, be supported, even to the extent of fulfilling his request to have a mother imprisoned. These measures seem highly inappropriate and are indicative of how a rights-based discourse continues to infiltrate the operation of the law. For this reason alone, this new model of family life needs to be scrutinised in relation to the practices and values of parents themselves.

Practising Post Divorce Family Life

This brings us to our empirical evidence on how family life following parental divorce or separation is being negotiated and practised in the wake of recent legislative changes. We conducted two rounds of in-depth, qualitative interviews with a sample of 60 parents (31 mothers, 29 fathers from 60 families), who had recently separated or divorced.[6] The parents came from a wide socio-economic constituency and their separations ranged from the privately ordered and non-conflictual through to the legally ordered and highly conflictual. A complex variety of family arrangements and practices were in evidence, which fell into three broad patterns: co-parenting, custodial parenting and solo parenting.

Co-parenting (practised in 10-12 families over the study period) is a pattern of shared parenting which entails a conscious balancing of parental care and parental authority. The parents negotiate a schedule for how the child's time is to be shared out across the two households (perhaps a shared week on a 3-4 or 2-5 day split, or alternate weeks at each house). They may also negotiate some shared activities, strategies for joint decision-making, and constraints on the parenting of new partners. Whatever the precise arrangements, the child not only has two parents, but (at least) two carers and two homes and the parents are fully engaged with each other over the upbringing of their children. In all but one case in our sample, this sharing of parenthood required a conscious blurring of the gendered patterns of care and economic support that had operated before the divorce or separation. The co-parenting model of family life promoted in family law thus has more than ideological significance: it is a lived reality for a minority of parents both within our sample and in the wider population (Macoby and Mnookin, 1992).

Custodial parenting (practised in 37-42 families over the study period) entails a clear imbalance in the way parental care and authority are allocated between the parents. It thus arises as a natural extension of the gendered practices of parenting/economic support operating prior to the separation. The residential parent (usually the mother) takes on substantially more of the responsibilities for day-to-day care than the non-residential parent, whose parenting is reconstituted as 'contact' and undertaken on a clearly delineated part-time basis. As a result of her caring responsibilities, the mother holds the balance of power in terms of decision-making; she has 'custodial' authority and she may opt to share this authority with a new partner. In effect, while a child sustains a relationship with two parents, he or she has one main carer and one main home, and the parents are much less likely to be engaged with each other over their children's upbringing.

Within this broad custodial pattern a subgroup of parents (between 8 and 15 in our sample) may operate as solo parents. As in a custodial arrangement, parental care and authority are vested in the residential parent (usually the mother) so that the children have one carer and one home. But they no longer necessarily retain their links with the other parent. The non-residential parent (usually the father) plays little or no part in the children's lives, so that the children have a distant or non-existent relationship with him. The father may no longer be able to achieve a clean financial break because of the activities of the Child Support Agency, but he is disengaged from his children as well as from his former partner. This pattern is most likely to arise where non-residential fathers drift out of their children's lives as they forge new commitments. But it is not simply a default pattern; it may also be the result of conscious choice on the part of one or both parents and /or the child, particularly where it is seen as a protective measure for the stability of the child or the child's primary carer.

Taken together these custodial and solo patterns of parenting indicate the resilience of the lone parent/reconstituted model of family life, at least in the sense of the persistence of the notion of a 'custodial' parent who alone exercises parental authority. If this model has been replaced by co-parenting in legal thinking, it has not been superseded in practice (and may well not be while parenting prior to separation remains gendered). However, the drift into solo parenting as non-residential fathers opt out of their children's lives may well be diminishing. Certainly, the parents in our study held on to the ideals of ongoing contact 'for the children's sake' although, in practice, this was contingent upon the nature of the relationships between family members.

These three patterns have been discussed and illustrated elsewhere (Neale and Smart, 1997; Smart and Neale, 1999) but we draw out some salient points here. Firstly, none of these patterns is more productive of consensus than the others. Solo parenting is not necessarily imposed on one parent by another, particularly where previous relationships have been tenuous, children are very young, or where reconstituted families are being formed. Co-parenting, on the other hand, may fuel conflicts, particularly where the pattern is the product, not of a shared ideology, but of legal, financial or physical coercion or unresolved tension over who is to be the custodial parent (Neale and Smart, 1997; see also Goldstein, 1991; Johnston *et al*, 1991; Saposnek, 1991).

Family law seems to assume that co-parenting will foster collaborative relationships but our evidence suggests that if there is a causal link at all, it operates only in the other direction; collaborative, caring relationships *may* support the development of co-parenting arrangements and help to sustain them over time. Thus we found no simple correlation between the organisational structure of post divorce family life and the nature of the relationships between family members. Secondly, these patterns of parenting are not static but change over time. Approximately half of our sample moved from one pattern of parenthood to another over the study period, with further changes occurring subsequently. Even where parents stayed within the same basic pattern, contact or residence arrangements might alter or new partners arrive or depart. This notion of change as a constant feature of family life is somewhat at variance with the rather static notions of family life assumed within family law.

Finally, the variety of patterns in evidence, which straddle the legal models of family life outlined above, indicates that one pattern is not necessarily superior to the others. They are all viable as a means of structuring post-divorce family life, albeit that each entails certain advantages and disadvantages for family members. Co-parenting for example, preserves a child's close ties but the lives of partners are bound up with each other in a way that may make the arrangement particularly demanding and fragile. Under solo parenting, these pros and cons are reversed, while a custodial pattern may represent a compromise. Parents do not necessarily aspire to an optimal structure for their family lives but may formulate 'good enough' solutions which fit their own particular circumstances. From this point of view, family life is likely to be characterised by a diversity of forms, making the legal struggle to impose one form alone a misguided aim.

The Ethics of Care and Justice

Moving beyond these structural considerations we also wanted to explore the moral codes which underpin these varied practices and to investigate how changes over time are negotiated. Some parents spoke of their family practices in terms of an ethic of care:

> Meg [first interview]: The other day, Dan [former spouse] said, 'we are a family' and we try very hard for the children to understand that although we aren't partners, we don't live together any more, we are still very much, to them, the family. I never though it would be possible for us to get along so well.
>
> Meg [second interview, 16 months later]: I think the very, very important thing is to respect each other and show commitment that you are - although you don't love one another - you care about the children you are bringing up together ... and that's what's moving out of our relationship now. ... I saw Dan on his own and me on my own and this constant hand in glove situation ...

> [but] he's decided on a long term relationship and the children now have to fit in around that ... He's no longer there for the children, that reliability has disappeared. He now knocks when he comes in, I receive letters that are left for me. It's to distance me. [Co-parent with custodial episodes]

Meg subsequently explained how she had, through careful negotiations, persuaded Dan to maintain his commitment to his children by retaining his house near the family home and joining the children there once a week. His reliability was reinstated but he had established firmer boundaries around his relationship with Meg in order to secure his new partnership. While Meg did not regain the sense of 'family' that she had previously valued, she remained on good terms with Dan.

While Dan modified his commitment to his first family over time, Leon moved in the other direction, from a custodial to a co-parenting arrangement. His children stayed with him on alternate nights, leaving him no time for life outside of the family:

> Leon: I [was] doing the usual stereotype father role, come in from work, play with them, watch TV ... play golf. [But] I made a conscious decision ... that I was going to see my children grow up. You have to think, 'well, how do I want it to be in five years time?' and then, 'well, what do I need to do to make sure it happens?' No one has a right to custody. You have to prove that you are a responsible parent. ... She was saying, 'dads don't need the custody, you can see them ... on a weekend. You're always working anyway.' ... She didn't want me around too much. I'd lost their respect and I had to win back the respect. Now her mum says, 'oh you're a good father to them.'
>
> I think it's water under the bridge why you got divorced and the financial side because you can't [co-parent] without considering each other's needs ... and never pull each other down ... [otherwise] nobody wins in the end. My mum said, 'think of the children all the time'. ... I came to terms with that and had to put myself on one side. I realised that there was no point in pushing anything through the courts. ... The only way was for me and Jill to sort it out together. ... Every little thing is give and take. [Co-parent, formerly non-custodial parent]

In these accounts, the parents value the day to day practices and responsibilities of bringing up children. The changes in arrangements are gradual and privately ordered, driven by ongoing, measured negotiations that are bound up with the shifting realities of parental care and other life circumstances. They are also concerned with *how* these practices are put into effect. They articulate the notions of caring, respect and trust in their families, which extend beyond parent/child relationships to the relations between the parents themselves. In these ways they work within an ethic of care rather than an ethic of justice. The ethic of care defines moral situations, neither in terms of right and wrong, nor by reference to universal standards of objectivity, but in terms of the interdependence and value of relationships, the avoidance of harm and the preservation of the dignity and worth of others (in this context, other family members) (Gilligan, 1982; Benhabib, 1992).

As a general philosophy, the ethic of care was articulated by the majority of parents in our study, but particularly by the mothers (29 mothers, as opposed to 11 fathers). But not all parents recognise it, let alone use it, at least not in the sense of showing concern for their former partners as well as their children. The dominant ethical framework articulated by the fathers in our study was one of justice, which was quickly invoked at times of conflict. These fathers spoke in terms of their status as fathers, their natural rights to their children, their right (as a universal principle) to equal treatment with mothers and other fathers, and in terms of the duties of mothers (and children) to respond to these rights.

> George: I can't go up and see him any time I want, it's got to be done through an appointment, so where does your parental rights come in? [Non-custodial parent]

Many fathers might do little more than grumble about their perceived loss of rights. They might try to negotiate, keep tensions within manageable levels and, like George, use the courts as a last resort. The ethic of justice could be held in check by the desire not to damage relations of care:

> Ron: I'm now having to fork out money to get something that's mine by birthright. ... [But] the solicitor helped me with this. The only rule of thumb [over arrangements] is that it has to be in my son's welfare. But that must also take into account the parents and that's why I've hesitated from bringing any kind of legal action into it. ... I feel as though ... I'm having to back off all the time in order for his welfare to be better looked after. [Unmarried non-custodial father]

A minority of fathers, however, were more assertive about their rights:

Anthony: I made her aware of the legal standpoint. I says, 'You have a duty as a caring parent' - which is a joke - 'to inform me of his schooling and his medical records.' I says, 'By statute.' And then I throw the law at her. [Non-custodial parent]

Gordon: You don't *make* parents. You *are* that child's parent. You have biological rights, far beyond any human laws. ... If it's going to take another four hearings to [settle the case] the judge ought to be prepared to put her in prison. ... [They are] supposed to prevent crime by punishing people who commit crime. ... I've nothing to lose by causing all kinds of mayhem, damage and fear and I simply think that if the courts don't help me ... . [Non-custodial parent, formerly no contact parent]

Gerry: I've become very powerful because I simply do not communicate ... I totally ignore her. She knows I've got total control, there's nothing she can do or say. ... I feel out of control and not able to make decisions unless I go through the legal process. I told her I'd pursue her through every court in the land, relentlessly, and that's what she doesn't like, because she knows I'll always be on her back. [Custodial parent, formerly non-custodial, leading to court ordered interim shared residence]

In these scenarios what drives changes in arrangements are struggles over parental authority rather than the negotiation of parental care. The changes are likely to involve coercion or be legally ordered and imposed rapidly on one parent by the other. These fathers worked with the assumption that relationships could be forced rather than nurtured, and they were particularly unwilling to negotiate. The very idea was demeaning to them, as if it negated their rights to act autonomously and without accountability. Instead, they made frequent use of the courts as a way of increasing their demands on the mothers or wearing down their resistance. A small minority also took the law into their own hands. Gordon for example, used a variety of forms of harassment to gain contact with his son, who lived with his mother and stepfather, and to then tell him of his 'real' parentage. Gerry removed his daughter from the mother (formerly a full time carer) on the grounds of neglect, and used coercive means to regain the family home.

From the perspective of an ethic of justice, these actions might appear understandable. The fathers saw themselves as up against the situational power of the residential mothers and the challenge was to overthrow this power in order to establish their 'rights' to their children. The very fact that they wanted to see their children and spend more time with them endeared them to a legal system which was working under a co-parenting/biological ethos, and their desperate actions, if not exactly condoned, could be explained in terms of their frustrations, and consequently treated sympathetically. But from the perspective of an ethic of care, these fathers' positions were less tenable and their actions damaging to relations of care for their children.

Some mothers in our study had been on the receiving end of behaviour that was driven by such assertions of rights. The fathers in these cases countered the situational power of the mothers by wielding forms of debilitative power over them, acting and interacting in ways that were demeaning or undermining of the mothers and which mothers experienced as an effacement of their sense of self (Smart and Neale, 1999).

> Diane: When Paul first went I felt - and all the professionals, everybody - thought that the best thing for children is to have a good relationship with the absent parent and I was all for that at the beginning. Whatever animosity I felt towards him, I thought, 'well, he'll always be their father'. But having seen what he's like, and having seen the things he does and says to them. ... The week he left he said to Bobby, 'mummy's trying to steal all my money so I won't have enough money to get a place and you won't be able to come and see me'. And I thought, 'how can he tell his own children that?' ... It was impossible to have a reasonable conversation with him, he just wouldn't be reasonable. [Solo parent - formerly custodial]

What Diane had experienced was not a one-off incident but a sustained personal vendetta against her over many months which took the form of oppressive actions (e.g. abusive letters and phone calls), a refusal to negotiate or communicate over arrangements or child care, and the manipulation of the children. This subtle oppression was damaging her mental health and disturbing the children. In her move towards solo parenting she was supported by her solicitor, who curtailed the father's contact, and by the court which, having taken the children's views into account, advised the father to postpone his contact application.

Diane's case was heard just after the implementation of the Children Act; had it occurred a year or two later, Diane might not have found the courts so sympathetic to her case. Indeed she might have been labelled 'implacably hostile', or seen as a manipulator who had induced 'parental alienation syndrome' in her two young children (Maidment, 1998). This was the experience of Kate who, in 1994, also requested a legal cessation of contact for her pre school age child:

> Kate: There's a very strong movement for father's rights, which, I used to think, 'great'. But I think they end up abusing it because it's not talking about a father's responsibility and whether this person is healthy for this particular child. ...
>
> He was getting more and more aggressive and paranoid, kicking doors down in front of James and making him watch. ... So I couldn't have gone on. And yet, at the same time, it almost is still going on. He accosts me in the street, trips me up and kicks me. He takes every opportunity to abuse me verbally in front of James, saying, 'mummy doesn't love you, she's bad'. I'm being constantly undermined. It's a nightmare. [Co-parent with custodial episodes]

Kate endured sustained physical violence as well as the subtly corrosive form of debilitative power that Diane had been subjected to. She felt this had almost obliterated her sense of self and her ability to parent, as well as being highly damaging for her child. But, since the court refused to support her, the only way she could stop the violence was to acquiesce and return to a co-parenting arrangement which gave the father daily contact with her and her son.

These mothers placed value on relations of care within their families but were unable to establish or sustain such relations following separation because their former partners acted in ways that were antithetical to this ethos. Diane's move to solo parenting enabled her to re-establish relations of care with her children. Kate was less fortunate. Family law recognises and takes situational power into account in regulating family life; it is on this basis that it perceives mothers to be advantaged and fathers to be disadvantaged so that more 'sharing' becomes the answer. However, the wielding of these other forms of power (usually, but not inevitably, by fathers), which can destroy relations of care in families, is not properly recognised in the regulation of family life.

We have argued elsewhere (Smart and Neale, 1999) for the importation of an ethic of care into legal practice and policy because it has the potential to transcend the impasse between the competing claims of the discourses of rights and welfare. Care is as much about justice (the right thing to do) as are rights. It also resonates with a welfare approach in that it seeks to minimise harm and sustain positive relationships. Our evidence suggests that an ethic of care is of fundamental importance to many parents, and to their children (Neale *et al*, 1998), and should not be glossed over in family law.

Negotiated Family Practices and Relationships

> [T]he aim of policies should be to facilitate flexibility in family life, rather than shape it into a particular form.... to ensure that people have maximum opportunity to work out their own relationships as they wish to suit the circumstances of their own lives. It is not the proper role of governments to presume that certain outcomes would be more desirable than others (Finch, 1997, p.130).

This quotation from Janet Finch returns us to the main theme of this chapter. Along with Sevenhuijsen (1998), Finch points to the dangers of positing ideal models of the family as the basis for developing policy, particularly where these models are too rigid to accommodate the diversity and fluidity of family life. The models outlined earlier in this chapter are precisely of this sort. They privilege the static, structural features of family life: institutional status (legal marriage or legal parenthood), organisational structure (bounded nuclear household or cross household); and the positional status of family members (articulated through the discourse of rights, which weighs up the relative merits of mothers and fathers, and the discourse of welfare which dictates that only the child counts). What these models lack, and what our empirical evidence privileges, are the negotiated practices and relationships of family life.

The key emphasis on practices, with how parenthood is practised on a day-to-day basis, grounds our thinking in the actualities of family life. It is the *doing* of family life which assumes significance (Morgan, 1996), rather than who is doing what, and within what organisational or institutional framework. By focusing on practices rather than structures, a wide variety of family forms can assume equal validity, including those based on non-biological parenthood and same sex relationships. A focus on practices requires us to attend to the social aspects of parenthood, with how parenting is put into effect, and to pay rather less attention to the bare bones of its biological origins. It brings the activity of caring *for* children into clear focus (rather than collapsing this activity into the wider category of caring *about* them). In all these ways it is possible to transcend the model of the biological family which is the current concern of the law.

The second key concept, that of relationships, is bound up with how family life is practised, in particular with the notions of caring, moral responsibility, interdependency, respect, trust and commitment. Working within a normative framework, it becomes possible to explore the patterns of reciprocal care which operate in families and the moral codes and normative guidelines which are constructed as guides to practice (Finch, 1989, Finch and Mason, 1990; Clark, 1991). Whether a child is being co-parented or solo parented, for example, becomes less of an issue than how caring operates within these patterns. The positional status of family members also assumes less importance; rather than prioritising individual 'worth', or setting the needs/rights of family members in opposition to each other, each family member can be viewed as part of a nexus of caring relationships. Importance might then be attached to the means of preserving relations of care (which is not the same as preserving biological kin ties) and, in the process, to identifying what might be destructive of such relations.

To date, such considerations have been accorded little importance in relation to post-divorce family life simply because divorce has been perceived almost entirely within a social problems framework, and interpreted in dysfunctional terms as decline, disorder and a descent into uncaringness and immorality. From our perspective, however, divorce and separation can properly be recognised as an entry into a new moral order where ethics are not abandoned but are painstakingly reworked in a variety of ways (Smart, 1991).

The third key concept, that of negotiation, combined with that of practices, acknowledges the dynamics of family life. Negotiation implies that family practices and relationships are not fixed or taken for granted, they are accorded not as of right, but have to be worked at, discussed and re-negotiated over time. This perspective, then, accommodates fluidity and change, not only at discrete turning points such as the point of separation or divorce but as a gradual and ongoing process. In Giddens' terms, intimate relationships have a contingent quality which, of necessity, requires us to think beyond the 'for life' model of the romantic love complex (for partners) and the 'for life' model of genetic ties (for parenthood) (Giddens, 1992).

We have tried to show some of the limitations of the ideological models that underpin the operation of family law and of the discourses that feed into them. A greater recognition of the actualities of practices, relationships and negotiations within legal policy might go some way to countering these limitations. But we are not suggesting that these qualitative perspectives in themselves should assume the status of a legal model. On the contrary, as Finch (1997) reminds us, it would be inappropriate for family policy to start laying down the law to people about how to relate to each other. Instead, these perspectives might allow for a more nuanced understanding of parental disputes and the reasons parents have for wishing to practice their family lives in particular ways or to change things. They might also allow greater flexibility in the search for legal solutions to these disputes. Perhaps, in the process, they might lead to the (re)discovery of different way of valuing family life beyond divorce or separation.

Notes

1. The ideas in this chapter are explored more fully in Smart and Neale (1999).
2. As Brinton once famously observed, 'bastardy and marriage in this world are quite complementary - you cannot have the one without the other' (cited in Maclean and Eekelaar, 1997). We are rapidly moving to a state where both will have diminished legal and social significance.
3. Children themselves might well refute this negative view of their lives (Neale *et al*, 1998). In fact, the research evidence for what children need following divorce appears to have been heavily skewed in order to reach this negative construction of their needs (Neale and Smart, 1998).
4. The Act has stopped short of making mediation compulsory, since this goes against the philosophy of the service, but it has introduced a number of measures to induce parents to use it, including withholding legal aid unless parents can give good reason why mediation is unworkable for them.
5. This can be seen, for example, in the proposals for institutionalising the entry into parenthood through the introduction of new parenting contracts, the signing of which will be bound up and socially sanctioned with new civil ceremonies (LCD 1998a, 1998b).
6. The parents were from the Yorkshire region, had one or more children under the age of 16, and were recruited into the study via their solicitors, support groups or adverts in works' magazines. The divorces all come under the jurisdiction of the Children Act, but some parents had separated in the late 1980s shortly before the implementation of the Act in 1991. The study period ran from the time of separation (ranging from the late 1980s to the early 1990s) through to the second round of interviews conducted in 1995-6. Our work was supported by the ESRC, award number R002345.

References

Beck, U. (1992), *Risk Society: Towards a New Modernity*, Sage, London.

Benhabib, S. (1992), *Situating the Self*, Polity Press, Cambridge.

Brophy, J. (1989), 'Custody Law, Child Care and Inequality in Britain', in C. Smart and S. Sevenhuijsen (eds), *Child Custody and the Politics of Gender*, Routledge, London, pp.217-242.

Burghes, L., Clarke, L. and Cronin, N. (1997), *Fathers and Fatherhood in Britain*, Occasional Paper No. 23, Family Policy Studies Centre, London.

Burgoyne, J. and Clark, D. (1984), *Making a Go of It: A Study of Stepfamilies in Sheffield*, Routledge & Kegan Paul, London.

Clark, D. (ed) (1991), *Marriage, Domestic Life and Social Change*, Routledge, London.

Cockett, M. and Tripp, J. (1994), *The Exeter Family Study: Family Breakdown and its Impact on Children*, Exeter University Press, Exeter.

Dennis, N. and Erdos, G. (1992), *Families without Fatherhood*, Institute of Economic Affairs, London.

Dewar, J. (1992), *Law and the Family*, 2nd ed, Butterworths, London.

Eekelaar J. and Clive, E. (1977), *Custody after Divorce*, Centre for Socio-Legal Studies, Oxford.

Finch, J. (1989) *Family Obligations and Social Change*, Polity Press, Cambridge.

Finch, J. and Mason, J. (1990), 'Divorce, Re-marriage and Family Obligations', *Sociological Review*, vol 38, pp.219-246.

Finch, J. and Mason, J. (1993), *Negotiating Family Responsibilities*, Routledge, London.

Finch, J. and Morgan, D. (1991), 'Marriage in the 1980s: A New Sense of Realism?', in D. Clark (ed) *Marriage, Domestic Life and Social Change*, Routledge, London, pp.55-80.

Finch, J. (1997), *The State and the Family*, Lecture to inaugurate the Institute of International Social Sciences, University of Edinburgh, 30 October 1996, Institute of International Social Sciences, Edinburgh.

Giddens, A. (1992), *The Transformation of Intimacy*, Polity Press, Cambridge.

Gilligan, C. (1982), *In a Different Voice*, Harvard University Press, Cambridge, MA.

Goldstein, J. (1991) 'In Whose Best Interest?', in J. Folberg (ed) *Joint Custody and Shared Parenting*, 2nd ed, Guilford Press, London, pp.16-25.

Goldstein, J., Freud, A. and Solnit, A. (1979), *Beyond the Best Interests of the Child*, 2nd ed, Free Press, New York.

Goode, W. (1965), *Women in Divorce*, Free Press, New York.

Johnston, J., Kline, M. and Tschann, J. (1991), 'Ongoing Post Divorce Conflict in Familes Contesting Custody', in J. Folberg (ed), *Joint Custody and Shared Parenting*, 2nd ed, Guilford Press, London, pp.177-205.

LCD (Lord Chancellor's Department) (1993), *Looking to the Future: Mediation and the Ground for Divorce*, Cm 2424, HMSO, London.

LCD (Lord Chancellor's Department) (1998a), *Court Procedures for the Determination of Paternity and the Law on Parental Responsibility for Unmarried Fathers*, Consultation Paper, Lord Chancellor's Department, London.

LCD (Lord Chancellor's Department) (1998b), *Parental Responsibility to be Conferred on Unmarried Fathers*, Press Release 201, 2 July, Lord Chancellor's Department, London.

Macoby, E. and Mnookin, R. (1992), *Dividing the Child: Social and Legal Dilemmas of Custody*, Harvard University Press, Cambridge MA.

Maclean, M. (1994), 'The Making of the Child Support Act of 1991: Policy Making at the

Intersection of Law and Social Policy', *Journal of Law and Society*, vol 21, pp.505-519.

Maclean, M. and Eekelaar, J. (1997), *The Parental Obligation*, Hart Publishing, Oxford.

Maidment, S. (1998), 'Parental Alienation Syndrome - A Judicial Response?', *Family Law*, pp.264-266.

Mitchell A. (1985), *Children in the Middle - Living with Divorce*, Tavistock, London.

Morgan, D. (1991), 'Ideologies of Marriage and Family Life', in D. Clark (ed), *Marriage, Domestic Life and Social Change*, Routledge, London, pp.114-138.

Morgan, D. (1996), *Family Connections*, Polity Press, Cambridge.

Neale, B. and Smart, C. (1997) 'Experiments with Parenthood?', *Sociology*, vol 31, pp.201-219.

Neale, B. and Smart, C. (1998) *Agents or Dependants? Struggling to Listen to Children in Family Law and Family Research*, Working Paper no. 3, Centre for Research on Family, Kinship and Childhood, University of Leeds.

Neale, B., Wade, A. and Smart, C (1998), *'I Just Get On With It': Children's Experiences of Family Life Following Parental Separation or Divorce*, Working Paper no.1, Centre for Research on Family, Kinship and Childhood, University of Leeds.

Piper, C. (1993), *The Responsible Parent*, Harvester Wheatsheaf, Hemel Hempstead.

Piper, C. (1996), 'Divorce Reform and the Image of the Child', *Journal of Law and Society*, vol 23, pp.364-382.

Richards, M. (1982), 'Post-Divorce Arrangements for Children: A Psychological Perspective', *Journal of Social Welfare Law*, vol 69, pp.133-151.

Saposnek, D. (1991), 'A Guide to Decision Making About Joint Custody: The Needs of Children of Divorce', in, J. Folberg (ed), *Joint Custody and Shared Parenting*, 2nd ed, Guilford Press, London, pp.29-40.

Sevenhuijsen, S. (1998), *Citizenship and the Ethics of Care*, Routledge, London.

Smart, C. (1984), *The Ties that Bind*, Routledge, London.

Smart, C. (1989), 'Power and the Politics of Child Custody', in C. Smart and S. Sevenhuijsen (eds), *Child Custody and the Politics of Gender*, Routledge, London, pp.1-26.

Smart, C. (1991), 'The Legal and Moral Ordering of Child Custody', *Journal of Law and Society*, vol 18, pp. 485-500.

Smart, C. (1997), 'Wishful Thinking and Harmful Tinkering: Sociological Reflections on Family Policy', *Journal of Social Policy*, vol 26, pp.1-21.

Smart, C. and Neale, B. (1997), 'Arguments against Virtue: Must Contact be Enforced?', *Family Law*, pp.332-336.

Smart. C. and Neale, B. (1999), *Family Fragments?*, Polity Press, Cambridge.

Smart, C. and Sevenhuijsen, S. (eds) (1989), *Child Custody and the Politics of Gender*, Routledge, London.

Thery, I. (1989), 'The "Interests of the Child" and the Regulation of the Post Divorce Family', in C. Smart and S. Sevenhuijsen (eds), *Child Custody and the Politics of Gender*, Routledge, London, pp.78-99.

Thery, I. (1993), *Le Demarriage*, Editions Odile Jacob, Paris.

Wallerstein, J. and Kelly, J. (1980), *Surviving the Breakup*, Basic Books, New York.

3 Children and Divorce: A Private Affair?

JEREMY ROCHE

Introduction

In this chapter I explore the ways in which the law positions children caught up in divorce. I examine the competing images associated with children and divorce and the uneasy relationship between the languages of the modern children's rights movement and the contemporary 'privatised' divorce agenda. Within this agenda, shaped by adult concerns to protect children, the child is viewed as the victim of relationship breakdown and, whatever else happens, such children must not be drawn any further into the legal divorce process than is necessary or have the responsibility of making choices thrust upon them.

In what follows I review some of the tensions within the literature on children's rights in order to set a context for the discussion of children and divorce. On divorce the child's welfare is central to the decision-making of courts and professionals and an 'adult' consensus has emerged around the need to keep children out - albeit for their own good. Those subscribing to this consensus include lawyers, court welfare officers and mediators as well as academic commentators. However there are some discordant voices. These range from the deliberations of the Scottish Law Commission which has promoted the idea of the child being possessed of rights even in the privacy of the home, to the ability of the child under the Children Act 1989 to initiate legal proceedings, to emerging demands that children (especially the older child) be seen as citizens entitled to participate in the deliberations that will shape their lives. And all of these have thrown up resistances, for example, the courts' response to children applying for leave to apply for a section 8 order under the Children Act 1989. I conclude by considering the tensions between children's rights and the democratisation of family life on the one hand (Beck,1997) and, on the other, the practices of excluding children, as a class, from certain kinds of conversations.

Children's Rights

There is a compendious volume of literature on the subject of children's rights. Archard (1993) provides a useful review of this literature drawing together much of the writing under two headings: 'liberationist' and 'caretaking'[1] (see also Freeman,1983). The 'caretaking' thesis (which ultimately belongs within a welfare discourse) argues that children 'should not be free to make autonomous decisions' (Archard, 1993, p.52). This denial of the right to self determination is justified on the basis that children lack the requisite rationality to be able to make intelligent decisions and because they are emotionally immature. And, as Archard points out, the caretaker thesis 'not only argues that caretakers can choose for their children. It suggests how they should choose' (1993, p.53). While there are different wordings used, it is clear that 'welfarism' emphasises the point of view of adults concerned with the child's welfare and protection and the need to protect them, even from themselves. Thus the core problem with welfare is its objectification of the child: the potential for 'welfarism' eroding rights is ever present. The Pindown affair provides a powerful example of this:

> Pindown, in our view involved elements of isolation, humiliation and confrontation to varying degrees. We have no doubt that children were humiliated in many ways. In addition during confrontational 'meetings' numerous children were harangued and referred to in grossly abusive terms. Pindown was intrinsically unethical, unprofessional and unacceptable (Levy and Kahan, 1991, p.127).

This practice, which included the denial of access to education and contact with the family, lasted almost six years: at the end, some of those involved could still not see why the practice was so controversial. The failure to properly address the liberty rights of children is part of the explanation. Welfarism, because entailing action for the good of 'others', permits action which otherwise could not be taken. Those professionals involved in Pindown believed that they were acting for the best - children would benefit from this regime of sanctions and rewards. Such objectification of children can only be sustained in the absence of the language of children's rights, if you do not have to listen to what children have to say about their situation or respond to their self-defined interests.

The liberationist position is that adult rights should be extended to children of all ages (Holt, 1975). Those writing from within the liberationist position argue that children lose out as a result of the firm separation of child from adult (Farson, 1974) and that the justifications for the 'dividing line' between adulthood and childhood do not stand up to scrutiny. The 'remedy' is to abolish all legal distinction between child and adult with children exercising rights as and when they are in a position practically to do so. And in so doing, the many excesses which characterise adult/child relations, for example abuse, would be avoided. In other words children's best protection is to give them the same rights as all citizens, though the argument for doing so is not based on a protectionist position.

Archard observes that the dispute between the child liberationists and caretakers boils down to two linked issues: the arbitrariness of the distinction between adulthood and childhood and the presumption of children as incompetent. He writes (1993, p.58):

> The child liberationist is correct to argue that a distribution of rights on the basis of age *alone* would be unfair. It would be morally arbitrary and unjust to deny children rights merely because they were younger than adults. It would be as arbitrary and wrong as denying rights to humans who were shorter than average, had fewer hairs or a lower pitch voice than others ... the denial of rights to children is not based solely on age. It is done on the basis of an alleged correlation between age and some relevant competence.

So, Purdy argues that the 'child liberationist' position is to be rejected not because age is important in itself but because there are 'morally relevant differences between children and adults' and children are not positioned so as to be able to take 'prudential and moral action' (Purdy, 1994, pp.226-7). Others' objections to children's rights centre on the question of family authority; for many commentators this was the issue raised by the Gillick case rather than access to contraceptive advice and treatment and underage sex or the growing powers of doctors (*Gillick v West Norfolk and Wisbech Area Health Authority* [1986] AC 112).

In addition, rights in general, and children's rights in particular, have been attacked on the ground that such language is indicative of a morally impoverished view of the world and the place of children within it - what is needed is not rights but more emphasis on the obligations owed to children (O'Neill, 1992). And, with reference to the practical value of engaging with 'the law', there is an argument which sees the language of rights and the paraphernalia of law as a distraction and at times harmful (King and

Trowell,1992).

However even those who see themselves as being committed to children's rights in the sense of their liberty rights can disagree over what should happen in a particular instance.[2] A good example of this was provided at an Institute for Public Policy Research (IPPR) seminar the author attended along with others committed to children's rights in 1993. I recall two things standing out in the discussion. First while we were all committed to children's rights it was obvious through the discussion that our definitions of children's rights and their importance varied. Second, towards the end of the seminar, discussion moved onto a custody dispute before the Austrian Supreme Court involving a 12 year old boy. The boy's father was a disciplinarian and would physically chastise the boy despite such punishment being contrary to Austrian law. The mother applied for custody on the basis of the father's use of corporal punishment but the boy wanted to remain with his father. The participants in the seminar were divided about what should happen: some gave priority to the boy's wishes, others to the issue of corporal punishment. The example illustrates an awkward truth about children's rights: the language of children's rights, like that of welfare, is always caught within wider debates about ourselves and society, debates almost exclusively pursued and set by adults.

So, on the one hand, there is a literature which seeks to promote the idea and practice of children's rights and, on the other, writing which expresses concern over the undermining of authority within the family, the neglect of a convincing ethical language upon which to ground demands for rights and the negative costs (relating to time, resources and psychological well-being) associated with the law and the legal process.

Rights and Participation

Today much writing on children's rights places emphasis on their participation in decisions which are going to have a major impact in their lives; to talking with them and listening to what they have to say and respecting, and at times acting on, their self-defined interests and needs. At first sight such participation is seen as 'resolving' the tension between children's liberty and welfare rights; however it resolves the tension by side-stepping it. It is no longer a question of whether the child's right to self determination should prevail over adult concerns about the child's welfare. Rather the child acquires a right to be included in the decision-making process; this new right to a conversation avoids choosing between the child's self determination, which Farson sees 'at the heart of children's liberation' (1974, p.27) and paternalism. Now the idea of acting in the child's best interests carries with it a responsibility to consider and, where appropriate, act on the child's wishes and feelings. Thus the languages of welfare and rights meet. The child's right to participate, as opposed to making the decision, is integral to their welfare as well as respectful of their liberty rights.

This right underlines the interconnectedness of our lives through the metaphor of conversation and the social reality of including children. Nedelsky (1991) has argued that rights are about relationships and Minow (1987) has urged that we rethink rights in such a way that they are no longer seen as just being about state-citizen relations but about our interdependencies. The exercise of individual rights does not require autonomy; 'the only precondition is that the community is willing to allow the individual to make claims and participate in the shifting of boundaries' (1987, p.1885). The emphasis on participation within contemporary children's rights writing is a recognition of the inter-connectedness of our lives as adults, parents and children. In a subsequent text Minow (1990, pp.297-298) has observed:

> Including children as participants alters their stance in the community, from things or outsiders to members ... by signalling deserved attention, rights enable a challenge to unstated norms, to exclusion, and the exclusive perspectives. Rights discourse implicates its users in a form of life, a pattern of social and political commitment.

One of the key articles of the United Nations Convention on the Rights of the Child (UNCRC) concerns the child's right to participate (art.12). Recently there has been a number of publications (all under the auspices of the IPPR) organised around the theme of children's participation.[3] These range across such diverse settings as making health care decisions (Alderson and Montgomery, 1996), juvenile crime (Allen, 1996) and child protection (Schofield and Thorburn, 1996). Courts and others entrusted with making decisions about and for children are committed to their wellbeing and increasingly this entails taking their views into account (Roche, 1997). Much has been made of the ways in which the Children Act 1989 can be seen as enhancing the participation of children in a range of decision-making contexts - but in that of divorce the language and imagery of participation is markedly absent. One reason for this is that, for some, the language of rights for children, including 'a right to participate', is concerned ultimately with their welfare. Liberty rights for children are more problematic and more so when the context is one of family life and relationship breakdown.

Family Privacy

Some writing is explicitly hostile to the children's rights project on the basis that it undermines the integrity of the family (Burrows, 1998). Just as the language of the 'best interests' of the child was used to legitimate a range of state sanctioned interventions into family life, likewise today the language of children's rights is seen as a kind of late twentieth century 'trojan horse'. Arguments around the parental right to chastise their child and to bring up their children as they see fit, free from the risk of state interference save in clearly defined circumstances, connect with wider arguments on state power, images of 'big brother' (or the 'nanny state') and the right of families and the communities within which they live their lives to live these lives differently. Mount (1982, p.1) observes:

> The family is a subversive organisation. In fact it is the only consistently subversive organisation. Only the family has continued throughout history and still continues to undermine the state. The family is the enduring permanent enemy of all hierarchies, churches and ideologies.

Mount views the family as the place where diversity and dissent can flourish. Likewise, Arendt argued against what she saw as the 'politicisation of childhood' (1958). Arendt saw the realm of the private as private and as properly separate from the world of the political and the social. It is only in the private sphere, a sphere hidden from public gaze, that the child can be brought up as the child's parents, and not the state, see fit. State intrusion into the private carries with it the unacceptable risk of indoctrination. It was for this reason in part that she criticised the involvement of African American children in the desegregation campaign in the USA in the 1950s (Arendt, 1959). Thus, according to this argument, we all have an interest in the law recognising the multiplicity of communities within society and the different values held by such communities - the politics of identity make too prescriptive a vision of 'the good family' and 'good parenting' politically problematic.[4]

Yet it is not a question of 'privacy' versus 'no privacy', rather it is a recognition of two interconnected issues. First the law is always there (Olsen,

1985). The state is deeply involved in the production and reproduction of healthy, functioning families through approved professional practice and legal regulation. The meaning of privacy has changed (McGillivray, 1997). The family has become self-governing - or at least the 'successful family' has done so. How has this been achieved? Rose observes (1989, p.208):

> The new relational technologies of the family are installed within us, establishing a particular psychological way of viewing our family lives and speaking about them, urging a constant scrutiny of our inherently difficult interactions with our children and each other. Each normal family will fulfill its political obligations best at the very moment it conscientiously strives to realize its most private dreams.[5]

The 'prize' of such success is privacy; for the 'unsuccessful family', which in the post divorce context would be indicated by the 'implacably hostile mother' and the 'parent who alienates', what awaits is the possibility of coercion, for example, in an extreme case involving the imprisonment of the residential parent - see *A v N (Committal: Refusal of Contact)* [1997] 1 FLR 533; *Z v Z (Refusal of Contact: Committal)* [1996] 1 FCR 538.

Second, because 'coercive interventions' are exceptional events the boundary between the complexities of family life and State practices are ambiguous and contested. For example, is sex education in schools legitimately part of the school curriculum or is it an unwarranted interference with parental authority? With such deep anxieties operating it is perhaps hardly surprising that the question of how the law and professional practice should position children caught up in the divorce of their parents is so contentious.

Children and Divorce

> In this case, whilst no doubt the mother is a good mother in one sense of the word in that she looks after the children well, giving them love and, as far as she can, security, one must remember that to be a good mother involves not only looking after the children, but making and keeping a home for them with their father. ... In so far as she herself by her own conduct broke up that home, she is not a good mother (per Lord Denning MR in *Re L* [1962] 1 W.L.R. at pp.889-890).

According to the law report the mother, who had left her husband and two children for another man, in reply to a question about why she had changed her mind about letting her children have contact with the other man, said 'Well, I did not realise that everybody would want to be so very difficult about things'.

The Transformation of Divorce

Today, by and large, people are not quite so difficult. Of course this case was decided in the early 1960s and much has changed since. One of these changes is that today encouragement and support is given to the parents to agree for themselves what is to happen to the children on divorce (see Piper, this volume): unless they are unable to agree or are determined to take it to court, it will not be the law's business.

This is one piece from a dramatically changed divorce jigsaw; from 1966 to 1996 divorce has been transformed from a public issue to a private matter. In 1966 divorce itself was still clearly a public matter in the sense that an independent judicial arena had to satisfy itself that the grounds for divorce had been made out and that disputes over arrangements regarding property, finance and children would be heard by a court of law. Arguably the real revolution in the regulation of divorce came about not simply as a result of the substantive changes contained in the Divorce Reform Act 1969 but also the procedural changes of the 1970s - most notably the introduction of 'special procedure' for all undefended divorce petitions. The Family Law Act 1996 in the context of a rapid growth in mediation services since the late 1980s has continued this process of rendering divorce a matter of private ordering.

There have been other significant changes in this period. First, disputes over what are now termed residence and contact appear to have intensified (Bailey-Harris *et al*, 1998, chapter 4). In the 1990s we have seen the development of the 'implacably hostile' parent and the parent who 'alienates' the child's affection for the other parent. The Children Act 1989 has not succeeded in taking the heat out of disputes around children on divorce despite its introduction of a concept of 'parental responsibility' which would endure beyond the end of the marriage. So why are there still fights over children on divorce? One reply might be that the law can only do so much, another relates to the second change.

Domestic relations are undergoing significant change in that the social and emotional meaning invested in children by both parents is shifting. Fathers are playing a greater role in child care and child rearing with the result that fathers are disputing where the children should live on divorce and it is no longer quite as clear as it once was as to with whom the child should live. Being cautious in assessing the 'new father' position does not mean that we ignore research which supports the idea that men are thinking differently about their role as fathers and their relationship with their children (Collier, 1995; Lupton and Barclay,1997). While men may be just 'being there' for their children (Lupton and Barclay, 1997, p.121) rather than assuming wider responsibility in the domestic sphere, significant change is taking place within domestic relations (White,1994).

Third, new professionals are offering their services to enable those caught in divorce to disentangle their affairs with the 'minimum of bitterness' - an industry largely fuelled in its early days by a concern over the welfare of children affected by divorce combined with a critique of law and legal institutions (Bottomley, 1984; Bottomley and Roche, 1988; Piper, 1993). Now the range of professionals involved in mediation has increased and mediation is seen as one of a number of mechanisms to assist couples in negotiating practical and fair agreements at the end of the marriage.

Fourth, the children's rights movement has had an impact on the way in which some adults and interested professionals think about family matters. This has entailed an emphasis on communicating with children, 'ascertaining their wishes and feelings' (see Piper this volume), representation and advocacy (Timms, 1995; Timms, 1998; Children's Rights Office, 1995). However the impact of this 'movement' has been limited and it has not fundamentally displaced the welfarist agenda. For instance the *National Standards for Probation Service Family Court Work* (Home Office, 1994) require the court welfare officer to see the child (unless there are strong reasons for not doing so) though they also make it clear that children should 'never be forced to express a view'. In divorce the family is going through a painful transition and one in which the parents, who are directly caught up in the emotional turmoil of the breakdown of the relationship, are presumed by legislators and mediators to know what is best for their children. Running alongside this emphasis on parental agreement, the key to a successful divorce, there is a strong preference for continuing parental responsibility in the sense that both parents should be enabled to continue as parents, albeit in radically different circumstances.[6] Throughout this a consensus has emerged that the child should not be directly involved in the legal process.

The Position of Children

It is revealing to think about how children and divorce are not talked about; the languages of democracy and citizenship are absent. There is no talk of the 'liberty rights' of children - the private world of the family is no place for the languages of democracy (cf. Beck, 1997). Further, there is little talk about the extra needs that children might have beyond those of adjustment to their new circumstances and general references to the poverty that awaits many divorced women and children living with them. The Law Commission (1990) in its statement of the objectives of a 'period of consideration and reflection' as part of the new divorce process provides the following 'health warning'(para.5.25)

> the parties will have to consider the consequences of a separation or divorce order before it actually happens. This will entail the often painful exercise of deciding whether or not the home should be sold, with whom the children are to live, how much contact the other parent is to have with the children, and how their furniture and other possessions should be divided. This will be in addition to learning to adjust emotionally, socially and psychologically to the dramatic change of circumstances in their lives.[7]

In England and Wales the issue is how best to 'protect' the child from the legal process; a consensus has been fashioned that lawyers and the courts should be avoided if possible.[8] The provisions in the Children Act 1989 which provide for children to apply for section 8 orders with the leave of the court have been narrowly interpreted (see *Re SC (a minor) (leave to seek residence order*) [1994] 1 FLR 96). In section 8 order applications, where the rules are silent on the question of the child's attendance, the courts have discouraged their presence and have done so in the name of their welfare.[9] The Children Act Advisory Committee Handbook of Best Practice in Children Act cases states with reference to the final hearing that 'except by direction of the court, children should not attend a hearing' (1997, para 58).

Yet lawyers do offer two things that might be important to children: partisanship and confidentiality. The lawyer is not professionally committed to a particular vision of post-divorce family life.[10] The child is the client and the lawyer is there to act on behalf of his or her client.[11] Such action might take a number of forms ranging from entering into negotiations with one or both parents, 'mediating' between the child client and relevant adults, and, if it gets that far, representing them in court. Throughout this process they are 'on the client's side' and can act constructively to resolve a dispute. Second the communications between lawyers are covered by professional privilege and only in very exceptional circumstances can such confidences be broken - this might be of great importance to the child who might feel much easier dealing with a 'child-friendly' lawyer than a professional concerned for their welfare. As Leach (1994, pp.222-223) has observed:

> How much children manage to say, and how much notice adults take of what they say in any type of legal case, is open to question ... As long as it is assumed that children are less likely to know for themselves where their best interests lie than adults are to know for them, just finding adults who will listen to children is not enough. How, for example, can children talk freely, even to people who will take the trouble to tune in to them, if those people will not grant them the confidentiality - and therefore the control of the results of their own confidences - that is the right of every adult?

Leach goes on to recognise the special appeal of advice lines such as Childline - their anonymity allows the child to retain control (1994, p.223). The drive towards keeping lawyers out and relying on mediation services and the court welfare service to protect the interests of children caught up in divorce contrasts with the way in which children are positioned by the law when not involved in private law matters.

In the criminal justice system we can see a distinctive positioning of the child in operation. In *Re R and Others (Minors) (Wardship: Criminal Proceedings)* [1991] 2 FLR 95 allegations of serious sexual offences against the father in relation to his three older daughters had been made and the father's solicitors wanted the leave of the wardship court to interview the 12 year old son and to call him as witness in the criminal proceedings. The Court Appeal held that where a child was a ward of court and the police wished to interview the ward, while application for leave to do so must be made, it was not for the wardship court to use its jurisdiction to interfere with the performance by the criminal courts of their lawful duties. In the course of giving the judgment of the court Lord Donaldson of Lymington MR, stated that: 'Children, whether wards of court or not, are citizens owing duties to society as a whole (including other children) which are appropriate to their years and understanding'. And in *R v Highbury Corner Magistrates' Court ex parte Deering* (1996) 161 J.P.N. 168 the applicant had sought judicial review of the refusal of the magistrates' court to issue a witness summons to a nine year old boy. The magistrates refused to do so, relying on section 44 of the Children and Young Persons Act 1933, holding that it would be detrimental to the boy's welfare. The Divisional Court allowed the application on the basis that the child was a witness to the alleged incident and it was for the trial court, not the magistrates, to balance the interests of the defendant against those of the child.[12]

It can be argued that the operation of the criminal justice system raises different issues than those raised by divorce. There is a compelling public interest in seeing that offenders do not escape punishment because of legal procedures; personal liberty and public safety might be at issue. Yet the ease with which the language of citizenship is deployed is revealing. The movement from a position in which the child is seen as vulnerable, in need of protection and who should not be required to express a view to that in which they are valuable witnesses, whose welfare will be properly considered by the criminal court and who might be required to give evidence is significant. It is a movement from 'private victim' to 'public citizen' and it is one which is arranged entirely by adults acting to particular and varying agendas. It is not that children are not able to express a view, or give a clear account of what happened or what their wishes and feelings are, it is that the family justice system does not think that it is a good idea that they should be asked to do so to a lawyer. The quiet but insistent message of the system is that such communications (if any) are properly made to the court welfare officer or mediator. The Family Law Act 1996 with its endorsement of mediation and the private settlement of disputes seems to carry the risk of marginalising the voice of the child (see Piper, in this volume).

These professional concerns, which have a resonance for adults in particular settings, might appear less compelling from a child-centred standpoint informed by the language of children's rights. Sawyer has commented (1997, p.7):

> The right to have one's position advocated is the essence of the legal process. The child's involvement as a mover of the action in the proceedings will very possibly be minimal if his or her wishes and feelings are only put to the court through the medium of the court welfare officer's report; in that context the child's wishes and feelings are not advocated but presented, and in the context of their parents' dispute rather than from a child-centred standpoint.

It seems that it is inevitable that the child, while a central consideration in the divorce process, will remain on its margins - divorce is, and will remain, an adult affair.

Participation and the Democratisation of Family Life

As adults we take it for granted that we will participate in key decisions in our lives; we might not 'get our way' but we will be players most of the time. With children it is different; there is no automatic expectation of participation. Of course some 'good parents' might encourage participation within the family, but in civil society children do not count. Held (1991, p.20), writing on citizenship, has argued:

> If citizenship entails membership in the community and membership implies forms of social participation, then citizenship is above all about the involvement of people in the community in which they live; and people have been barred from citizenship on grounds of class, gender, race and age among many other factors. Accordingly, the debate on citizenship requires us to think about the very nature of the conditions of membership and political participations.

The inclusion of children in such spaces and conversations would change things. For children it is the family that represents the most significant space within which they act in society. Does the language of citizenship cease to have any purchase at the front door?[13] The Scottish Law Commission did not think so. They noted (1992, paras 2.62-64):

> The question as we saw it was whether a parent or other person exercising parental rights should be under a similar obligation to ascertain and have regard to the child's wishes and feelings as a local authority was in relation to a child in its care ... There are great attractions in such an approach. It emphasises that the child is a person in his or her own right and that his or her views are entitled to respect and consideration...On consultation there was majority support for a provision requiring parents in reaching any major decision relating to a child, to ascertain the child's wishes and feelings so far as practicable and give due consideration to them having regard to their age and understanding ... any respondents clearly regarded such a provision as an important declaration of principle.[14]

In contrast, the recent furore over children 'divorcing' their parents testifies to the judicial and social unease over the child as a possible legal subject within the private sphere. In the *Observer* Polly Ghazi issued the following warning to parents:

> Parents who turn up their noses when their children bury themselves in Viz, Smash Hits or Just 17 may be making a big mistake. The magazines may soon contain advertisements for a booklet entitled Your Say in Court, which could have a significant effect on family relationships. Aimed at 10 to 16 year-olds it provides a step-by-step guide on how to 'divorce' parents (*Observer*, 25/7/93).

Such information is seen as a threat to family life; of course it is possible to see in children's rights an enrichment of the family. It is in this context that Beck's notion of the democratisation of family life is important (1997). While Beck sees authority relationships in the 'post-familial family' as fluid and multiple he also notes that 'not much fantasy is necessary to imagine how later generations could rub their eyes in amazement' at the 'serfdom' of children. In Sweden the language of citizenship is increasingly applied to children - whereas in many other countries the 'private enslavement' of children by their parents 'is scarcely noticed' (1997, p.161).[15] In Sweden the child is given the right to act on their own in accordance with their age and developmental status. In his consideration of the changing nature of authority in family relationships and divorce Beck cites Orfali:

> The child must therefore have the status of a party in all proceedings that pertain to their guardianship and residency and visiting rights; moreover, they must be able to call upon legal representation. In the proceedings they can decide through a court-appointed representative which of the parents they wish to live with, even if their decision contradicts an amicable settlement of the parents ... The child thus has the same claim to be heard and defended as any other citizen (Orfali,1993, p.494).

In the UK the Children's Rights Office, insisting upon respect for children's civil rights within the family, has pursued a similar argument (1995, p.28):

> Nobody wants decision making about family matters to go to court, but if children's rights to involvement in decision making and to respect for their

> evolving capacity are to be taken seriously, they must have the right to be heard in all judicial and administrative procedures which affect them.[16]

Eekelaar notes that 'any rights based approach to social policy [must] have regard to claims which people make and to provide opportunities for claims to be made' (1992, p.228). Without such claims and the opportunity to make them the language of rights dissolves into that of welfare. Eekelaar continues (1992, p.228):

> No social organization can hope to be built on the rights of its members unless there are mechanisms whereby those members may express themselves and wherein those expressions are taken seriously. *Hearing what children say* must therefore lie at the root of any elaboration of children's rights. (emphasis in the original)

The question then arises as what happens to such conversations and here the issue of adult power reasserts itself. Eekelaar argues that a commitment to children's rights for all children requires a 'hypothetical judgement' on the part of the adult (1992, p.229):

> Adults' duties towards young children cannot be convincingly perceived as reflecting rights held by the children unless it can be plausibly assumed that, if fully informed of the relevant factors and of mature judgement, the children would want such duties to be exercised towards them.

Yet this is problematic; we are caught up in a number of competing constructions of childhood (Trinder, 1997; Gittins, 1998). Furthermore, uncertainty and ambiguity are part of the child welfare landscape (see Parton, 1998) . In order to avoid the ever-present threat of the collapse of his children's rights position into a welfare discourse Eekelaar argues that hypothetical judgement 'stipulates a process which requires serious attention to be given to what the child in question, of his or her gender, ethnicity and other personal and social characteristics, is likely to have wanted if fully informed and mature'. The language of rights, participation and citizenship might open up new possibilities precisely because they are fluid and changing - it might permit a construction of childhood in which children themselves come to play a part. Then we might be enabled to rethink the legitimacy of not just the language of children's rights but their participation in a different range of contexts and we might develop new practices of listening and action which are shaped by the voices of children.

Conclusion

Over 100 years ago Parliament endorsed what was already established good practice in disputes over the custody of children. Section 4 of the Custody of Children Act 1891 provided that:

> Nothing in this Act contained shall interfere with or affect the power of the Court to consult the wishes of the child in considering what order to be made, or diminish the right which any child now possesses to the exercise of its own free choice.

Throughout the nineteenth century the courts hearing habeas corpus applications involving children had developed the practice of 'examining the child'. In *R v Clarke* (1857) 7 El & Bl 186 Lord Campbell CJ said (pp.196-197):

> As a general rule, it is admitted that, if a child under the age of seven years is brought up, the court ought at once to order the child to be delivered to the guardian. But the contention is that, between the ages of seven and fourteen, the Court ought to examine the child and ascertain whether it has the mental capacity to be competent to make a choice, and, according to the degree of mental capacity which it is found to possess, to hand it over to the guardian, or to liberate it and desire it to go where it pleases ... although we do not find the exact age defined within which the Court, on a habeas corpus, will order the child to be delivered up to the parent or guardian without examination, we do find cases where this course has been adopted, the child being above seven years of age.[17]

Today, when the child does get to speak what does the law hear? The words of the child are filtered through the lens of concern of mediators and other welfare professionals operating the current family justice system. And despite the rhetoric of the UNCRC and of children's rights in general children are either caught within a protectionist discourse or a culture of disrespect: they are victimised or demonised. The law is implicated in this. The words of the child are inherently suspect. They are the victim of 'parental alienation' (Willbourne and Cull, 1997; Maidment, 1998) or do not know their own best interests, or are not in a position to know them. For example, in *Re B (Change of Surname)* [1996] 1 FLR 791 which involved an appeal against the decision by a circuit judge to refuse the mother's application to change the surname of three children, all three children wanted the change of name to take place. Wilson J sitting in the Court of Appeal stated (at pp.794-795):

> [O]rders nowadays which run flatly counter to the wishes of normal children aged 16, 14 and 12 are virtually unknown to family law. But in my view there is a big distinction between, for example a residence or contact order made in the teeth of such opposition and the order made by the judge here, which left the existing prohibition in force.

At the end of the twentieth century what is to happen to children caught up in the divorce of their parents will be left to their responsible parents to decide. Of course, later some children may seek the leave of the court to make an application for section 8 order, for example to change the contact arrangements or to reside with the other parent. However in the divorce context the difficulty children have in acquiring a voice is considerable. Family privacy renders hearing their voice problematic and the family justice system is making this increasingly difficult. Perhaps the child is doomed for some time to remain a legal object (O'Donovan, 1993). Images of the complexity and fragility of family relationships have been deployed to close down children's access to lawyers and the courts.[18]

Perhaps it is only the experience of other jurisdictions or within the literature of science fiction (Stainton Rogers and Stainton Rogers, 1992) that can open up to us the possibilities of children (particularly the older child) being social agents at moments and in circumstances of their own choosing. The visibility and speech of children will not only alter their worlds but ours too: in this McGillivray is correct when she sees children's rights as a beginning not the end (McGillivray, 1994). We need to be able to hear the unfamiliar and the law could provide one framework within which the many voices of childhood can be heard on matters that move and concern them In the context of divorce this might require that children should have access to safe and partisan advice and support.

Notes

1. These terms link respectively to 'liberty rights' and 'welfare rights'.
2. Jenks observing that 'the child is always revealing of the grounds of social control' (1996) captures the sense that debates about children are never simply just that - there is always more at stake. In arguments about childhood and children's rights we are arguing about ourselves and our place in the world: it is an argument about politics.
3. These have been published under the IPPR's Participation and Consent series.
4. Of course the family is not outside of society; the values of parents and the organisation of family life are historically and culturally located. Families are constantly changing both in terms of how they are seen, how they operate and the practical, emotional and symbolic investment and responsibilities that family members anticipate and assume.
5. Jenks makes a related point when he observes that when 'Donzelot tells us that the child has become the meeting place of the political contract and the psychological complex he is developing a wider argument about the functioning of control in modern life. The contemporary political state no longer addresses the polity as a whole but rather treats the family as its basic unit of control' (1996, p.80).
6. Of course this is expressed *inter alia* as contact being 'a right of the child' - see the discussion in chapter 5 of this volume.
7. It is clear that, by requiring the parties to the divorce to address the practical problems that the disentanglement of the relationship will entail, some may be encouraged to remain together - 'perhaps with the help of counselling, find some way of re-negotiating their relationship so that they and their children can have a future together' (para 5.26).
8. In Scotland a different approach has been taken. Proceedings which might affect the child must be intimated to the child. In an action for divorce where the child has indicated that he or she wishes to express a view the court must order such steps to be taken as it considers appropriate to ascertain the views of the child. The child's views can be ascertained in a number of ways e.g. in writing or personally to the sheriff. These views must be recorded although they need not be made available to the parties.
9. However under the Children Act 1989 the ascertainable views of the child must be made known to the court - this will be done via either an affidavit, a solicitor representing the child's views to the court and/or a report from a social worker, welfare officers or guardian *ad litem*.
10. Though, as other chapters in this volume point out, they may well be greatly influenced by particular ideas about good and bad parenting.
11. However note Sawyer's work (1997) where she states that even those lawyers who saw themselves as being committed to children's rights were at times uneasy about children becoming involved in the legal process. Kroll makes a more general observation regarding this kind of work (1995, p.91): 'Working with children is painful. It is often about loss, anger, rejection, neglect and sadness; it is also often about limited options and second rate solutions. It touches private life in tender places, it is unbearable and it makes us feel hopeless, helpless, sad and angry. Many workers admit to keeping children at a distance in an attempt to avoid feeling these feelings, to protect themselves from the pain, and to preserve a sense of competence'.

12. In the criminal justice context not only can children give evidence they can be required to do so - the concern about distress and familial relations, about putting a burden on the child, is gone.
13. In her examination of the family and the question of justice Moller Okin has argued (1989, pp.184-185) that, in her imagined 'genderless society', children, as well as men and women, would benefit: 'It is undeniable that the family in which each of us grows up has a deeply formative influence on us. This is one of the reasons why one cannot reasonably leave the family out of the "basic structure of society", to which the principles of justice are to apply The enhancement of justice that accompanies the disappearance of gender will make the family a much better place for children to develop a sense of justice'.
14. Section 6 of the Children (Scotland) Act 1995 imposes such a duty on parents and provides that children over 12 years of age are presumed in law to be old enough to express a view.
15. Beck also notes that 'equality of rights for the child certainly collides with the protection of the family and requires or allows the deprivatisation of privacy to a certain extent' (1997, p.162).
16. With reference to divorce the Scottish Law Commission recognised that parental agreement in itself did not mean that the child's views were irrelevant: 'the fact that two adult parties to say a divorce action are content with proposed arrangements for the child does not necessarily mean that it is any less important to have regard to the child's views. It seems to us that it would be difficult to justify a provision which appeared to regard the child's views as of less importance merely because the application was, or ended up being, unopposed. The child is the central figure in these matters. He or she is the person most directly affected' (1992, para 5.26).
17. Where the court refused to examine the child in order to determine whether he should be delivered up to the mother. See also *R v Greenhill* (1836) 4 Ad & E 624, 640 per Lord Denman C.J.
18. In a very different context Sir Stephen Brown in *Re V* [1995] 2 FLR 1010 has stated:

    > In the family context this, in my judgment would have the potential effect of destroying the family relationships. This family is not going to be assisted in the present state of the law by this course. This is a problem which has to be worked out with goodwill by all the parties involved.

    This case concerned an 18 year old physically disabled young man who was in dispute with his mother as to where he should reside.

References

Alderson, P. and Montgomery, J. (1996), *Health Care Choices Making Decisions with Children*, IPPR, London.

Allen, R. (1996), *Children and Crime Taking Responsibility*, IPPR, London.

Archard, D. (1993), *Children, Rights and Childhood*, Routledge, London.

Arendt, H. (1958), *The Human Condition*, University of Chicago Press, Chicago.

Arendt, H (1959), 'Reflections on Little Rock', *Dissent*, vol 6(1), pp.45-56.

Bailey-Harris, R., Davis, G., Barron, J. and Pearce, J. (1998), *Monitoring Private Law Applications Under The Children Act*, Research Report to the Nuffield Foundation, University of Bristol.

Bainham, A. (1990), 'The Privatisation of the Public Interest in Children', 53 *Modern Law Review*, vol 53 (2), p.206.

Beck, U (1997), 'Democratisation of the Family', *Childhood*, vol 4(2), pp.151-168.

Bottomley, A. (1984), 'Resolving Family Disputes: A Critical View', in M.D.A. Freeman (ed) *The State, the Law and the Family*, Tavistock, London.

Bottomley, A and Roche, J. (1988), 'Conflict and Consensus: A Critique of the Language of Informal Justice' in R. Matthews (ed) *Informal Justice?*, Sage, London.

Burrows, L. (1998), *The Fight for the Family. The Adults behind Children's Rights*, Family Education Trust, Oxford.

Children's Rights Office (1995), *Building Small Democracies. The Implications of the UN Convention on the Rights of the Child for Respecting Children's Civil Rights within the Family*, Children's Rights Office, London.

Collier, R. (1995), '"Waiting Till Father Gets Home": The Reconstruction of Fatherhood in Family Law', *Social and Legal Studies*, vol 4 (1), pp.5-30.

Eekelaar, J. (1992), 'The Importance of Thinking That Children Have Rights', in P.Alston, S. Parker and J. Seymour (eds) *Children, Rights and the Law*, Clarendon, Oxford, pp.221-235.

Farson, R. (1974), *Birthrights*, Collier Macmillan, London.

Freeman, M.D.A. (1993), *The Rights and Wrongs of Children*, Francis Pinter, London.

Gittins, D. (1998), *The Child in Question*, Macmillan, Basingstoke.

Held, D. (1991), 'Between State and Civil Society', in G.Andrews (ed) *Citizenship*, Lawrence and Wishart, London.

Holt, J. (1975), *Escape from Childhood. The Needs and Rights of Children*, Penguin, Harmondsworth.

Jenks, C. (1996), *Childhood*, Routledge, London.

King, M. and Trowell, J. (1992), *Children's Welfare and the Law, The Limits of Legal Intervention*, Sage, London.

Kroll, B. (1995), 'Working with Children', in F. Kaganas, M. King and C. Piper (eds) *Legislating for Harmony, Partnership under the Children Act 1989*, Jessica Kingsley, London.

Levy, A. and Kahan, B. (1991), *The Pindown Experience and the Protection of Children*, Staffordshire County Council.

Lupton, B. and Barclay, L. (1997), *Constructing Fatherhood Discourses and Experiences*, Sage, London.

McGillivray, A. (ed) (1997), *Governing Childhood*, Dartmouth, Aldershot.

Maidment, S. (1998), 'Parental Alienation Syndrome - A Judicial Response', *Family Law*, pp. 264-266.

Minow, M. (1987), 'Interpreting Rights: An Essay for Robert Cover', *Yale Law Journal*, vol 96(8), pp.1860-2017.

Minow, M. (1990), *Making All the Difference: Inclusion, Exclusion and American Law*, Cornell University Press, Ithica.

Mount, F. (1982), *The Subversive Family*, Jonathan Cape, London.

Nedelsky, J. (1993), 'Reconceiving Rights as Relationship', *Review of Constitutional Studies*, vol 1(1), pp.1-26.

O'Donovan, K. (1993), *Family Law Matters*, Pluto, London.

O'Neill, O. (1992), 'Children's Rights and Children's Lives', in P. Alston, S. Parker and J. Seymour (eds) *Children, Rights and the Law*, Clarendon, Oxford, pp.24-42.

Okin, S.M. (1989), *Justice, Gender and the Family*, Basic Books, New York.

Olsen (1985), 'The Myth of State Intervention in the Family', *University of Michigan Journal of Law Reform*, vol 18(4), p.835.

Orfali, K. (1993), 'Modell der Transparenz die schewische Gesellschaft' in P. Aries and G. Duby (eds) *Geschichte des privaten Lebens*, Fischer Verlag, Frankfurt.

Parton, N. (1998), 'Risk, Advanced Liberalism and Child Welfare: The Need to Rediscover Uncertainty and Ambiguity', *British Journal of Social Work*, vol 28, pp.5-27.

Piper, C. (1993), *The Responsible Parent: A Study in Divorce Mediation*, Harvester Wheatsheaf, Hemel Hempstead.

Purdy, L. (1994), 'Why Children Shouldn't Have Equal Rights', *International Journal of Children's Rights*, pp.223-241.

Roche, J. (1991), 'The Children Act 1989: Once a Parent Always a Parent?', *Journal of Social Welfare and Family Law*, pp.345-361.

Roche, J. (1997), 'Children's Rights: Participation and Dialogue', in J. Roche and S. Tucker (eds) *Youth in Society*, Sage, London.

Rose, N. (1989), *Governing the Soul: The Shaping of the Private Self*, Routledge, London.

Schofield, G. and Thorburn, J. (1996), *Child Protection. The Voice of the Child in Decision Making*, IPPR, London.

Stainton Rogers, R. and Stainton Rogers, W. (1992), *Stories of Childhood - Shifting Agendas of Child Concern*, Harvester Wheatsheaf, Hemel Hempstead.

Timms, J. (1995), *Children's Representation. A Practitioner's Guide*, Sweet and Maxwell, London.

Timms, J. (1998), 'The Needs of Children Involved in Family Breakdown', *Family Mediation*, vol 8(1), pp.16-17.

Trinder, L. (1997), 'Competing Constructions of Childhood: Children's Rights and Children's Wishes in Divorce', *Journal of Social Welfare and Family Law*, vol 19(3), pp.291-305.

White, N. (1994), 'About Fathers: Masculinity and the Social Construction of Fatherhood', *Australian and New Zealand Journal of Sociology*, vol 30(2), pp.119-131.

Willbourne, C. and Cull, L. (1997), 'The Emerging Problem of Parental Alienation, *Family Law*, pp.807-808.

Williams, P. (1995), *The Rooster's Egg On the Persistence of Prejudice*, Harvard University Press, Cambridge, Mass.

4 The Wishes and Feelings of the Child

CHRISTINE PIPER

Introduction

'The ascertainable wishes and feelings of the child' is hardly a phrase which trips easily off the tongue. Yet it has become increasingly prominent in discourses about the family in the 1990s, since its assumed creation by the Children Act 1989. The Children Act provided the courts, for the first time in the UK, with a welfare checklist on which one item to be taken into account is the child's wishes and feelings. That Act also placed duties on local authorities and voluntary bodies to do likewise in a range of specified situations.[1] Nevertheless, neither the phrase nor the professional practice it implies was an invention for the purposes of the Children Act 1989 or the Children (Northern Ireland) Order 1995.

As Brenda Hoggett - then a Law Commissioner and now Mrs Justice Hale - pointed out, section 1(3)(a),[2] the sub-section setting out the requirement to 'have regard' to ascertainable wishes, 'mirrors a provision which has been part of adoption law for some time' (Hoggett, 1993, p.175).[3] In Scottish legislation the phrase can be found in the Social Work (Scotland) Act 1968 section 20 which imposed a duty on social workers and voluntary organisations north of the border similar to that imposed 21 years later on the English and Welsh. In addition, the power, if not the duty, to consult a child to ascertain her views is to be found, as Roche pointed out in the previous chapter, in legislation as far back as the Custody of Children Act 1891, section 4. Even a brief 'crash course' publication by the College of Law over 20 years ago includes, as point five of 10 'guidelines' in the law of custody and access, the statement that 'the child's wishes can be taken into account in deciding what is best for his welfare' (Lowe, 1975, p.15). The weight to be given to children's wishes generally and in particular circumstances has, therefore, been the subject of reported cases from the English and Scottish[4] courts long before the Children Act 1989.

The Welfare Context

These pre-Children Act provisions from legislation and case law can clearly be placed in the context of widening the range of 'further and better particulars' in order to determine the best interests of the child concerned. What has raised the profile of 'wishes and feelings' is, as Roche's chapter made clear, the development of an international children's rights discourse, with an emphasis on the voice and the autonomy of the child. Legislators in the UK had incorporated Article 13 of the Hague Convention on the Civil Aspects of International Child Abduction into the Child Abduction Act 1985, allowing for an authority to refuse to order the child's return to a particular jurisdiction if 'the child objects [and it is] appropriate to take account of its views'.[5] Parliament was, therefore, mindful not only of complying with Article 12 of the United Nations' Convention on the Rights of the Child but also the recommendation of the Council of Europe in that body's document, *Parental Responsibilities* (1984 Part II), that there should be an independent duty on the court to take account of the child's views in all matters affecting the child (see the Law Commission (1988, p.20, n.66)).

Discussion about legislative change in the 1980s revolved around the perceived polarities of child welfare or parental autonomy as against child rights. For example, the Law Commission had discussed the matter of the wishes of the child in its Working Paper on *Custody* (Law Commission, 1986, paras 6.40-6.44), asking consultees about two issues: whether the duty to ascertain and consider the child's wishes should be part of a welfare checklist or a separate duty and whether the duty should apply only to contested cases. In its Report the Law Commission (1988) said that, whilst consultees had been almost unanimous in favour of statutory recognition of the child's views, the concerns about the 'dangers in giving them too much recognition' (para 3.23) 'all point towards including the child's views as part of a statutory checklist, which in practice will be limited to contested cases' (para 3.24).

And so the Children Act 1989 and the Children (Northern Ireland) Order 1995 impose the duty to 'have regard to' the 'ascertainable wishes and feelings of the child' or to ascertain and 'give due consideration to' the child's wishes on, *inter alia*, the courts via a checklist (in section 1 and Art 3(3) respectively) which is used to apply the welfare paramountcy requirement.[6] As the former Lord Chancellor, Lord Mackay of Clashfern, has since stressed,

> While the Act provides for the court taking account of the views of children, giving them weight according to the circumstances, it does not put the children in a position to decide on those matters. That is an important point to underline in connection with the philosophy of the Children Act.[7]

Therefore, whilst the inclusion of references to the child's wishes has been seen as a development which 'marks an important adjustment in the balance of power between children and adult society' (Bainham, 1993, p.60), its symbolic importance - in the law of England, Wales and Ireland - is in the addition of the child's perspective to the operation of the welfare test. Whether it affects power differentials depends on how it operates in practice: a question this chapter will address.

This dominance of a welfare discourse in relation to the child's wishes and feelings is in contrast to the approach of the Scottish Law Commission (1992). That Commission not only discussed the different implications of using the terms 'wishes and feelings' or 'views' and 'maturity' or 'understanding' (paras 2.60-2.64),[8] but also stated quite firmly that 'the child's own views ... we believe, ought to be taken into account in their own right and not just as an aspect of welfare' (para 5.23). They argued against limiting the provision's scope to contested private law proceedings as in the Children Act 1989: 'It seems to us that it would be difficult to justify a provision which appeared to regard the child's views as of less importance merely because an application was, or ended up being, unopposed' (para 5.26). Four years earlier the (English) Law Commission had had no such difficulties: 'If the parents have agreed on where the child will live and made their arrangements accordingly, it is no more practicable to try to alter these to accord with the child's views than it is to impose the views of the court' (1988, para 3.23).

In contrast to Scotland, therefore, participation by the child in decision-making in the rest of the UK has been located firmly within a welfare discourse linked only to a 'caretaking' version of children's rights. Participation - this new right to a conversation - has side-stepped, but not resolved, the tension between liberty and welfare rights (Roche, in this volume).

The Family Law Act 1996

Marriage Saving and Child Saving

The Family Law Act 1996, as clearly as the Children Act 1989, locates the wishes and feelings of the child in a welfare context. Contributions made by members of both Houses of Parliament, in debates and in the committee stages of the Bill, reveal that most saw the ascertaining of views as being part of their project to protect the child from the dangers of divorce. In the House of Lords, within the context of a widely expressed view that 'divorce is a disaster under any circumstances for any child', and a professed belief that 'children should come first' in the provisions of the Bill (Baroness Faithful and Lord Irvine of Lairg respectively, Hansard, HL vol 568, col 813, 22 Jan 1996), the aim was to ensure that all involved should be 'constantly vigilant as to the welfare of the child' (Lord Simon of Glaisdale, Hansard HL vol 568, col 911, 23 January 1996). Perhaps they endorsed concern generated by research which showed that the child's ability to adjust to change on divorce is affected by feelings of powerlessness that they may have in relation to the process and outcome of divorce.[9] But there was also evident in the debates a clear strand of thinking that linked this 'child saving' approach to 'marriage saving'. The Law Commission Report (1990, para 2.19) and the Consultation Paper on divorce reform (1993, para 5.11) noted that 'The children themselves would usually prefer the parents to stay together' and the following contribution - made in the debate on proposed amendments that would have imposed duties on, *inter alia*, parents and a new court children's officer to take account of the children's views - clearly rests on this assumption:

> It is surely not impossible that if there is a clear and definite obligation laid by the Act on the need to take account not only of the interests but of the views of a child ... it may be just possible that it could make the warring parents address themselves to this enormously important aspect of their marriage and pay just a little more attention to it. If, by putting this on the face of the Bill, we produced in only a handful of cases a balancing factor which perhaps tipped the couple away from divorce, then I believe that that in itself would totally justify the amendment ... (Lord Murray of Epping Forest, Hansard, HL vol 568, col 913, 23 Jan 1996).

When the Bill finally returned to the House of Commons, the government - to 'save' the Bill - accepted, *inter alia*, a new clause which became section 11.[10] Considering wishes and feelings was then presented as part of a clear child-saving reform: '[The amendments] provide for even greater protection of children's interests - and children are, of course, the innocent victims of divorce' (Mr Streeter, Hansard HC col 591, 17 June 1996).[11]

Section 11

Section 11, replacing - except in relation to nullity proceedings - section 41 of the Matrimonial Causes Act 1973 (MCA), places a duty on the divorce court to 'have particular regard', inter alia, to 'the wishes and feelings of the child' (s11(4)(a)). Perry argues that section 11 of the Family Law Act 1996 'is the first time that provision has been made for the child's views to be taken into account whenever the court is considering the arrangements for children at divorce' (1996, p.13). Whilst this is true there are grounds for querying the exact scope - and therefore significance - of section 11.[12] On a strict reading it would appear that the welfare principle and the checklist (sections 11(3) and (4)) apply only to the decision[13] - which currently can be made under section 41 of the MCA - whether to take the exceptional course (see Bromley and Lowe, 1992, p.367) of not granting a divorce until the children arrangements are 'approved'.[14]

However, the parliamentary debates on this provision would suggest that the intention (though not adequately conveyed in the wording of the Act) was to apply the checklist to the decision - now in section 11(1)(b)[15] - as to whether to exercise Children Act powers (Bird and Cretney, 1996, pp.79-82). This decision is not currently subject to a checklist.

There may be some difficulty in implementing the checklist. As a result of the Family Proceedings Rules 1991 the current procedure relating to the MCA section 41 is largely a paper exercise completed by the district judge. The latter has the power to ask for further details or a welfare report but the decision whether to do so is done on the information in the statement of arrangements provided to the court. For the procedure to remain as a paper exercise in the majority of cases, the statement of arrangements would have to include information about the wishes and feelings of the child, begging the question as to how they would be ascertained and recorded. One of the possibilities being considered by the Lord Chancellor's Department is to require a parent to state in his or her application for a divorce order whether the children of the family have been consulted (Bird and Cretney, 1996, p.81).

If the court decides it should exercise its powers under the Children Act in respect of 'any children of the family' then a further question is raised. The court can make orders (for example, section 8 residence or contact orders) of its own motion in family proceedings - which now include proceedings under the 1996 Act - but, again strictly speaking, the checklist in the Children Act does not apply.[16] However, it is likely that the Children Act and Family Law Act checklists will be influential, given the recent statement of the Court of Appeal that the Children Act checklist 'remains a most useful aide-memoire' in cases where consideration of the checklist is not mandated.[17]

Encouraging Parents

The duty imposed on the court by the Family Law Act to have regard to the child's wishes is symbolically important because neither the Children Act 1989 nor the Family Law Act 1996 impose a statutory duty similar to that in the Children (Scotland) Act 1995 section 6(1), whereby those with parental responsibility making major parenting decisions should have regard to the views of the child.[18] Instead, '[t]he primary strategy deployed in the Family Law Act is for professionals to encourage parents to consider children's wishes and feelings' (Trinder, 1997, p.292). This encouragement is to be undertaken at several stages.

First, the regulations relating to information meetings must make provision for information to be given to parent(s) about 'the importance to be attached to the welfare, wishes and feelings of children' (s8(9)(b)). Secondly, a solicitor may have a similar duty: the Lord Chancellor is empowered to make rules requiring a legal representative of a party to a marriage to inform the party that 'in relation to the arrangements to be made for any child the parties should consider the child's welfare, wishes and feelings' (s12(2)(a)(iii)). Thirdly, there are also specific duties on state funded mediators: the Code of Practice for mediators funded by the Legal Aid Board must require them 'to have arrangements designed to ensure that the parties are encouraged to consider - the wishes and feelings of each child' and whether the child should attend mediation to express those wishes (s27(8)). In addition, those mediators subscribing to the Code of Practice of the UK College of Family Mediators, 'must encourage the participants to consider their children's own wishes and feelings' and may discuss with parents 'to what extent it is proper to involve the children themselves in the mediation process in order to consult them about their wishes and feelings' (Code of Practice, 1998, para 4.16).

The extent to which professionals ascertain children's views or encourage parents to do so is, therefore, crucial to the influence of the Act in promoting the idea that children should be heard, so it is to professional practice that the next section of this chapter turns. In the light of the operation of similar provisions in the Children Act 1989, how likely is it that the child's wishes will be heard and considered under the Family Law Act 1996?

Practice under the Children Act 1989

The Court

The main focus of the duties in the Children Act 1989 is the court. In contested section 8 applications the judge must be made aware of the child's wishes and can ascertain this directly or ask a probation officer to report on matters relating to the welfare of the child.[19] In addition, under section 41 the court can, but rarely does (Monro and Forrester, 1995, chapter 15), appoint a *guardian ad litem* who, under Rule 11 of the 1991 Rules, must ascertain the child's wishes.

The judiciary have not generally been encouraged to ascertain wishes themselves: '[T]he judge can see the child in his or her private room, but this is a procedure which must be adopted with caution' (Balcombe LJ, 1994, p.11). Whether or not with caution, some judges do see children.

> Booth J has recently stated judicially that justices should hardly ever see a child privately ... I do not know what status the doctrine of precedent in English law affords these observations, but they will be bold magistrates who decline to follow them. Perhaps anomalously, a judge has greater freedom. Personally, I will always agree to see a child, of whatever age, if the child has expressed a wish to see me. ... For my part I think, unfashionably, that judges and magistrates should see children more often and not be intimidated into thinking that only trained experts should be allowed direct access to their minds (Collins, J, 1994, pp.396-397).

It would, however, be an unusually bold *child* who would ask to see a judge, even if in a position to do so. It is, therefore, usually the court welfare officer who is asked to provide information about the welfare and wishes of the child. However, 'a common refrain' of research results and academic critique has been the inadequacy of court welfare officers in their role as advocate of the child's views (Trinder, 1997, p.293). Research conducted in the early 1990s found the question of ascertaining the wishes and feelings of the child to be 'a thorny and delicate issue and one that generates frequent disagreement amongst welfare officers both within and between areas' (James and Hay, 1993, p.96) to the extent that, in one research area, officers saw children alone in only 4% of cases (p.101).[20] This may have been due to a lack of clear guidance (Jones, 1992) which has been at least partially remedied by the *National Standards for Probation Service Family Court Welfare Work* (Home Office, 1994). These state that, in the course of compiling welfare reports, 'All children should be seen by the court welfare officer unless there are strong grounds for not doing so' (para 4.17).

Recent research is more favourable: 42% of respondents always, and 47% mostly, saw children at the report stage and, when children were consulted, 87% were seen separately from their parents (Hester *et al*, 1997, pp.30-31). However, there were differences in the weight given to the child's views - a finding supported by a small scale qualitative study which found that, despite a high degree of verbal agreement on certain key principles, consensus broke down into two very different approaches (Trinder, 1997, pp.294-301).[21]

As the previous chapter has pointed out, in section 8 proceedings very rarely are these deficiencies and problems circumvented by the child being separately and directly represented in court by a solicitor (see Piper, 1998; Sawyer, 1995 and 1997) or by the appointment of a guardian *ad litem* for the child.[22] As a result, despite positive changes in the 1990s, 'The methods provided whereby children's wishes are conveyed to the court are so inefficient and arbitrary that it is almost a matter of coincidence whether the court receives a clear idea of what these are' (Fortin, 1998, p.168). Many court welfare officers would, of course, contest the underlying assumption of that statement that the child has a clear view to be discovered and communicated. My concern is, rather, that, for the majority of children whose parents separate it is irrelevant whether or not a court requests a welfare report and how that request is complied with. Only a small proportion of parental disputes over residence and contact lead to the compiling of a welfare report and yet, as the next section will argue, in the current system for managing divorce, the potential for a court hearing leads to a belief among solicitors that the child's wishes are not their concern.

Solicitors

It is accepted that solicitors are currently the first port of call for those seeking divorce but there is a widespread view that this dominant role will, or ought, to be reduced when the Family Law Act divorce provisions are implemented. However, there are also compelling arguments for the view that they will retain a significant role (Cretney, 1997; Cretney and Masson, 1997, pp.374-383). Only the parent intending to make a statement of marital breakdown must attend an information session (though the other parent must attend if he wishes to contest matters regarding their child). Mediation will not be compulsory for privately funded clients whilst clients seeking Legal Aid funding may be deemed unsuitable for mediation and be granted Legal Aid for representation, as, indeed, might those suitable for mediation.[23] For the foreseeable future the solicitor may therefore remain as the main or sole professional contact for one or both of the parents involved and may, consequently, be the main conduit for ideas about the importance of the child's views. There is no duty on the solicitor to ascertain or take into account the child's wishes within the Children Act 1989 or its Regulations and section 11 of the Family Law Act 1996 places the duty on the court only though, as noted above, the Lord Chancellor may make rules requiring a solicitor to encourage clients to take note of their children's wishes. The development of 'franchising' of firms for family law work by the Legal Aid Board is, however, placing a non-statutory pressure on solicitors.

A growing number of franchised solicitors are subject to the transaction criteria imposed by the Legal Aid Board. The requirement to note the views of the child in relation to proposed arrangements for residence and contact on divorce first appeared in the checklists for 'Getting Information from the Client' and 'Advising on This Information' (Sherr *et al*, 1992, pp.14 and 19). This can now be found in the criteria in Part 4 of the Family Transaction Criteria (Issue No. 2, February 1995) - for use when 'arrangements for residence/contact of children affected by the relationship under s8 of the Children Act 1989 are not agreed': 'Unless the child(ren) are very young (pre-school age), does the lawyer have any understanding of the child(ren)'s views as to the current/proposed arrangements for contact/residence?' (para 128, see also para 132.1). The criteria also impose a comparable duty in relation to a negotiated agreement (para 153.2).

There is a dearth of empirical evidence for evaluating the role of solicitors specifically in relation to this issue[24] and so this section will rely on the Brunel University research which did aim, *inter alia*, to shed light on solicitors' attitudes to the acquisition, use and influence of children's views.[25] That research[26] included interviews with 22 solicitors who worked in firms franchised for family work and 14 who did not. The franchised solicitors were asked whether the requirement to record the views of the child in relation to residence and contact 'caused difficulties' for them and they were asked to explain the reasons for their answers. The remaining solicitors were asked whether and why they did or did not usually ask clients about the views of their children.

The results showed that over two-thirds of the franchised solicitors felt the requirement caused them difficulties. A handful of franchised solicitors expressed either ignorance of or hostility to the requirement or felt guilty that they ignored it, but most solicitors commented on how they fulfilled the requirement. Surprisingly their explanations were very similar whether or not they had initially said the criterion caused them difficulties. In other words, solicitors explained it was a difficulty because they were (only) recording the parent's view of the child's wishes or that it was not a difficulty because they simply recorded the client's views. Similarly they either did not feel the need to take the requirement too seriously because it would be done by the court welfare officer or they felt unhappy at ascertaining wishes because it was 'properly' the court welfare officer's job.

(i) Relying on the Views of the Parent All but five of the franchised solicitors said that they mostly recorded only the views of their client and some of these clearly found this quite unproblematic: 'No [it doesn't cause a difficulty] ... I mean, parents are usually forthcoming with that'. Five of the 14 non-franchised solicitors also indicated a lack of concern on this issue: recording the views of the client was hearsay 'but there we are', 'there's always going to be an element of bias'. Other solicitors expressed their dislike of having to rely on 'asking the client what somebody else's views are': 'you're very reliant on your client (a) being *aware* of what the children's views are and then (b) being totally upfront about it.' The remaining non-franchised solicitors were also uneasy about recording information they believed to be unreliable because of the inability of children to tell parents what they 'really' wanted or the potential for deliberate distortion by parents:

> [W]hat happens is, you know, the ... children come in with the mother - or their

> father - and they're simply going to go along with the parent that's come in to see me.

> [Y]ou get the parent saying this but ... I approach it on the you know 'Well you would say that wouldn't you' syndrome that the parents tends to reflect what they think, what they want, the child to say.

A revised statement of arrangements in line with the provisions of section 11[27] of the Family Law Act 1996 would, on the basis of this research, result only in solicitors recording - without query - parental views of the wishes and feelings of the child.

(ii) Relying on the Court Welfare Officer Over half the franchised solicitors justified their reliance on parents' views by explaining: 'No [it doesn't cause difficulties] I simply ask the client what his or her views are ... obviously the court welfare officer will be appointed later'. Their answers, together with those of the non-franchised solicitors, were predicated on the belief that the child's wishes were not 'needed' until the court had to adjudicate and a welfare report was ordered: 'I think the court welfare officer will get to the bottom of the position so far as the child is concerned'. They believed that legally 'usable' information about the child's wishes, that is information that was 'true' and 'unbiased', could only be collected by the court welfare officer: 'the only way I can give it any *serious* consideration is through an independent person such as the court welfare officer' and 'I would have to rely on the court welfare officer to determine objectively what those wishes would be'.

In addition, what could be detected in almost half of the responses[28] was an anxiety about apparently ever-changing professional boundaries.

> I think one has to be clear about what you're doing - who you're acting for. If you're acting for one of the parents and you start embarking upon a quasi-legal counselling, therapy, God knows what, session with a child, where do you finish up? What does it do to your professional relationship with the parent? I think there are very good professional reasons for being *extremely* cautious.

Though some expressed concern that interviewing children was 'really hard', for others this lack of confidence and/or appropriate skill was not the source of anxiety: 'I'll interview the children in Children Act cases - I'm a member of the Children's Panel so I don't have a problem with that. ... [in matrimonial cases]

I'm acting for the client not the children.' They fear having, in effect, two clients with conflicting interests.

(iii) Welfare But Not Wishes There is no question that 'the new cadre of specialist family lawyers who are characterised as "good"' (Neale and Smart, 1997, p.378) is concerned to promote the welfare of the child. They may even prejudice their ability to retain clients by their insistence that the child's welfare requires an agreed parental solution and contact with both parents: 'I was acting for mum, but I came very close to losing her because she didn't want to hear what I was telling her' (Neale and Smart, 1997, p.394). This particular construction of welfare - what Roche referred to in the previous chapter as 'a strong professional preference for a particular outcome for children' - has led lawyers and social workers to internalise fears of harming the child and undermining parental responsibility by seeking the views of the child. These fears have not only been recurrent themes in criticisms of the views of child liberationists since the 1970s (Fortin, 1998, p.5) but they have also fed into political agendas. Particular notions about harming children have given impetus to the child-saving element of the divorce reform debate - so necessary for the passage of legislation. The concern not to undermine parental control has buttressed political ideas about personal responsibility and the family - the ideological framework for reducing state intervention and expenditure. Given, therefore, that professional concerns have been strengthened by interaction with the political and moral discourses of the last two decades, it is not surprising that these fears have become an almost insuperable obstacle to ascertaining the views of children.

Don't Ask the Children

Wishes as Harmful

The problem flagged up by the Law Commission - that the benefit to the child of being heard will be outweighed by the burden of expressing wishes[29] - has constituted a powerful argument against asking the child for her views.

> Obviously there are dangers in giving [the child's views] too much recognition. Children's views have to be discovered in such a way as to avoid embroiling

> them in their parents' disputes, forcing them to 'choose' between their parents, or making them feel responsible for the eventual decision (Law Commission, 1988, para 3.23).[30]

This is also echoed in the *National Standards for Probation Service Family Court Welfare Work*: 'Children should never be made to feel as if they are taking responsibility for decisions about them which properly belong with adults' and officers are enjoined to 'be alive' to any pressure being placed on the child (Home Office, 1994, paras 4.17 and 4.18). Others have argued that this balancing exercise is too difficult to achieve. For example, a solicitor and court welfare officer have asked: 'How does the practitioner explain to the child that he is willing to listen to his opinion but simultaneously reassure him that adults are responsible for the ultimate decision?' (Bennett and Armstrong Walsh, 1994, p.93). Solicitors are also unenthusiastic: 'Sometimes clients will bring their children in - I don't recommend that because I think it puts undue pressure on the children ... "go on, tell her Billy .. tell her you want to live with me" - but I think that's to be discouraged' (Piper, 1997, p.799).

A twist on this argument is that ascertaining views and then not acting upon them may be even more damaging to the child than exclusion entirely from the decision-making process. Mrs Justice Booth points to a further pitfall: 'But a child may also impart some new information to a judge which that judge is bound to pass on to the other parties ... To the child that may well seem a nasty breach of confidence ...' (1993, p.652).

As the previous chapter and earlier sections of this chapter reveal, it was a concern for the child's welfare, not rights, which led to the inclusion of the child's wishes and feelings in checklists tied to the welfare paramountcy principle in both the Children Act and the Family Law Act. This welfare context for ascertaining views, together with a dominant construction of the risk of harm to the child of divorce (see Kaganas in this volume), has created the need for a decision as to whether the child is sufficiently mature (and the family situation is one appropriate for an expression of the child's views) that he or she will be 'empowered' and not burdened by expressing views. As we have seen, solicitors, judges and many court welfare officers avoid having to make this distinction.

Parental Responsibility

The Law Commission's recommendation that the duty to consider the child's wishes should be restricted to contested court hearings was in line with the growing political importance of a concept of parental responsibility. The parental 'right' to make decisions is now very strongly supported by norms upholding the 'rightness' of the exercise of parental responsibility and incorporating the idea that the exercise of parental responsibility is, of itself, beneficial for children. There is a consensus that the exercise of parental responsibility and, in particular, its exercise in the pursuit of 'joint' decision-making, is a major, if not the main, factor in promoting the welfare of the child. An early formulation of what was then a new idea is to be found in the following statement by two probation officers:

> Our philosophy is quite simple: we believe that the basis of a child's best interest lies in an agreement between the parents regarding the arrangements for their child. ... This philosophy entails fundamental shifts in practice: it involves ... a shift from the welfare officer deciding between who or what is best towards parental agreement (Howard and Shepherd, 1982, p.87).

This shift has been achieved: 'The best interests of the children are served by getting the parents to agree. It's as simple as that' (court welfare officer quoted in James, 1995, p.266). There is, in effect, a 'presumed logical sequence in the [Children] Act which places parental responsibility first' and only where there are disputes 'the hitherto unassailable notion of parental responsibilities is progressively eroded by the best interests of the child, perhaps directly articulated by the child as his or her "ascertainable wishes"' (Simpson, 1991, pp.392-393).

This particular normative construction of parental responsibility has gained strength from the dominant message about the harm caused by divorce. There is almost a presumption that children *will* be harmed by divorce. A recently published poem by a mediator about 'lonely, frightened, tearful' children makes the parents' potential culpability very clear:

> And in this the children suffer,
> Lose foundations, world in tatters,
> Fearful, lost with loveless future,
> These the victims, little children. ...

Have we something better for them?
Can we give them hope and future
Talking with their warring parents? ...
But in the end it's their decision:
- Nurse their hurt, or love their children.
(Mottashed, 1998).[31]

What this piece also makes clear is that, in the dominant story about children and divorce, the extent of the potential harm depends on whether their parents manage the divorce 'properly'. 'All hope is not lost. Many researchers believe that in some cases children have emerged self-reliant, compassionate, and courageous if parents handle the divorce responsibly' (Bias, 1996, p.113). Parents must act firmly, together, and in agreement and this must not be jeopardised by 'interference' from the views of their children.

What this means in professional practice is indicated by a case described by two court welfare officers. They refused to see a child separately to ascertain his wishes and feelings but talked to him only in front of his parents who they therefore felt were forced to accept responsibility and make a decision themselves (Cantwell and Scott, 1995; see also Piper, 1998). In effect the court welfare officers constructed the family meeting - where the child was present but not asked directly about wishes and feelings - as a site of expression of views. In professional practice, therefore, the expression and consideration of the child's views are sidestepped because the welfare context for ascertaining the child's wishes is taken to justify its subordination to the rights and wishes of parents.

Mediators May Consult the Children

The 'old' divorce professionals, whose practice has so far been described, often do not ascertain and consider the child's wishes: the expectation - evidenced in professional documents and parliamentary debates - is that the mediator, the 'new' divorce professional, will do so. This belief has hastened the development of techniques and processes through which to consider children's views in mediation (NFM, 1994) and a theoretical solution has been found to the 'conceptual impasse' caused by the need to admit the voice of the child into a parent-centred process (Fisher, 1996, p.14). The solution is consultation[32] (Roberts, 1997, pp.141-142), either directly within mediation or indirectly by mediators helping parents with ways to listen to their children. Not all mediators wish to use direct consultation - '*On occasions* it may also be appropriate for children to attend in order to voice their feelings on possible future plans which will affect their lives' [emphasis added][33] so techniques to encourage two-way communication between parents and children are also under development, drawing on practices used by professionals in child care and child health (NSPCC, 1997).[34]

However, mediators work within the same discursive constraints as the 'old' divorce professionals: parental responsibility and particular notions about the risks of talking to children 'inappropriately' again provide barriers to asking children what they think. Despite the optimism of some of our legislators, listening to children and allowing them to influence outcome will not automatically occur in the new divorce process. As Roberts summarises the NFM (1994) research findings:

> All mediator respondents, despite strong differences of approach, were agreed that the decision-makers were the adults, not the mediator nor the children, and then an approach of caution in relation to children was appropriate (Roberts, 1997, p.145).

Conclusions

This chapter, and that by Roche in this volume, explore the two theoretical contexts for the idea of ascertaining and considering the child's wishes - that of rights and that of welfare/best interests. In most of the UK children's views are heard firmly within a welfare discourse. The Children Act 1989 and the Family Law Act 1996 provide a legal framework which means that views are ascertained as part of process in which adults decide what is best for the child and, within the context of divorce, try to protect the child from a particular set of perceived risks of harm. Those risks, predicated on the influential image of the child as vulnerable victim of divorce, whose present happiness and future stability is seen to depend on harmonious joint parenting, can be reduced or removed only by the encouragement of parental decision-making and control.

It is not, therefore, surprising that the messages surrounding the issue of ascertaining and considering the wishes and the feelings of children in relation to arrangements being made for them by adults are confusing ones. At one level, as evidenced by the speeches of politicians, by professional guidance, by the signing of Conventions and by the proliferation of books and courses, there is apparent adherence to a conceptual framework of children's rights. At the level of talk about divorce however, the views of the child have been placed firmly within a child-saving agenda which itself has sometimes been used to pursue marriage and money saving agendas. The impression has been given that children and their wishes are a top priority in divorce and indeed Mr Llwyd, the MP who was a promoter in committee of the amendment which eventually became section 11, wanted that to be so: 'It is therefore vital that children's voices are heard loudly - not in a peripheral manner or as an afterthought, but central to the process' (Hansard HC col 586, 17 June 1996). The problem is that the current political, moral and professional ideologies make that very difficult. This undercurrent of non-engagement with the children of divorce whilst the rhetoric suggests something different, must be brought to the surface before there can be any real hope that more than a very small minority of children feel they have been heard.

Notes

1. For example, the Local Authority must give due consideration to the child's views in decisions about the child being 'looked after' by the Authority (ss 20, 22 and 26) as must voluntary organisations and children's homes under sections 61 and 64; police constables have 'to discover' the views of the child who has been taken into police protection under section 46(3)(d). Similar provisions are to be found in the Children (Northern Ireland) Order 1995 in, *inter alia*, articles 21, 26-28 and 45.
2. The comparable provision for Northern Ireland is in Art 3(3) of the Children (Northern Ireland) Order 1995. The Child Care Act 1991 imposes a similar duty on the courts (section 24) and health boards (section 3.2(b)) in the Republic of Ireland.
3. Now Adoption Act 1976 s6.
4. See Scottish Law Commission, 1992, p.53.
5. For a discussion of the operation of this provision see Sachs, 1993.
6. In the Republic of Ireland there is no statutory welfare checklist but there is a general duty on the courts to apply the paramountcy principle and 'to give due consideration' to the child's wishes (Child Care Act 1991 section 24).
7. Hansard, HL Vol 576 No 29, Col 1091, 11 December 1996 in a debate on a motion 'to call attention to the role of the family' moved by Lord Northbourne.
8. See Roche in this volume.
9. See Simpson (1991) for a discussion of the findings of research which was based on interviewing children of divorced parents about their feelings of distress, anger etc. Whether the publicised findings are an accurate reflection of the generality of research in this area, however, is debatable in relation to the 'powerlessness' of the child. McLoughlin and Whitfield used an interview sample from which it might not be

possible to generalise but, in that sample, 67% of the adolescents said that they had been kept informed of what was going on and 81% believed their views had been given sufficient consideration (1984, p.164). The debate on the detrimental effects of divorce on children also has not always reflected the generality of research findings (Piper, 1994).

10. See Read and Marsh (1996) for a discussion of voting patterns in the passage of the Family Law Bill.
11. The measure included no duty to seek out the views of the child but, as Eekelaar (1994, p.60, n51) points out, Article 12 of the United Nations Convention on the Rights of the Child, does not impose such a duty.
12. Subsections 1 and 2 of section 11 reproduce the effect of provisions in the amended section 41 of the 1973 legislation: it is subsections 3 and 4 which are new.
13. The new power is in section 11(2) which lists the situations when the court 'may direct that the divorce order or separation is not to be made until the court order otherwise'.
14. This interpretation is based on the fact that section 11(3) states: 'In deciding whether the circumstances are as mentioned in subsection 2(a), the court shall treat the welfare of the child as paramount', and section 11(4) states, 'In making that decision, the court shall have particular regard' to the checklist. Subsection (2)(a) says 'the circumstances of the case require [the court] or are likely to require it to exercise any of its powers under the Children Act 1989 with respect to any such child' but that section (11(2)) deals with the decision to delay the making of a separation or divorce order. It is section 1(1) which deals with the decision simply to exercise Children Act 1989 powers or not.
15. Section 11(1) states that 'In any proceedings for a divorce ... the court shall consider ... whether ... it should exercise any of its powers under the Children Act 1989'.
16. The section 8 order would not be the result of a contested application, and a direction under 37 (for the local authority to investigate the child's circumstances) is not an order under part IV (see Children Act 1998 section 1(4)). Whilst the s1(3) checklist does not strictly apply, the Lord Chancellor assumed it would in relation to residence and contact (see Bird and Cretney, 1996, p.82).
17. *Re B (Change of Surname)* [1996] 1 FLR 791. Conversely, it is not clear that all parts of the checklist are given specific consideration (in disputed applications) in the light of a further Court of Appeal statement in *B v B (Residence Order, Reasons for Decision)* where it appeared to be necessary to affirm that, 'It is certainly not a good reason for not carefully considering all the matters in the checklist, simply that neither party makes "complaints" against the other' ([1997] 2 FLR 602 at 608).
18. Unlike the Law Commission (1988) the Scottish Law Commission found majority support from their consultees for such a duty to be placed on parents (1992, paras 2.64 and 2.65).
19. Using the power in section 7 of the Children Act: See Rule 13 of the Family Proceedings Court (Children Act 1989) Rules 1991.
20. A similar view of Swedish practice is given by Saldeen: 'For example there have been instances where the [court welfare] investigator has only met the child once or not met the child at all' (1996, pp.447-448)).

21. The two teams researched who were working within a systemic family therapy framework aimed to shield the child from the burden of decision-making and encourage instead parental decision-making, believing in any case that children could not convey their 'real wishes' because of the context of inter-parental hostility. The remaining two teams believed, by contrast that it was 'vital' to see the child separately to ascertain her needs and to 'allow the child to let off steam' (p.298). Both approaches were, therefore, working within a welfare context.
22. In the small minority of cases where a guardian *ad litem* is allocated their role is now governed by Standard 5 of the *National Standards for the Guardian ad Litem and Reporting Officer Service* (1995, Department of Health/Welsh Office) which states that the *Guardian* must 'make explicit efforts' to ascertain the child's wishes' (para 5.6).
23. Those applying for Legal Aid for representation and found to be suitable for mediation must then decide, with the mediator's 'help', 'whether instead to apply for mediation' (section 29).
24. See Piper (1996b) for a review of research on divorce solicitors generally. See also Neale and Smart in this volume and research by Sawyer (1995, 1997). Research currently underway and not fully reported includes that by Sara Mclean for the Legal Aid Board and that by Bristol University in relation to section 8 applications, funded by the Nuffield Foundation (see Bailey-Harris *et al*, 1998).
25. This research is reported in Piper (1997).
26. See Kaganas and Piper in Chapter 9 of this volume for details of the sample and methodology.
27. 'Parenting plans' are currently being piloted by the Lord Chancellor's Department. These entail more detailed information from parents.
28. From 11 solicitors working in franchised firms and 5 in non-franchised.
29. As Fox Harding expresses it: 'The ambivalence in child liberationist writing about whether the enlargement of children's rights should, or could, be accompanied by a commensurate increase in their responsibilities has also created an unfortunate space in which it is possible for children to have inappropriate responsibility for themselves thrust upon them by default' (1996, p.148).
30. See also the Scottish Law Commission (1992, para 5.27).
31. Bill Mottashed is a mediator with the Somerset Mediation Service.
32. See Best (1995) for a discussion of training modules.
33. From an information leaflet distributed by a team of mediators trained by the Family Mediators Association, whose front page 'title' - 'A sensible approach ...' - is indicative of the way that mediation is being portrayed and promoted.
34. The techniques used to focus on and consult with children may put more psychological pressure on one parent than the other with a consequent effect on power differentials within mediation (Piper, 1993, pp.191-201).

References

Bailey-Harris, R., Davis, G., Barron, J. and Pearce, J. (1998), *Monitoring Private Law*

Applications Under the Children Act: A Research Report to the Nuffield Foundation, University of Bristol.

Balcombe LJ (1994), 'The Voice of the Child', *Family Mediation*, vol. 4(1) 11).

Bennett, S. and Armstrong Walsh, S. (1994) 'The No Order Principle, Parental Responsibility and the Child's Wishes', *Family Law*, p.91.

Best, R. (1995), 'Direct Consultation with Children: A Progress Report on Training Modules', *Family Mediation*, vol 5(3), p. 8.

Bias, T. Di (1996), 'Some Programs for Children', *Family and Conciliation Courts Review*, vol 34(1), pp.112-129.

Bird, R. and Cretney, S. (1996), *Divorce The New Law*, Family Law, Bristol.

Booth, J. (1993), 'Closing Address to the Lawyers for Children Conference', 24 September 1993 in *Family Law*, p.652.

Cantwell, B. and Scott, S. (1995), 'Children's Wishes, Children's Burdens', *Journal of Social Welfare and Family Law*, vol 17(3), p.377.

Collins, Judge Paul (1994) 'The Voice of the Child', *Family Law*, p.396.

Cretney, S. (1997), 'Lawyers Under the Family Law Act' *Family Law*, p.405.

Cretney, J. and Masson, J. (1997), *Principles of Family Law* (6th Edition), Sweet and Maxwell, London.

Douglas, G., Murch, M. and Perry, A. (1996), 'Supporting Children When Parents Separate - A Neglected Family Justice or Mental Health Issue', *Child and Family Law Quarterly*, vol 8, p.121.

Eekelaar, J. (1994), 'The Interests of the Child and the Child's Wishes: the Role of Dynamic Self-Determinism', *International Journal of Law and the Family*, vol 8, pp.42-61.

Eekelaar, J. (1992), 'The Importance of Thinking that Children Have Rights', *International Journal of Law and the Family*, vol 6, pp.221-235.

Fisher, T. (1996), 'The Rights of the Child in Mediation and Divorce', *Child Care Forum*, vol 9, p.14.

Fortin, J. (1998), *Children's Rights and the Developing Law*, Butterworths, London.

Fox Harding, L. (1996), 'Recent Developments in "Children's Rights": Liberation for Whom?' *Child and Family Social Work*, vol 1, pp.141-150.

Freeman, M. (1983), *The Rights and Wrongs of Children*, Francis Pinter, London.

Franklin, B. (1986), *The Rights of Children*, Blackwell, Oxford.

Hester, M., Reason, C. and Radford, L. (1997), *Domestic Violence: A National Survey of Court Welfare and Voluntary Sector Mediation Practice*, University of Bristol, Bristol.

Hoggett, B. (1993), *Parents and Children* (4th Ed), Sweet and Maxwell, London.

Home Office (1994), *National Standards for Probation Service Family Court Welfare Work*, Home Office, London.

Howard, J. and Shepherd, G. (1982), 'Conciliation - New Beginnings', *Probation Journal*, vol 29, p.87.

James, A. and Hay, W. (1993), *Court Welfare in Action*, Harvester Wheatsheaf, Hemel Hempstead.

James, A. (1995), 'Social Work in Divorce: Welfare, Mediation and Justice', *International Journal of Law and the Family*, vol 9, pp.265-274.

Jones, E. and Parkinson, P. (1995) 'Child Sexual Abuse, Access and the Wishes of Children' *International Journal of Law and the Family*, vol. 9(1), p.54.

Jones, S. (1992), 'The Ascertainable Wishes and Feelings of the Child', *Journal of Child Law*, vol 4(4), p.181.

King, M. (1999), '"Being Sensible", Images and Practices of the New Family Lawyers', *Journal of Social Policy* (forthcoming).

King, M. and Piper, C. (1995), *How the Law Thinks About Children* (2nd Ed), Arena, Aldershot.

Kroll, B. (1996), *Chasing Rainbows*, Russell House Publishing, Lyme Regis.

Law Commission (1986), *Custody. Working Paper* No. 96, HMSO, London.

Law Commission (1988), *Report on Guardianship and Custody Law* No 172, HMSO, London.

Law Commission (1990), *The Ground for Divorce* No. 192, London, HMSO.

Lord Chancellor's Department (1993), *Looking to the Future: Mediation and the Ground for Divorce*, Cm 2424, HMSO, London.

Lord Chancellor's Department (1995), *Looking to the Future: Mediation and the Ground for Divorce*, Cm 2799, HMSO, London.

Lowe, R. (1975), *Marriage Breakdown and Children*, Crash Course Lecture 1997, The College of Law, London.

McLoughlin, D. and Whitfield, R. (1984), 'Adolescents and their Experience of Divorce' *Journal of Adolescence*, vol 7, pp.155-170.

Monro, P. and Forrester, L. (1995), *The Guardian ad Litem* (2nd ed), Family Law, Bristol.

Mottashed, W. (1998), 'Mediation 1998', *Family Mediation*, vol 8(1), p.4.

NFM (National Family Mediation) (1994), *Giving Children a Voice in Mediation*, NFM, London.

NSPCC (National Society for the Protection of Cruelty to Children) (1997), *Turning Points: A Resource Pack for Communicating with Children*, NSPCC National Training Centre.

Perry, A. (1996), 'Children and the New Divorce Law' *Childright*, No. 131, p.12.

Piper, C. (1993), *The Responsible Parent: A Study in Divorce Mediation*, Harvester Wheatsheaf, Hemel Hempstead.

Piper, C. (1994), 'Looking to the Future for Children', *Journal of Child Law*, vol 6(3), pp.98-102.

Piper, C. (1996a), 'Divorce Reform and the Image of the Child', *Journal of Law and Society*, vol 23(3), pp. 364-382.

Piper, C. (1996b), 'Norms and Negotiation in Mediation and Divorce', in M. Freeman (ed) *Divorce, Where Next?* Dartmouth, Aldershot.

Piper, C. (1997), 'Ascertaining the Wishes and Feelings of the Child: A Requirement Honoured Largely in the Breach?' *Family Law*, p.796.

Piper, C. (1998), 'Child Advocacy', in Y. Craig, (ed), *Advocacy, Counselling and Mediation in Casework: Processes of Empowerment*, Jessica Kingsley Publications, London.

Pitrusu, M. (1998), 'Research Findings on the Parent and Child Counselling Services of the South East London Family Mediation Bureau', *Family Mediation*, vol 8(1), p.19.

Read, M. and Marsh, D. (1996), 'The Family Law Bill: Conservative Party Splits and Labour Party Cohesion', *Journal of Parliamentary Affairs*, p.263.

Roberts, M. (1997), *Mediation in Family Disputes*, (2nd ed), Aldershot, Arena.

Sachs, T. (1993), 'The Views of the Child in Abduction Cases: Re R and S v S', *Journal of Child Law*, vol. 5(1), pp.43-44.

Saldeen, A. (1996), 'The Rights of Children to Speak for Themselves and Obtain Access to Information Concerning their Biological Origins etc.,' in A. Bainham (ed) *International Survey of Family Law*, International Society of Family Law.

Sawyer, C. (1995), 'The Competence of Children to Participate in Family Proceedings', *Child and Family Law Quarterly*, vol 7(4), pp.180-195.

Sawyer, C. (1997), 'The Mature Child - How Solicitors Decide', *Family Law,* pp.19-21.

Sherr, A., Moorhead, R. and Paterson, A. (1992), *Transaction Criteria*, Legal Aid Board, HMSO, London.

Scottish Law Commission (1992), *Report on Family Law*, Report No. 135.

Simpson, B. (1991), 'The Children Act 1989 and the Voice of the Child in Family Conciliation', *Family and Conciliation Courts Review*, vol 29(4), pp.385.

Timms, J. (1997), 'The Tension between Welfare and Justice', *Family Law*, pp.38-47.

5 Contact, Conflict and Risk

FELICITY KAGANAS

Introduction - The Family Law Act 1996

Increasingly in recent years public debate, fuelled by concern about juvenile delinquency, by New Right theory, and by the fathers' rights and new fatherhood lobbies (Smart, 1989), has focused on the detrimental effects on children of relationship breakdown. Children are thought to sustain harm not only as a result of the trauma and upheaval of their parents' separation but, more importantly, they are thought to be damaged by losing contact with the non-resident parent. Father absence, in particular, has been blamed for educational and socio-economic underachievement, anti-social activity and delinquency, sexual promiscuity and confused sexual identity (see, for example Dennis and Erdos, 1992). In addition, it is thought that conflict between parents compounds the damage: both trauma and the risk of loss of a parent are thought to be exacerbated by parental hostility and inability to co-operate. The Family Law Act 1996 is framed, therefore, to address these most pressing problems of divorce. It is designed, through the promotion of mediation, to encourage conflict-free resolution of disputes about children. And it seeks, through stating explicitly how the welfare of the child will best be served (section 11(4)(c)), to ensure that those disputes are resolved in a way that enables links between children and both parents to be preserved.

The legislation not only re-enacts the paramountcy principle enshrined in section 1 of the Children Act 1989 (section 11(3) Family Law Act 1996), it also specifically provides for a presumption that contact is in children's best interests. The welfare of the child, it states, is best served by regular contact with those with parental responsibility and other family members and by the maintenance of as good a continuing relationship with his parents as possible (section 11(4)(c)). The legislation goes on to put in place procedures designed to implement its goals and, at every stage of the divorce process, to remind parents of the desirability of co-operation and contact. The priorities of the lawmakers are to be made clear to the parties early on at the information meeting, projected to be the initial 'port of call'.

While the precise content of the information to be supplied in terms of section 8(9) awaits the outcomes of various pilot projects, sections 1[1] and 11 leave little room for doubt that the importance of avoiding conflict and the benefits of contact will be impressed on parents under subsections (b) and (c) of section 8(9). The function of the information meeting, it seems, is unlikely to be simply the neutral transmission of information. Indeed, unless the information is confined to giving a bald repetition of the words of the section or notification of the availability of legal advice and support services, it is difficult to imagine how it could be so. It appears that the information meeting may prove to be the forum in which norms are purveyed concerning what are considered appropriate ways of safeguarding children's welfare. Thus moral pressure may well be exerted on both fathers and mothers; they are likely to be left with the clear understanding that 'good' parents agree arrangements for children and that one of the things they agree on is contact. Further pressure may be applied by solicitors and mediators (section 1) and, finally, by the courts.

In most cases, it is likely that it will be mothers who will be the target of all these efforts. It is likely that it will be mainly mothers who attend information meetings; the majority of divorces are initiated by women[2] and, unless the other party makes or contests an application concerning children or finances, he need not attend (section 8(5)).[3] Fathers who do not seek contact will not attend except in those cases where they make the statement of marital breakdown. The gender neutral language of the legislation does suggest that fathers may be apprised of its general principles by solicitors and mediators and that they may be instructed by the courts to see their children, but current practice makes this appear unlikely (see below).

The Background to the Family Law Act 1996

The legislation endorses what are already strong trends in family law. For a number of years now, the courts have placed greater and greater emphasis on contact between children and their absent fathers. By the 1970s, the judiciary was endorsing the 'immense value' (*M v M (Child: Access)* [1973] 2 All ER 81, 85) to children of access and, in a statement that has echoed down the years, Wrangham J in *M v M* declared it to be a right of the child:

> I for my part would prefer to call it a basic right in the child rather than a basic right in the parent. That only means this, that no court should deprive a child of access to either parent unless it is wholly satisfied that it is in the interest of that child that access should cease, and that is a conclusion at which a court should be extremely slow to arrive (p.85).

This formulation of access or contact as a right of the child has often been reiterated[4] and, in *Re R (A Minor) (Contact)*[1993] 2 FLR 762, 767, the Court of Appeal said that the principle that contact is a right of the child is underlined by the UN Convention on the Rights of the Child[5] and confirmed in the parental responsibility provisions of the Children Act 1989. Recent decisions show an increasing readiness to 'enforce' this right by means of a court order. Judges have articulated what is in effect 'a very strong presumption in favour of maintaining contact between a child and both parents' (*Re M (Contact: Welfare Test)* [1995] 1 FLR 274, 281).[6] Balcombe J said in *Re H (Minors) (Access)* [1992] 1 FLR 148, 152 that the question the court has to ask is whether there are 'any cogent reasons why ... children should be denied the opportunity of access to their natural father'. It is not necessary to ask whether there are any positive benefits to be gained by that contact. And in *Re F (Minors) (Denial of Contact)* [1993] 2 FLR 677, 684 the court referred to 'the normally compelling rule of law, and indeed of nature, that children should not be deprived, save for good reason and in exceptional circumstances, of the benefit of contact with a natural parent'.

So strong is the presumption that contact is in children's best interests that an attempt in one case to introduce a more individualised balancing exercise into the decision-making process has had no impact on subsequent decisions. In *Re M (Contact: Welfare Test)* [1995] 1 FLR 274, 278-9, Wilson J sought to apply the checklist in section 1(3) of the Children Act 1989 to the question of contact in order to determine whether the 'fundamental emotional need of every child to have an enduring relationship with both parents ... is outweighed by the depth of harm' which the child 'would be at the risk of suffering' if a contact order were made. However in *Re O (Contact: Imposition of Conditions)* [1995] 2 FLR 124, 128, Sir Thomas Bingham MR reasserted the presumption, saying that it is 'almost always in the interests of the child' to have contact with the non-resident parent.

The presumption has steadily increased in strength in recent years.[7] An examination of the case law reveals that courts are increasingly reluctant to refuse contact. The fact that the child has no recollection of the non-resident parent and that there has been little contact in the past does not nowadays preclude an order *(Re F (Minors) (Contact: Mother's Anxiety)* [1993] 2 FLR 830; *Re D (Contact: Reasons for Refusal)* [1997] 2 FLR 48, 52).[8] The courts are also proving more and more reluctant to deny contact on the grounds of disruption to the child.[9] Children's opposition to contact is not decisive either and it has been said that courts should not be unduly perturbed by the prospect of distress being caused to children by contact;[10] 'upsets' resulting from contact are deemed to be 'usually minor and superficial' (*M v M*, 1973, p.88).[11] Even in cases where the child has been abused by the father, contact, albeit normally supervised, may be ordered.[12] Certainly resistance on the part of caretaking mothers too has largely been discounted as a reason for refusing contact orders.

The Implacably Hostile Parent

Mothers who have sought to oppose contact for any reason have, in recent years, felt that they have been placed under considerable pressure to withdraw their objections. This pressure emanates from solicitors, mediators, court welfare officers and courts. Bailey-Harris *et al* report that district judges, court welfare officers and solicitors all 'tend to be suspicious of mothers who oppose contact' (1998, p.35). Smart and Neale (1997, p.333) illustrate the 'robust' approach taken by solicitors who set out to 'lay down the law' to mothers[13] while Piper (1993, p.118) observes that for mediators, 'contact was an overriding "good", regardless of its content and any drawbacks'.[14] And although the courts make it clear that they expect parents to come to an agreed settlement, in those cases that do come before them, they will, as we have seen, normally order contact. The order is directed at the residential parent and the courts have not shied away from making orders that almost resemble mandatory injunctions in the steps it prescribes for those parents.[15] Moreover, courts are increasingly prepared to threaten a change in the child's residence if contact is resisted[16] and to imprison residential parents who disobey orders.[17]

If a caretaking mother opposes contact she is seen to be undermining the potential for the creation of a 'good' post-divorce family both because she is fomenting conflict and because she is 'robbing' her child of a relationship with the non-resident parent. She is described as 'implacably hostile' and is chastised by professionals and by courts alike (see *Re W (A Minor) (Contact)* [1994] 2 FLR 441). The court in *Re O* made it clear that '[n]either parent should be encouraged or permitted to think that the more intransigent, the more unreasonable, the more obdurate and the more unco-operative they are, the more likely they are to get their own way' (*Re O (Contact: Imposition of Conditions*) [1995] 2 FLR 124, 129-130). Even risks to the mother's health are not considered as sufficient reason to refuse contact.[18] And in those cases where the court finds that the hostility is such that the child will be harmed if contact were ordered, the courts make it clear where the mother's duty lies. So, for example, in a case where the father had been violent to the mother, intimidated her, drank excessively and took drugs, the court, after indicating its belief that he was now a reformed character, expressed the hope that the mother would come to realise that it would be best for the child to be brought up in the knowledge of both parents (*Re D (A Minor) (Contact: Mother's Hostility)* [1993] 2 FLR 1, 8).[19]

Indeed, until recently, the courts did not consider a history of violence as a legitimate reason for the mother to oppose contact. So, for example, in *Re P (Contact: Supervision)* [1996] 2 FLR 314,[20] the Court of Appeal made an order for supervised contact in favour of a father who had allegedly threatened to kill the children and who had been jailed after attempting to strangle the mother. The court concluded that the evidence before it did not support the 'proposition that the possible detriment to the children of not seeing their father is outweighed by the possible detriment to them through a threat to their mother's health caused by stress and anxiety' (p.325). The mother was not so affected that she was rendered incapable of caring for the children and there was no evidence that they were adversely affected by contact. There was also, said the court, the 'danger' that if it did not order contact, the intransigent parent would get her own way (p.330).

This approach appears to be changing with judicial awareness of the growing body of research into domestic violence and contact. In *Re D (Contact: Reasons for Refusal)* [1997] 2 FLR 48,[21] the Court of Appeal accepted that the father presented a risk of physical harm to the child, or of physical harm to the mother to the extent that the child would be indirectly harmed. The court declined to treat this as a case involving an implacably hostile mother, pointing out that the way the term is used is sometimes misleading. Hale J indicated that it should not be used to describe mothers whose fears 'are genuine and rationally held' (p.53) and dismissed an appeal against a refusal to order contact.

Similar views are expressed by another judge in an article published in

1997. His Honour Judge Victor Hall (1997) suggests that the overriding importance accorded to contact by welfare officers, legal advisers and courts might be misplaced in cases involving a violent father; consideration should be given to the consequences to mothers and children of such orders. In addition, he points out, it should not necessarily be assumed, as courts often do,[22] that it is the mother who is to blame for her children's resistance to contact; it may be that children have witnessed 'inappropriate' behaviour on the part of their fathers (1997, p.814).[23]

Nevertheless, although the 'legitimate complaints' (p.818) of women and the wishes of children should be treated seriously, Hall concludes:

> Contact with the absent parent is and remains the norm that we should strive for. Obduracy without cause is still to be deprecated in the vast majority of cases. The interests of the child do, in most cases, require frequent contact with the other parent (p.818).

Explaining the Presumption

The designation of contact as a right, and the creation of what amounts to a presumption in favour of granting it, in effect largely removes the question of contact from the arena of contested fact into the realm of legal principle. This in turn largely removes any need for courts to justify their decisions to award contact other than by reference to legal principle. Nevertheless there are judicial pronouncements that provide some insight into the reasoning of the courts.

Hall (1997, p.813) explains that the basis of the assumption that contact is in a child's best interests is that 'the child would be harmed if contact with the absent parent is denied'. The transformation of contact into the right of the child did indeed take place within the framework of the welfare principle. In *M* v *M* (1973) Wrangham J cited with approval an earlier decision[24] to the effect that to deprive a 'good parent' of access is to make a 'dreadful' and 'Draconian' order that could have 'lifelong consequences' for both parent and child (p.85). Latey J in turn stressed the advantages of keeping in touch so that the absent parent does not lose interest and, in consequence, fails to make the emotional and material contributions to the child's development that would otherwise be made (p.88).

In characterising contact as the right of the child rather than purely as the right of the parent, the judgments in *M* v *M* clearly seek to shift the focus of the law's concern from the interests of parents to those of the child; they place the welfare of the child at the centre of judicial deliberations. However, the decision goes further than that. That contact is described as a right has the effect that the otherwise indeterminate concept of the welfare of the child is invested by law with a particular content: as a general rule contact is a desirable 'good' for children. Moreover, the court appears to be suggesting that not only is contact beneficial for children but that lack of it can be detrimental; implicit in the judgments are notions of harm and loss to the child. The 'right' of contact accorded to the child then may be seen as a legal device designed to ensure that courts faced with contact cases make decisions favouring contact, so benefiting children and averting loss or other forms of harm.

These notions of loss and harm are made explicit in later cases. For example, in *Re O* the court, after indicating the desirability of contact went on: 'The reason for this scarcely needs spelling out. It is, of course, that the separation of parents involves a loss to the child, and it is desirable that that loss should so far as possible be made good by contact with the non-custodial parent, that is the parent in whose day-to-day care the child is not' (*Re O (Contact: Imposition of Conditions*) [1995] 2 FLR 124, 128). In *Re P* the court referred to '[t]he possible detriment to the children of not seeing their father' (*Re P (Contact: Supervision*) [1996] 2 FLR 314, 325). In *Re J (A Minor) (Contact)* [1994] 1 FLR 729, 736, Balcombe LJ noted that it was necessary 'to balance that harm [of making a contact order] against the harm that will undoubtedly be caused to [the child] by being deprived of contact with his father'. In *A v N (Committal: Refusal of Contact)* [1997] 1 FLR 533, consideration was given to the risk of 'long-term damage' to the child if there were no contact with the father (pp.537, 540). And in *Re M* [1998] 1 FLR 727, 732, the court described as 'surprising' the finding of an assistant recorder that the child concerned would not suffer emotional harm if there were no contact with the father.

Conflict-free Contact as a Priority for the Legal System

The courts have long declared themselves in favour of access (see Maidment, 1984, pp.241-2; Bailey, 1994, pp.394-395),[25] but such statements were apparently not indicative of any great concern within law about contact between children and their absent parents (Maidment, 1984, p.242).[26] It seems that until the 1980s, courts dealt with access in a 'perfunctory' manner and, in the 'overwhelming majority' of cases, access was left to the parents to arrange as they wished (Maclean and Eekelaar, 1997, p.50). Its elevation into a priority for law,[27] along with the goal of reducing conflict, has been coterminous with the growth of child welfare knowledge focusing on these matters and courts have turned to this body of knowledge in justifying their decisions. Even in 1973, Latey J in *M* v *M* (p.88) invoked not only 'common sense' and 'human experience', but also referred to 'medical and other expert discovery' favouring contact. And after the publication of research studies such as that of Wallerstein and Kelly (1980), judicial recourse to child welfare discourse has increased. In *Re P*, for instance, Wall J warned that 'internecine warfare' between the parents over contact would damage the children: 'They will find it very difficult as they grow up to develop a normal relationship with a member of the opposite sex. Their own sense of self-worth will be damaged. The chances of their growing up to be normal and decent human beings will be seriously affected' (*Re P (Contact: Supervision)* [1996] 2 FLR 314, 332). And in *Re F (Minors) (Contact: Mother's Anxiety)*, Balcombe LJ referred to 'the risk, well documented by medical and legal literature and cases, that the children could be damaged by not having the right to know their own father' ([1993] 2 FLR 830, 834).

Those governmental bodies charged with devising legislation too refer extensively to the findings of research in the field of child welfare science. In a Consultation Paper, the Lord Chancellor's Department (LCD) sketched out the aims of what was to become the Family Law Act 1996. In relation to children, it stated:

> **4.4** A considerable amount of research has been carried out on the effects of divorce on children .... Conflict between parents has been linked to greater social and behavioural problems among children .... When parents separate the loss often results in low self-esteem in children who feel they are the cause of the parent leaving. When conflict continues through a separation and divorce, the effects on the children can be very damaging.
>
> **4.5** What is important about this research is not that it confirms what we must all already know - namely the awful trauma children suffer when their parents are in conflict or when they split up - it is that this trauma can be reduced in certain circumstances. A major factor is the reduction of conflict between their parents.

> **4.6** .... It is clear that most children will benefit from maintaining a good relationship with both their parents ....
>
> **4.7** Continuing and peaceful contact arrangements with which both parents and children are happy are essential and are likely to influence the child's wellbeing. Conversely, no contact or acrimonious contact will have a negative effect. (LCD, 1993)

Within pronouncements such as these, one can detect the influence of the work of researchers such as Wallerstein and Kelly (1980), Hetherington *et al* (1982) and Richards (1982). And, certainly, the Exeter Family Study (Cockett and Tripp, 1996) as well as other research findings coloured parliamentary debates during the passage of the Family Law Act 1996 (see Hansard HL, 22 Jan 1996, cols 805, 808, 825). Even solicitors' advice to clients is characterised by slippage between legal and child welfare discourse (King, 1999).

The version of the research studies that has shaped the dominant discourse about divorce and contact is clearly a simplified one. In this version, divorce damages children and, in order to limit that damage it is essential to ensure that conflict is reduced or eliminated and that contact is maintained. The more nuanced and complex features of the research are absent. For example, Wallerstein and Kelly reject the imposition of any 'presumptive pattern' of post-divorce parenting and remark that parents 'may have little interest in their children; they may demean or exploit their children; they may use the children to establish a permanent foothold in the divorced partner's life' (1980, pp.310-311). Richards refers not only to reduction of conflict and the benefits of contact but also to the need for affordable housing, the need to ensure an adequate income for post-divorce households with children, and the need to provide emotional and practical support for caretaking parents (1994, p.252). A recent review of research in the field confirms that it is characterised by greater complexity and greater uncertainty than the law allows. Rodgers and Pryor (1998, pp.4-5), observe that, '[t]here is no simple or direct relationship between parental separation and children's adjustment, and poor outcomes are far from inevitable'. Nor can it be assumed, they say, that the disadvantages to children identified by researchers are attributable to the separation (p.5). And although they ultimately favour contact (pp.7, 16, 46), they note that the loss or absence of a parent does not appear to have a very significant effect on children (pp.6, 40) and that it is the quality and not the frequency of contact that matters, (pp.6-7). Furthermore, they identify factors such as the ability of parents to recover from the psychological distress as being important for children's ability to adjust (p.6).

Moreover, there is conflicting research in this field. Yet little credence is attached to studies that contradict what Maclean and Eekelaar (1997, p.50) term the 'new orthodoxy'. The most frequently cited of these, written by Goldstein, Freud and Solnit (1973, 1979), and which recommended that the question of contact be left to the caretaking parent, met with a hostile reception (see, for example, Freeman, 1983, p.218). Others, (for example, Furstenberg, Morgan and Allinson (1987)), which found that contact had no consistent influence on children's well-being, have attracted little attention.

In addition, the response within politics and law to research documenting the failure of fathers to exercise contact has been muted. Reasons postulated by researchers for the cessation of contact are not confined to maternal intransigence and focus also on fathers' voluntary withdrawal. This is attributed by Goode (1956, p.315) to, among other things, expense, travelling time and a loss of familiarity with the child's activities. Simpson *et al* (1995) point out that some fathers are unable to relate to their children without maternal mediation (pp.9, 62-63). In a more recent study, Wallerstein and Lewis (1998) found that relationships between non-resident fathers and their children were affected by factors unrelated to the fallout from marriage failure. Fathers became unavailable to their children because their psychological state and dominant mood led them to withdraw, because their new partners were hostile to contact, because they felt uneasy during visits as children grew to adolescence, and, simply, because they lost interest in their children (pp.374-375).

Wallerstein and Lewis's research is out of step with the conventional wisdom surrounding contact in other respects too. They found that regular contact did not prompt the majority of fathers in their study to support their children financially.[28] Moreover, where fathers insisted on contact, children found rigid adherence to arrangements distressing; none of these children had a good relationship with their fathers after reaching adulthood (pp.376-378, p.381). The authors conclude that their findings:

> raise doubts about the policy expectations of recent years that the child of divorce can be expected to maintain a close relationship with both parents during the postdivorce years if the anger between the parents can be contained (p.374).

Child Welfare Knowledge and Law

Bailey-Harris *et al* comment that the body of knowledge forming the basis on which legal decision-making is made in the context of private family law is 'speculative and uncertain' (1998, p.41), 'ill-understood, and probably unsuited to such massive generalisation' (p.44). King, in turn, points to the contingency of child welfare knowledge (1997, p.55) and doubts, except in cases of extreme physical abuse, that it is ever possible to identify the 'right' causes of harm to children or to find the 'right' measures to combat it (1997, p.34). Nevertheless, as we have seen, the law has, by selectively invoking certain research findings, evolved a very definite and clear model of the 'good' post-separation family.

To some extent, this process of selection can be explained in terms of the necessity for law of reducing complexity. King and Piper (1995) argue that reductionism and the simplification of child welfare knowledge is an inevitable consequence of law's autopoetic nature. Law cannot incorporate external discourses, they say, without reconstructing them in a way that 'makes sense' within law (p.50), enabling it to codify events as lawful or unlawful. These legal reconstructions of the complex discourse of child welfare are 'necessarily simplistic because law by its very nature needs clear normative principles' (p.51).

The process of reconstruction is unavoidable; the law cannot ignore child welfare science and still purport to be applying principles and making decisions that serve the best interests of children. Law as a system of communication has nothing to say about what is good or bad for children. In contemporary society this is the preserve of experts within child welfare science, whose expertise confers on their work a claim to truth. Child welfare science alone can claim authoritatively to tell us what will best serve children's interests and which events or choices will lead to which outcomes for children.

Yet the need for clear normative principles legitimated by science does not of itself explain the way in which the law has reconstructed child welfare science in the context of contact. It has had to make choices from a range of available principles. It could, for example, have chosen to adopt the principle that contact should not be ordered against the wishes of the resident parent but chose, instead, the opposite. The reason for this must be that a decision to give the resident parent a veto would run counter to a dominant discourse surrounding contact which has been informed by political as well as child welfare imperatives. Currently, government and professional groupings, as well as popular culture reflected in the media, all espouse a particular understanding of the consequences of separation and divorce for children. This understanding has been accorded the status of taken-for-granted truth and cannot fail to impact on the legal system if it is to retain credibility. And the law, in making pronouncements consistent with the dominant discourse, confirms its 'rightness'. Within the dominant discourse and so, also, in the legally reconstituted version of child welfare science, children are damaged by divorce and, increasingly, it is thought that the damage or loss they suffer is exacerbated by conflict or lack of contact. The task for law, then, is to establish the rules and to make the decisions that will avoid or minimise this damage; the legal system must be able to retain public confidence by giving the impression that it can do what is right for children and avert the risks to which they might be exposed.

Risk Management

Contemporary society, says Niklas Luhmann, 'seeks to comprehend misfortune in the form of risk' (1993, p.viii) and embraces an 'ethic of ensuring the nonoccurrence of disaster' (p.xi). Rather than attributing calamity, as we might have done in the past, to witchcraft, magic, or the will of God (p.viii), we tend to think we are, to some extent, in control. The notion of risk, he comments, appears to promise that 'even if things do go wrong, one can have acted correctly' (p.13).

Luhmann draws a distinction between risks and dangers. Risks are those losses that are perceived as having been avoidable and that are attributed to decisions, to choices made between alternatives (p.16, pp.21-22). Dangers are those losses that are categorised as occurring other than as a result of decisions (p.22). Risks do not exist as objective truths awaiting discovery. Rather, Luhmann contends, they are produced (p.6). This refers to the 'process by which the factors that are seen as contributing to future loss become identifiable, as knowable, and once known, controllable through decisions' (King and Kaganas, 1998, p.238). From that point on, the loss is transformed from danger into risk and there arises an expectation that a right decision can be found.

As Douglas (1994) observes, science and expertise are central to the identification and quantification of risks. In the context of divorce, it is through child welfare science that the dangers to children have been recast as risk. That children are harmed or turn out badly is not the result of chance or fate, it is because their parents decide to divorce and because the right decisions concerning their future upbringing are not made.

Of course, some risks are considered permissible or worth taking and, according to Luhmann, politics is implicated in making those evaluations (1993, p.30). Law's selection then, from the body of child welfare knowledge, of those risks deemed to be unacceptable, is, in part, informed by politics. A political decision has been made to discourage divorce but not to prohibit it. The period of reflection in the Family Law Act 1996 is intended to give pause to couples contemplating divorce and, perhaps, to prompt them to reconsider their decision. If this fails, however, other political priorities apply. First, the state has to calm public fears, prompted by the high divorce rate and the increased numbers of 'single mothers', about the consequences to society of what is perceived to be the undermining of the role of men (Collier, 1995, p.7) and the demise of the family. This it does by constructing the 'good' divorce, one that will minimise the risk of underachieving, disturbed and delinquent children or children whose only financial support comes from the state. The 'good' divorce is harmonious and leaves room for a unit closely analogous to the intact family, with both parents taking responsibility for and co-operatively involved in raising their children. Second, in the interests of promoting individual responsibility and also, supposedly, of securing more enduring arrangements for children, parents must be encouraged to take responsibility for decision-making on divorce. Finally, the costs to the taxpayer of divorce must be kept in check lest they escalate out of control.

These are clearly the priorities that underlie the provisions in the Family Law Act 1996 promoting contact and mediation. However they have for some time infused the dominant discourse, particularly since the advent of the Children Act 1989 with its emphasis on parental responsibility and the notion that 'parenthood is for life'. Risks that do not fall within the political agenda have either been downgraded in importance or ignored. So, for instance, little attention is paid by law to the quality of contact or to its adverse impact on the mother's or the child's psychological state. Children's distress at contact is largely dismissed as transitory (*Re O,* 1995, p.129; *Re H (Minors Access)* [1992] 1 FLR 148, 151) and mothers' objections are characterised as 'flimsy' (*A v N*, 1997, p.541) or as based on 'exaggerated' fears (*Re P*, 1996, p.320). In the past, the courts considered risky a decision to order contact where the parents were in conflict or where the child's family unit would be destabilised.[29]

Now, it is a decision not to order contact that is considered risky. Little can be allowed to stand in the way of contact for, since it is designated as the principal remedy for what ails the children of divorced parents, to deny contact would be to leave them without a cure.

Interestingly, despite the importance ascribed to contact, the risks of paternal indifference or unreliability do not figure prominently in concerns about divorce.[30] The successful construction of problems depends in part on the availability of acceptable solutions (Manning, 1985, p.162) and it may be that to compel non-resident parents to see their children would be too politically unpopular. Or it may be seen as futile: 'the law is not good at enforcing personal relationships' (Hale, 1997, p.16). Certainly, the courts do not appear to be eager to take this course and have interpreted the legislation accordingly (Bailey-Harris *et al*, 1998, p.35). The risks of paternal abandonment are, it seems, not seen as controllable by coercion. It may be that they will be addressed in future through persuasion (s1 and s8(9) Family Law Act 1996). However, the signs are that, at present, neither solicitors nor mediators routinely advise non-resident parents to maintain contact. In relation to mediation, it has been said that mediation is geared towards achieving contact for fathers by persuading mothers to accede to it. Mediators only use arguments invoking joint parental responsibility in cases of dispute; 'where the father doesn't bother with access, no-one else bothers either' (Wegelin, 1984).[31] Solicitors also appear to direct their efforts primarily at defusing conflict and at overcoming mothers' resistance to contact. In the Brunel University study (n.13 above), 16 out of the 36 solicitors interviewed, when questioned about the advice they gave to clients concerning children's welfare, gave answers which stressed either the desirability of contact or the inevitability of an order in the event of a hearing. Out of those, only three mentioned advice pertaining to the father's exercise of contact.[32]

It appears, then, that certain risks, namely conflict and denial of contact to a father who wants it, are increasingly amplified, while others are largely discounted. And law is implicated in this process of amplification. Moreover, not only has there been a shift in the relative acceptability of different risks, the locus of responsibility for risk-taking has also changed. In the past, courts saw it as their responsibility not to expose a child to risk by, for example, ordering contact where there was conflict between the parents. Now, if the court is faced with such a case, it is no longer the contact order that is seen as the risky decision; it is the parents' decision to persist in maintaining hostile relationships.[33] More specifically, if the conflict centres around a mother's refusal to accede to contact, it is she who is placing her child at risk. In allocating responsibility for risky decision-making in this way, the law participates in the construction of images of 'good' fathers and 'good' mothers.

'Good' Fathers and 'Good' Mothers

The law does not appear to make any onerous demands on non-resident fathers in relation to contact. If a father seeks a contact order, the fact that he wishes to see his child suffices to place him in the category of 'good' fathers;[34] contact is deemed to be beneficial unless there are cogent reasons to decide otherwise. 'Good' mothers, on the other hand, not only must refrain from obstructing contact, they must ensure that their children do not resist it and that it is 'peaceful' (LCD, 1993).[35]

Mothers are branded as 'irresponsible' (*Re H (Contact: Principles)* [1994] 2 FLR 969) if they oppose contact, and, more seriously, are said to be exposing their children to 'serious risk of emotional harm' (*Re D (A Minor) (Contact: Mother's Hostility)* [1993] 2 FLR 1, 7). It has even been said that the harm sustained by a child as a result of a defiant mother's committal to prison flowed from her own decision rather than the court's:

> For it to be submitted that the hardship to the child is the result of the court imposing the committal order is wholly to misunderstand the position. This little child suffers because the mother chooses to make her suffer .... If she goes to prison it is her fault, not the fault of the judge who did no more than his duty to the child (*A v N,* 1997, p.541).

'Good' mothers, lest they otherwise place their children at risk, are expected to be self-denying, to sacrifice their interests to those of their children and to cope with the vicissitudes that contact may bring them. So, for example, in *Re P*, while the Court of Appeal criticised both parents for their mutual hostility, it went on:

> These observations apply to both parents, but the mother has a special burden in this respect, particularly given her mental state and the treatment the recorder found she received at the hands of the father. I remind her, and ask her to take on board, that what is ordered is contact of a very limited nature. She

> should be able to cope. Whatever she does, these children will want to know their father as they grow up, and if she continues to obstruct contact she will in my judgment simply be storing up trouble for herself (*Re P (Contact: Supervision)* [1996] 2 FLR 314, 332).

Not only must mothers 'cope' with contact, they have a positive duty to facilitate it (*Re O*, n.15). In *F* v *F* (n.17) a suspended committal order was made against a mother who, it was found, indoctrinated the children against the idea of contact and failed to use her influence and authority to counter the children's refusal to see their father. There was, the court affirmed, 'a clear obligation upon the mother to assist the children to come to terms with having contact with their father' (at p.242).

Within law, therefore, mothers are constructed as powerful gatekeepers who hold the key to their children's destinies and, ultimately, to social order. For law has incorporated the image of fathers as the 'producers of heterosexual children, the stabilizing anti-delinquency agent, and the bringer of realistic values and the desire for achievement' (Smart, 1991, p.486). It has designated mothers as the primary decision-makers in relation to contact; it is mothers who determine whether their children will be deprived of the benefits of paternal influence. Fathers, in turn, as Collier points out in this volume, are constructed as powerless, as the victims, like their children, of the capricious and vengeful conduct of their former partners. Their role in deciding whether or not to sustain contact, and their part, in some cases, in deploying contact to perpetuate conflict, receive little acknowledgement. In effect, they are left free to decide whether they want contact and, apart from exceptional cases, they receive the full backing of the courts if they do. It is mothers who are constructed as a problem[36] and it is mothers, therefore, who must be controlled. Those who resist are constructed as 'bad' and there are even suggestions that they should be seen by the courts as 'mad'.[37]

Conclusion

Bailey-Harris *et al* describe as 'remarkable' the way in which the idea that contact must be maintained has permeated legal culture (1998, p.42). They go on to express concern that what may amount to no more than 'pseudo-knowledge' or 'beliefs' (p.41) have been transformed into legal principles (p.44). However the ascendancy, and their translation into principle, of theories emphasising the importance of contact and the reduction of conflict is perhaps unsurprising.

It is imperative for law and for politics to heed child welfare science if they are to maintain legitimacy. And which theory from within that body of knowledge is invoked, which theory gains popular support and influences policy and practice, as King suggests, depends on whether that theory has 'the backing of powerful groups within society' and is 'consistent with the objectives of those groups' (1981, p.113). Research studies recommending conflict-reduction and contact have articulated objectives that have been consistent with those of government, those of professional groupings such as mediators and court welfare officers, and those of the New Right and fathers' lobbies; they fit neatly into the political and economic priorities that have dominated family policy since the 1980s. And the further simplification of the research so as to render conflict-free contact of overriding importance serves two purposes. First, as we have seen, reductionism is necessary for law. Secondly, it means that government, the legal system and the professionals can claim to be effective in the pursuit of children's welfare.

Divorce is considered to be a risky business. Government, law and the professionals are expected to act to eliminate those risks. In the simplified version of child welfare knowledge, it is those children who are exposed to conflict or who are cut loose from fathers who are deemed to be most at risk psychologically, emotionally and economically. These are the risks, then, that have to be controlled. In constructing resident parents, and more particularly mothers, as having the power and the responsibility for decisions surrounding contact, the law, and the professionals, have succeeded in characterising them as posing the main risk to children. This has meant that mothers must be persuaded to make the 'right' decisions and, if necessary, their power has to be wrested from them by the courts. To crack down on non-compliant mothers is not only justifiable, it is essential in order to safeguard the welfare of children.

Contact with non-resident fathers and the reduction of conflict have come to be constructed as the solutions to what are regarded as some of the most serious problems of divorce. By seeking to implement these solutions, and by minimising the significance of other problems, government, law and professional practice can give the impression of reducing the risks to children. In short, they can be said to be 'doing something' about the risks of divorce. It is unfortunate for mothers that 'doing something' about divorce has meant primarily 'doing something' about them.

Notes

1. Section 1(c)(ii) endorses the general principle that, on marriage breakdown, questions should be resolved in a manner designed to promote as good a continuing relationship between the parties and any children affected as is possible.
2. See, for example, Haskey, 1996, p.28.
3. The Act does, however, make provision for joint statements of marital breakdown, in the event of which both parties must attend a meeting (s8(4)).
4. See, for example, *Re S (Minors) (Access)* [1990] 2 FLR 166, 170; *(Re F; Minors) (Contact: Mother's Anxiety)* [1993] 2 FLR 830, 834.
5. For a critique of claims of this nature, see Fortin, 1998, pp.313-314, 327-328.
6. See also *Re A (Contact: Domestic Violence)* [1998] 2 FLR 171, 174.
7. Compare Weyland (1992) with Weyland (1995).
8. See also Bailey-Harris *et al*, 1998, p.35; *Re W (A Minor) (Contact)* [1994] 2 FLR 441. Compare *Re SM (A Minor) (Natural Father: Access)* [1991] 2 FLR 333. Compare, also *Re M (Contact: Welfare Test)* [1995] 1 FLR 274, 280, where the court regarded it as significant that the mother, on the advice of the court welfare officer, ceased for a time to press for contact and suggested that if she were insufficiently motivated to persevere through the initial difficulties, the value of restoring contact might be diminished.
9. See *Re R (A Minor) (Contact)* [1993] 2 FLR 762. Compare the earlier cases of *Re SM (A Minor) (Natural Father: Access)* [1991] 2 FLR 333; *Starling v Starling* (1983) 4 FLR 135; *Re W (A Minor) (Access)* [1989] 1 FLR 163. For cases where the risk of disruption was found to be so serious that contact was denied, see *Re H (A Minor) (Parental Responsibility)* [1993] 1 FLR 484; *Re B (Contact: Stepfather's Opposition)* [1997] 2 FLR 579.
10. *Re H (Minors) (Access)*[1992] 1 FLR 148.
11. However if there is a risk that forcing children to see their parents will lead to long term emotional damage, contact may be refused. See *Re M (Contact: Welfare Test)* [1995] 1 FLR 274; *Re F (Minors) (Denial of Contact)* [1993] 2 FLR 677.
12. See *Re H (Parental Responsibility)* [1998] 1 FLR 855; *L v L (Child Abuse: Access)* [1989] 2 FLR 16; *Re H (Minors) (Access: Appeals)* [1989] 2 FLR 174. Compare the earlier case of *S v S (Child Abuse: Access)* [1988] 1 FLR 213. It appears that there is a presumption, in cases where contact in some form or other is ordered, that if it goes well, it will be extended (Bailey-Harris *et al*, 1998, p.35).
13. See also Neale and Smart, 1997. A preference for a similarly persuasive style was discerned among solicitors interviewed in the course of a small research study conducted by the Centre for the Study of Law, the Child and the Family at Brunel University in the summer of 1996. For example, one solicitor said, 'If it's the mother I will say that unless there's an excellent or exceptional reason why the child should not have contact with the father, the court will generally order contact. He has a right to have contact with the child... . It's in the interests of the child to have contact with both parents'. Further on this study, see King, 1999.
14. See also Roberts, 1997, p.84.

15. See *Re O (Contact: Imposition of Conditions)* [1995] 2 FLR 124. Compare *Re D (Contact Orders: Conditions)* [1997] *Fam Law* 200 where the court held that it could not attach to a contact order conditions designed to protect the mother.
16. See *Re O*, n.15 above, at 130. But see also *Re B (Contact: Residence Order)* [1997] *Fam Law* 830.
17. See *A v N (Committal: Refusal Of Contact)* [1997] 1 FLR 533; *F* v *F (Contact: Committal)* [1998] 2 FLR 237.
18. See *Re F (Minors) (Contact: Mother's Anxiety)* [1993] 2 FLR 830, 834.The father, in this case, had been convicted of the assault of the mother and she suffered panic attacks, apparently triggered by the thought of the father's having contact with the children.
19. See also *Re J (A Minor) (Contact)* [1994] 1 FLR 729, 736.
20. See also *Re F*, n.18, above.
21. See, for the law in Scotland, *S* v *M (Access Order)* [1997] 1 FLR 980.
22. See for example *F v F* , n.17 above; Maidment, 1998.
23. Indeed, that children's recalcitrance is constructed as the result of maternal hostility is becoming increasingly apparent in the literature currently being produced by lawyers. There are growing calls for courts to be even more resolute in enforcing contact in cases of what is now termed 'parental alienation syndrome'. Psychologists, it is said, have found that mothers may appear to accede to contact while covertly influencing the child against it. This 'strategy of alienation' causes 'damage' to a child that is 'both insidious and long-term' and may even be 'tantamount to emotional abuse by the mother' (Willbourne and Cull, 1997, p.808).
24. *B v B* [1971] 1 WLR 1486, 1493.
25. Their reasons have changed over time. For instance Bailey (1994, p.394), reviewing judicial attitudes in the 18th century, says that it was considered ungentlemanly or immoral for fathers to refuse mothers access.
26. Writing in the first half of the 1980s, both Freeman (1983, p.215) and Maidment (1984, p.235) remark on the lack of interest within the legal system in the question of access.
27. Despite the non-intervention principle in section 1(5) of the Children Act 1989, Bailey-Harris *et al* (1998, pp.14-16) report a significant increase since implementation of the legislation in the number of contact disputes brought before the courts. They speculate on various explanations for this, including changes in the attitudes of fathers and changes in legal culture. One such change might be the prospect of almost certain success for fathers.
28. However, Maclean and Eekelaar, 1997, p.147 report that, in their study, they found a link between contact and the likelihood of financial support.
29. See *Starling v Starling* (1983) 4 FLR 135; *Re W (A Minor) (Access)* [1989] 1 FLR 163.
30. However, concern about paternal inconstancy has led the present government to consider introducing a 'child commitment ceremony' for unmarried fathers (The Observer, 5 April, 1998).
31. A Dutch writer cited by Davis and Roberts (1988) at p.114.
32. One said that he explained that contact should be regular and that its quality is more important than its frequency. A second said that she would gear the conversation towards pointing out that mum should allow contact and that 'dad should take it up'.

A third said that she 'might start counselling the absent parent ... about the importance of maintaining contact'.

33. In *Re P*, 1996, p.326, the court stressed that it was 'the conflict between the parents, not the contact, which causes the children's emotional suffering'. See also *Re C and V (Contact and Parental Responsibility)* [1998] 1 FLR 392, 399.
34. It is notable that in *Re R (A Minor) (Contact)* [1993] 2 FLR 762, Butler-Sloss declared that the test in *Re H* (1992) is the starting point *where a non-resident parent wishes to maintain contact.*
35. In a somewhat unusual case, a resident father was urged to 'put the hostility behind him' (*Re B (Residence Order: Status Quo)*) [1998] 1 FLR 368, 371. Nevertheless, it is the mother who is normally the resident parent and who bears this responsibility.
36. Fathers are seen as a problem only in relation to child support (Piper, 1995, p.358).
37. Willbourne and Cull (1997) report that '[c]ases of severe alienation come from a personality disorder or psychopathy' and moot the possibility of removing children from an alienating parent while she undergoes treatment (p.808). See also Rosenblatt and Scragg (1995) who suggest that mothers who are distressed by contact might be prescribed Prozac.

References

Bailey, M.J. (1994), 'England's First *Custody of Infants* Act', *Queen's Law Journal*, vol 20, pp.391-437.

Bailey-Harris, R., Davis, G., Barron, J. and Pearce, J. (1998), *Monitoring Private Law Applications under the Children Act 1989. Research Report to the Nuffield Foundation*, University of Bristol, Bristol.

Cockett, M. and Tripp, J. (1996), *The Exeter Family Study: Family Breakdown and Its Impact on Children*, University of Exeter Press, Exeter.

Collier, R. (1995), ' "Waiting Till Father Gets Home": The Reconstruction of Fatherhood in Family Law', *Social & Legal Studies*, vol 4, pp.5-30.

Davis, G. and Roberts, M. (1988), *Access to Agreement*, Open University Press, Milton Keynes.

Dennis, N. and Erdos, G. (1992), *Families Without Fatherhood*, Institute of Economic Affairs, London.

Douglas, M. (1994), *Risk and Blame. Essays in Cultural Theory*, Routledge, London.

Fortin, J. (1998), *Children's Rights and the Developing Law*, Butterworths, London.

Freeman, M.D.A. (1983), *The Rights and Wrongs of Children*, Frances Pinter, London.

Furstenberg, F., Morgan, S. and Allison, P. (1987), 'Paternal Participation and Children's Well-being After Marital Dissolution', *American Sociological Review*, vol 52, pp.695-701.

Goldstein, J., Freud, A. and Solnit, A. (1973), *Before the Best Interests of the Child*, Free Press, New York.

Goldstein, J., Freud, A. and Solnit, A. (1979), *Beyond the Best Interests of the Child*, Free Press, New York.

Goode, W.J. (1956), *After Divorce*, Free Press, New York.

Hale, B. (1997), 'Private Lives and Public Duties: What is Family Law For?', The Eighth ESRC Annual Lecture, 23 October.

Hall, V. (1997), 'Domestic Violence and Contact', *Family Law*, pp.813-818.

Haskey, J. (1996), 'Divorce and Children: Fact Proven and Interval Between Petition and Decree', *Population Trends*, No.84, pp.28-32.

Hetherington, E.M., Cox, M. and Cox, R. (1982), 'Effects of Divorce on Parents and Children' in M.E. Lamb (ed), *Nontraditional Families: Parenting and Child Development*, Lawrence Erlbaum, London, pp.233-288.

King, M., (1981), 'Welfare and Justice', in M. King (ed), *Childhood, Welfare and Justice*, Batsford, London.

King, M. (1997), *A Better World for Children*, Routledge, London.

King, M. (1999), '"Being Sensible". Images and Practices of the New Family Lawyers', *Journal of Social Policy*, (forthcoming).

King, M. and Kaganas, F. (1998), 'The Risks and Dangers of Experts in Court', *Current Legal Issues*, pp.221-239.

King, M. and Piper, C. (1995), *How the Law Thinks About Children* (2nd ed), Arena, Aldershot.

Lord Chancellor's Department, (1993), *Looking to the Future. Mediation and the Ground for Divorce. A Consultation Paper*, HMSO, London.

Luhmann, N. (1993), *Risk: A Sociological Theory*, R Barrett (trans), Walter de Gruyter, New York.

Maclean, M. and Eekelaar, J. (1997), *The Parental Obligation*, Hart Publishing, Oxford.

Maidment, S. (1984), *Child Custody and Divorce*, Croom Helm, London.

Maidment, S. (1998), 'Parental Alienation Syndrome - A Judicial Response?', *Family Law*, pp.264-6.

Manning, N. (1985), 'Reconstructing Social Problems', in Manning, N. (ed), *Social Problems and Welfare Ideology*, Gower, Aldershot.

Neale, B. and Smart, C. (1997), '"Good" and "Bad" Lawyers? Struggling in the Shadow of the New Law', *Journal of Social Welfare and Family Law*, vol 19(4), pp.377-402.

Piper, C. (1993), *The Responsible Parent*, Harvester Wheatsheaf, Hemel Hempstead.

Richards, M. (1982) 'Post-divorce Arrangements for Children: A Psychological Perspective', *Journal of Social Welfare Law*, pp.133-151.

Richards, M. (1994), 'Divorcing Children: Roles for Parents and the State', in M. Maclean and J.Kurczowski, (eds), *Families, Politics and the Law: Perspectives for East and West Europe*, Clarendon Press, Oxford.

Roberts, M. (1997), *Mediation in Family Disputes. Principles of Practice*, Arena, Aldershot.

Rodgers, B. and Pryor, J. (1998), *Divorce and Separation. The Outcomes for Children*, Joseph Rowntree Foundation, York.

Rosenblatt, J. and Scragg, P. (1995), 'The Hostile Parent: a Clinical Analysis', *Family Law*, pp.152-153.

Smart, C. (1991), 'The Legal and Moral Ordering of Child Custody', *Journal of Law and Society*, vol 18, pp.485-500.

Smart, C. and Neale, B. (1997), 'Arguments Against Virtue - Must Contact be Enforced?', *Family Law*, pp.332-336.

Simpson, B., McCarthy, P. and Walker, J. (1995), *Being There: Fathers After Divorce*, Relate Centre for Family Studies, Newcastle Upon Tyne.

Wallerstein, J. and Kelly J.B., (1980), *Surviving the Breakup: How Children and Parents Cope with Divorce*, Grant McIntyre Limited, London.

Wallerstein, J. and Lewis, J. (1998), 'The Long-term Impact of Divorce on Children. A First Report From a 25-Year Study', *Family and Conciliation Courts Review*, pp.368-383.

Weyland, I. (1992), 'Contact Within Different Legal Contexts', *Family Law*, pp.138-144.

Weyland, I. (1995), 'Judicial Attitudes to Contact and Shared Residence since the Children Act 1989', *Journal of Social Welfare and Family Law*, vol 17(4), pp.445-459.

Willbourne, C. and Cull, L. (1997), 'The Emerging Problem of Parental Alienation', *Family Law*, p.807.

PART III
HUSBANDS AND WIVES

6 From Women's Emancipation to Sex War? Men, Heterosexuality and the Politics of Divorce

RICHARD COLLIER

Introduction

This chapter is about one, increasingly prominent and problematic, aspect of the complex relationship between divorce reform and the social, cultural and symbolic representation of the heterosexual family 'in crisis': the relationship between men and the changing family. It seeks, specifically, to explore the discursive construction of the unspoken 'heterosexuality' of divorce, understood as a socio-cultural phenomenon; that is, society and culture do not exist outside divorce, shaping it externally, but are central to and productive of its very nature as a legal category and social experience. What follows presents an analysis of debates which have encircled and framed divorce reform during the period from the 1969 Divorce Reform Act (henceforth DRA) through to the 1996 Family Law Act (FLA).[1] The chapter focuses, in particular, on the interrelated conceptualisation of marriage, fatherhood and heterosexuality within contemporary debates. Certain assumptions about male heterosexuality have, I shall argue, not simply been contained within but have been *central to* the conversations presently taking place around reconfigurations of 'family', gender and social change at the end of the twentieth century.

In order to address these issues, and to move beyond the dominant paradigm through which divorce continues to be conceptualised by reference to ideas of 'collapsing', 'reforming' or 'reconstituting' families, it is necessary to engage with the complex - and, I shall suggest, under researched - nature of the *mutual constitution* of heterosexuality, marriage and divorce within a range of discourses concerned with constituting the in/outside of the boundaries of the 'family'. This chapter seeks, ultimately, to challenge the way in which a male subject has been encoded as, simultaneously, 'masculine' and 'heterosexual'. This is a subject which has historically signified a particular model of heterosexuality, a model which has appeared increasingly problematic as the 'sexual politics' of divorce have themselves become emblematic of some broader concerns, anxieties and tensions.

A Context: Heterosexuality, Divorce and the Changing 'Family'

The relationship between gender, law and the family has produced a vast literature, much of which provides a conceptual and practice-based critique of law from a range of feminist perspectives (see, for example, Smart, 1984; O'Donovan, 1985; Brophy and Smart, 1985; O'Donovan, 1993; Fineman, 1995). Yet despite this focus on gender politics, it continues to be rare to speak, specifically, of the *heterosexuality* of divorce. This may, in part, be due to what appears to be the tautological nature of the relationship. Marriage in Britain is, after all, an institution reserved for 'biological' men and women (Section 11(c) Matrimonial Causes Act 1973: henceforth MCA) and can thus be seen as the institutional embodiment of heterosexuality.

In recent years, however, in a range of disciplines, the study of heterosexuality *in its own right* has emerged as, in the words of one recent text, 'a new research agenda' (Wilkinson and Kitzinger, 1993; Maynard and Purvis, 1995; Richardson, 1996; Steinberg *et al*, 1997). Within the social sciences, the *heterosexual* family has surfaced as a contested terrain, a site of competing discourses. This work has sought to 'unpack' heterosexuality as a discursive, historical construct and to consider, in particular, its relationship to the ever-present Other of homosexuality. Yet, such an engagement remains rare in the fields of both family law and social policy.

In this chapter, I argue that heterosexuality is a concept which is of considerable potential analytic use in seeking to understand contemporary debates about marriage and divorce. What has emerged from within a diverse body of scholarship around the relationship between subjectivity, corporeality and gender(ed) identities is an, albeit sometimes implicit, theorisation of the heterosexual subject as a fluid 'performative practice', an understanding of being 'straight' as a dynamic 'project of the self' whereby the idea of the gendered self is conceptualised as a series of constantly shifting practices and techniques (Butler, 1990; Probyn, 1993). Within one strand of political-theoretical work on sexuality and identity - that informed by the different variants of 'queer theory' (Butler, 1990; Wittig, 1992; Butler, 1993; Warner, 1993; Sedgwick, 1994; Stychin, 1996) - the idea of there *being* a (hetero) sexed subjectivity has itself been seen as a process, not merely defined by private sexual acts, but as '... a public process of power relations in which everyday interactions take place between actors with sexual identities in sexualized locations' (Bell and Valentine, 1995, p.146; see also Smart, 1996a, 1996b).

The question arises as to what it might mean for the study of gender and divorce to fuse, to bring together, the problematisation of *heterosexuality* (understood as an always, already, contingent and performative practice) with a critical analysis of the pervasive idea that western societies are now experiencing a contemporary *crisis* in the family. A central theme within contemporary debates about the shifting boundaries of 'family' has been the changing demands on, and experiences of, men and their 'masculinities' both beyond, but also in, the heterosexual family. Within both the 'crisis of the family' and 'crisis of masculinity' discourses the issue of divorce has become a battleground around which these more general conversations about men's contribution to 'the social' are taking place. Whether it be from neo-liberal 'pro-family' perspectives, from sociological and historical research on fatherhood, in feminist, pro-feminist or explicitly anti-feminist thought, in media and popular cultural texts or at the level of social and family policy rhetoric, the legal regulation of men's relationships with women and children after divorce has emerged as a high-profile, pressing and unquestionably politically contentious issue.

Questions about the position and function of men in families are central to this debate. What is the nature of 'responsible' fathering after divorce? What should be the economic obligations associated with the non-residential parent (in the vast majority of cases the man)? Do 'families need fathers' at all? Is a father's, indeed is a *man's*, 'role', both during and after marriage, 'gendered'? What, ultimately, are men 'for' in constituting the familial at a time of profound economic, cultural and technological changes which are demanding new adaptations, new forms of attachment and, of course, the mobilisation of new subjective commitments to modes of belonging and integration such as legal 'marriage' and the heterosexual 'family'? (Giddens, 1992) .

Having established something of the theoretical and political context for this discussion of men, heterosexuality and divorce it is necessary, in order to begin to address these questions, to explore in more detail the nature of the debates which have taken place in Britain around the sexual politics of divorce. In the next section I shall discuss some of the ways in which men have historically been constituted as familial subjects focusing, in particular, on the construction of men as the 'new victims' of divorce reform. I will then proceed to address contemporary developments in family policy around divorce, paying particular attention to the reconstitution of fatherhood which has taken place during the 1990s.

Law, Power and the Construction of Men as the 'New Victims' of Divorce

> Men and victimhood now go together like bras and pyres did in the Sixties. Whether it's the catastrophic decline in sperm quality; fathers driven to suicide by the Child Support Agency; anorexic boys; or scary, Wonderbra-wearing bosses such as Demi Moore, masculinity appears to be in crisis (*Independent on Sunday*, 19 May 1996).

It has been a recurring theme throughout the divorce reform debates in Britain from 1969, the year of the DRA, through to the present day, that men have become the *new victims* of divorce. This is a notion which has grown in ideological significance in the shaping of broader debates around the family and social change. It is an assumption which rests, however, on a misleading reading of the relationship between law, power and the changing contours of heterosexual relating.

Each of the major pieces of divorce legislation following the 1969 DRA has resulted, I argue, from political, religious and public reassessments of and debate about, not just specific procedural laws and substantive concerns pertaining to transitions in legal status,[2] but also, perhaps above all else, shifting societal attitudes towards the institutionalisation of heterosexuality in the form of marriage. The period from the enactment of the DRA in 1969 through to the FLA 1996[3] has been marked by a noticeable transition in the ways in which the effects of divorce on women and men have been conceptualised. What is particularly interesting about this more recent period in family law, notably from around the mid-1980s, has been the way in which a number of social and economic changes have prompted a rethinking of men's 'role' in the family through the language of a transition in *gender relations*. This 'gender frame' has served to problematise many hitherto taken-for-granted aspects of men and their 'masculinity', in particular the nature of the paternal (presumed heterosexual) masculinity of the father. Developments such as rising rates of cohabitation and increasing numbers of births outside marriage, the increased 'visibility' of gay, lesbian and bisexual practices and cultures, the broader hegemony of the 'family crisis' idea (Midgley and Hughes, 1997) and a range of concerns around the implications of technologically transformed reproductive practices (Stanworth, 1987; Callahan, 1997; Steinberg, 1997) have each been interpreted as, variously, undermining, threatening or reconstituting the gendered performative practices of men and their 'masculinities' in the family and, in particular, in their role as fathers. In short, whilst women have been presented within a range of cultural artefacts as being *empowered* in multifarious ways (economically, socially, culturally, in work, education, in terms of physical, emotional and psychological health), men have been increasingly seen as 'losing out' to women as, within the period in question, a so-called crisis of the family has, increasingly, been interpreted *as* a crisis of paternal masculinity (cf. Fineman, 1995, pp.201-213).

In this construct of a masculinity 'threatened' by such changes, men's position as familial subjects has, implicitly, been conceptualised as something which is normatively *challenged.* At the same time a zero-sum calibration of power relations between men and women has been invoked whereby legislation perceived as empowering women has been seen as simultaneously *dis*empowering men.[4] In so doing, the existence of an ontologically fixed masculine subject been presumed - a man constituted as (relatively) powerful or powerless on the basis of (his) sex-status. Such a conceptualisation of the subject has tended to efface any recognition of the psychological complexity of human agency. In seeking to understand the rise of the 'new (male) victimhood' it gives no handle on *why* it should be that men feel themselves to be disempowered by legal changes, notwithstanding what might also appear to be objective evidence of men's continued economic, cultural and social empowerment relative to women. Nor does it explain why divorce arouses such feelings of anger and injustice in relation, not only to the former wife in particular, but also to women in general. Psychodynamically speaking, men's victimhood in divorce is a profoundly gendered phenomenon; it has deep psychological roots which are both reflected in and supported by legal and discursive constructions of heterosexual masculinities. Yet it is, nonetheless, a construct of men as victims which has been particularly evident in debates around divorce law reform.

'Feckless Fathers', 'Casanova's Charters' and 'Family Men'

By using the phrase 'women's emancipation to sex war' I am referring to what is, notwithstanding the above, an initially appealing assessment of this recent history. The legislative reforms of the DRA 1969 and MCA 1973 were widely interpreted as part of a broader 'emancipatory moment' marked by a concern to protect women, first and foremost, from the consequences of new liberalised divorce laws. In the parliamentary debates which preceded the reforms, clear assumptions about the nature of men's and women's familial subjectivities surfaced as, respectively, powerful and powerless. Although it was formally recognised that '... divorce law must be just to husbands as well as to wives' (Morton, 1956, para. 46) the combination of men's economic power relative to women, alongside the making of assumptions about men's 'natural' proclivities towards 'sexual (mis)adventuring', together served to constitute the (innocent) wife as the potential victim of divorce reform (albeit that this was a victim status mediated by assumptions about class and sexual propriety). Thus, a recurring image in the debates of the late 1960s and early 1970s was of the husband as a (potentially) adulterous man, a man who would, given the opportunity, discard his 'faithful' middle-aged wife for a younger and more sexually attractive woman. This idea underscored the widespread perception at the time of the DRA and MCA reforms as a 'Casanova's Charter' which would result in 'blameless' wives being repudiated by their husbands and left in economic difficulties (O'Donovan, 1993, pp.77-79). Whilst the social advantages deemed to result from the opportunity to regularise and improve the status of the children of new unions remained the paramount concern, a dominant theme of the debates nonetheless was that of recognising the implications of the loss of marital status for the 'innocent' wife.

In retrospect it was unsurprising that, by the early 1980s, increasing numbers of divorced men should have come to feel aggrieved with the reformed law and, in particular, with the nature of the financial and property settlements being made under the legislation. The financial protection for divorced women which the 1973 MCA had sought to secure had been premised on the belief that the primarily financial obligation marriage entailed was that of a husband's duty 'to maintain' his wife. The law had thus sought to ensure that a man should not be 'freed' from such an obligation.[5] Implicit in this aim was a construction of marriage as something from which the husband 'escapes' and of the husband himself as a man who must pay a 'price for his freedom'.[6] What was becoming clear by the 1980s, however, was that a combination of women's increased employment and other cultural and sexual-political realignments were together serving to undermine the economic and social basis of the original reforms. As a result it, was widely seen as 'unfair' for a husband to have to 'support' a former wife who not only was frequently capable of supporting herself but who would also, in many cases, have access to a second (male) partner's finances. Such a situation, it was argued, not only promoted a 'vicious circle of economic dependence on husbands';[7] it was also economically and psychologically damaging to women themselves who were being constructed as the dependents of men or, to use the term imported from North America, as 'alimony drones'.[8]

Without underestimating the significance of the grievances of divorced wives and second families as they figured in the debates which led up to the Matrimonial and Family Proceedings Act 1984 (MFPA), the figure of the divorced father emerged around this time as, in a number of respects, the new 'victim' of family law. Alongside the other injustices perceived to befall men as a sex-class in general, accorded a cultural legitimacy by the 'masculinity' problematic, this idea of the husband and father as victim was to gain an increasing cultural and political currency.[9] Meanwhile, both reflecting and promoting this new configuration, the political mobilisation of men's grievances within the context of divorce law reform took on a more organised, institutionalised and sophisticated form (Allan, 1982; Berotia and Drakich, 1993; Fineman, 1995; Collier, 1996). By the 1990s this 'new men's movement' has, internationally, embraced a political agenda far wider than the initial concern with men's rights on divorce (though divorce remains a primary, if not the, core concern: see, for example, Doyle, 1996).

Thus, what we have seen in the debates around divorce law reform from 1969 to the present day are some of the ways in which ideas about heterosexual masculinity have been made to signify certain features of the men/family relationship at particular moments. 'Family men' have appeared variously as 'Casanova's' and 'Lotharios', as 'beleaguered' and 'put upon' husbands, 'wholesome' and 'errant' fathers, 'good' fathers, 'absent' fathers, 'deadbeat' dads and, less visibly though arguably increasingly, as 'dangerous' or 'abusing' fathers. On one level these are images of familial and paternal subjectivities which draw on, and map onto, shifts in wider cultural understandings of masculinity, discourses which themselves must be located in the market imperatives of advanced capitalism (Mort, 1996). In the remainder of this chapter, I will argue that each of these images do not so much derive from but, rather, are only made possible by some fundamental ambiguities in the open-ended, contested nature of the encoding of men as 'familial' social subjects in the first place. And it is precisely the conceptual and political ambiguities inherent in men as familial subjects which have surfaced particularly clearly in the debates surrounding the recent legislative reforms.

(Re)reading the Male Heterosexuality/ies of Divorce Law Reform

What is taking place in Britain in the late 1990s is, Carol Smart (1997) has argued, no less than a clear and determined attempt to effect social engineering in the area of the family by using the law to '... change the very nature of post-divorce family life' (Smart, 1997, p.301). Smart sees the core provisions of three major pieces of legislation, the Children Act 1989 (henceforth CA), the Child Support Act 1991 (CSA) and the far-reaching divorce law reforms contained in the FLA 1996 as each, far from facilitating any adaptation to complex and rapid social change, as actively promoting a return to the 'traditional' family. And the way in which this reformation of the heterosexual family is taking place is, it is argued, through a reconceptualisation of *fatherhood.* In relation to both post-divorce and separation family economics (the CSA) and in relation to understandings of parenthood as a largely gender neutral (ungendered) practice (CA and FLA), an ideological shift has taken place in which what is in effect a new or reconstituted notion of 'fatherhood' has emerged. This what might be termed 'new' father is (a) to be economically responsible 'for life' for his 'first' family - financially, he is not to 'move on' unencumbered (the provisions of the CSA); and (b) he is considered, as part of the 'good father' ideal the law now seeks to promote, to be active in joint-parenting after divorce or separation. Together, the CSA, the CA and the FLA each contain measures which, Smart suggests, can be seen as being premised on this ideological commitment to *keeping fathers in touch* with children after divorce. In short, the key presumption of recent family law policy in Britain has been that, both economically and in terms of parenting involvement, 'fatherhood is for life'.

This model of the 'father as active parent' *appears* to be more in tune with contemporary demographic changes, cultural shifts and gender ideologies, a purported shift in 'what men do' perhaps epitomised in the notion of the 'new man' which assumed a currency during the 1980s and early 1990s (Hall, 1994). Yet, a number of questions can be asked of this 'new' kind of fatherhood. Central to the construction of paternal (hetero)normativity underlying the new fatherhood ideology is, I have argued elsewhere (Collier, forthcoming), an ultimately contradictory notion of men's familial 'responsibility', the tensions around which can be seen at a number of levels. The relationship between the concepts of 'parenting' and 'fatherhood' is far from clear, ideas of gender-specificity (the idea that there is something distinctive about a *man's* contribution to the familial) simultaneously both effaced and yet reproduced in different contexts. Whilst gender-neutrality is propounded in the form of 'parenting', the familial presence of the father continues to be constituted as desirable in 'official' family law policy in ways which continue to rest on reductionist notions of ontological (sexual) difference and normative (hetero)sexuality.[10]

There exists, moreover, a tension in the FLA with regard to the relationship between parenthood and heterosexuality as, in effect, an overarching heteronormativity is both reasserted and yet undermined by the recent reforms. Heterosexual marriage continues, on the one hand, to be the privileged foundational imperative of family law policy. An arguably *heightened* support for marriage underscores the FLA (Smart and Neale, 1997). At the same time, however, and in theory at least, the privileging of active gender-neutral parenting serves to displace the combination of masculine ontology, sexual division and normative heterosexuality - the trinity historically central to the discursive constitution of father-presence as socially desirable (Collier, 1995) - as the door is opened to 'transformations of intimacy' which embrace forms of 'confluent love' which do not *have* to be heterosexual (Giddens, 1992). However, it is in relation to another area -

the relationship between parenthood and the 'sexed' negotiation of divorce - that the problematic and contradictory nature of men as familial subjects within recent debates becomes particularly evident. For it is in relation to the bifurcation of parenting along lines of sexual difference that the tensions within the relationship between heterosexuality, marriage and divorce underlying the 'new fatherhood' ideal surface, perhaps, most clearly.

A 'Masculinised Discourse'?: Gender, Familial Responsibility and the 'Sexed' Negotiation of Divorce

It has been a recurring theme within family research across jurisdictions that men and women tend to position themselves differently within the discourses which surround divorce. Arendell (1995) suggests that the vast majority of men on experiencing divorce seek to preserve a sense of 'masculine' identity in the adoption of what is, in effect, a 'gendered' performative strategy, the discursive themes and actions of which constitute a distinctive 'masculinist discourse' in the negotiation of divorce and the end of heterosexual relationships. This idea of there being a distinctive 'masculinised' negotiation of divorce has been interpreted by others to be a key feature of contemporary debates which have characterised changes around marriage, divorce and 'family breakdown' as involving shifting power relations between men and women (c.f. Fineman, 1995; Smart, 1997; Smart and Neal, 1997). Central to this model is precisely the position identified above in which *conflict* over divorce is somehow seen as emblematic of broader social, cultural and economic shifts in relations of power between men and women:

> Related to both their victimization and belief in differences between men and women, divorce was understood as a battle - a 'war between the sexes' in general and with the former wife, in particular ... despite the situational ambiguity and stressful circumstances related to divorce, the men adhered to a definition of self that required a persistent demonstration, in action and comportment, of authority, confidence, and competency. They were not just being men, but were 'doing gender'... and because these identities had been brought into question by divorce in dramatic and far-reaching ways, they expended major efforts to re-establish and reassert their identities *as men* (Arendell, 1995, p.14: my emphasis).

The idea of the 'masculinised discourse' does not imply that women do *not* feel powerless on divorce. Rather, evidence suggests that women's feelings may be manifested in different ways (Smart, 1997). The model does, however, highlight ways in which the feelings of 'powerlessness' which arise on divorce must themselves be situated within experiences of heterosexuality which have *already* been sexed in terms of the hierarchical dualisms discussed above. As Fineman has warned, differences in the discursive constructions of motherhood and fatherhood, alongside the fact that men and women come before/to the law as already 'gendered' subjects living 'gendered lives' (1995, pp.47-51), means that family law itself can never be gender neutral. Approaching the negotiation of divorce and separation in terms of sex difference involves bringing to the surface the ways in which these gendered experiences of divorce are themselves then discursively produced. In Arendell's identification of men straining towards what is seen as being a coherent masculine identity, and in seeking to 're-establish and reassert their identities *as men*', it follows from the conceptualisation of the heterosexual subject above that such psychic investments will be played out both internally and externally (Jefferson, 1994: see further Sclater, this volume). For the individual *man* this is a search which is also taking place at a moment in the life-course (relationship breakdown) when the desire for authenticity and for a 'true' masculine self may well have a particular ontological resonance, a resonance further mediated by issues around class, 'race'/ethnicity, sexuality, fertility, 'potency' and physical ability.

When placed in this broader context, both the gendered subject implicit within the 'masculine discourse' model and the nature of the grievances being expressed within the men's rights/assertive-father discourse can each be seen to stand in, at the very least, an uneasy relationship to the new fatherhood ideal implicit within recent family law policy. The grievances being expressed by the assertive father, like the gendered negotiation of divorce, rest on clear-cut 'gender' roles derived from a belief in ontological differences between men and women. The new family policy, however, couched in the language of gender neutrality, cuts across the presumed biological basis of sexual difference and is, accordingly, seen by 'pro-family'/assertive father groupings as destructive of 'normal' marriage and undermining of the 'natural' social order. Yet *both* the father-right and new father discourses each draw on notions of men as active 'co-parents' which ultimately jar, in a number of respects, with what research suggests continues to be the 'everyday' material and emotional realities of divorce for the majority of women and men. That is, a distinct (though by no means clear-cut) contrast between men's and women's experiences with it being - most importantly - the material and emotional dependencies surrounding child care (and, increasingly, elder-care) which tend to mediate women's negotiations at moments of conflict within, or at the end of, heterosexual relationships (see further Smart, 1997, following Griffiths, 1995).

Without underestimating the economic imperatives of advanced capitalist societies, as mediated in specific national and governmental contexts, this point cannot be reduced to questions of public provision of child care. Experience across jurisdictions suggests it is by no means clear that men assume a greater share of child care responsibilities even when specific public provision is established (for example in the form of parental leave). In the UK context considerable evidence attests to the pervasive and deep-rooted nature of attitudes and behaviour which, notwithstanding the very real changes which have taken place in women's and men's familial roles, continue to reproduce quite traditional sexual divisions of labour. At the very least this pervasive dissociation from the dependencies of the familial on the part of men calls into question the material realities underlying the rhetoric of the new fatherhood. In short, although the law may be seeking to 'reconstitute' the relationship between men and children in a number of ways, it would appear that other economic, legal, cultural and social discourses continue to position men as social agents who are, if not effectively free, then are at least dissociated in a number of important respects from a range of familial, emotional and material encumbrances in relation to children. And, given the centrality of the figure of the child to the constitution of these sexed (as different) experiences of the material and emotional dependencies at divorce, it should perhaps not surprise that it has been in negotiations around conflicts over *children* that the nature of 'gender differences' should have surfaced most clearly. For, it is in the nature of this relationship between men and children that, ultimately, the limitations of the 'new' fatherhood itself are revealed.

Reconfiguring the Relationship Between Men and Children: Divorce, Heterosexuality and the 'Crisis' of the Social

To integrate questions of sexual difference is *not* to argue that women are inherently or biologically more 'connected' or 'relational' than men. It is, however, to address the complex, contingent and contested nature of the frame of heterosexual relating in which men and women have already been positioned differentially within the material, cultural and emotional discourses which surround ideas of divorce and 'family life'. Problematising the 'heterosexuality' of divorce, as it were, brings into focus aspects of the ways in which a normative model of male heterosexuality has itself been constituted via reference to the making of certain assumptions about paternal presence/absence, heterosexual marriage, economic status, emotionality and the nature of sexual difference. In order to transcend the dominant interpretation of legal reforms as being either 'pro' or 'against' the 'family', as either (and as necessarily) 'empowering' or 'disempowering' men or women, it becomes necessary to reconceptualise the concepts and systems of thought through which the categories which constitute the familial have been understood in the first place. This involves questioning not just the concept of fatherhood but also, in relation to the broader and multi-layered reconceptualisation of heterosexuality presently taking place, the idea of the child/childhood. Changes around the concept of the child have had, we shall see, a particularly powerful resonance for men who have *already* been positioned as 'masculine' within modernity in ways which set them apart from the embodied dependencies of the familial sphere.[11]

Conceptualising contemporary *men* negotiating divorce as subjects 'in process', engaged in a gendered reflexive project is lent a further resonance when it is recognised that the legal, social and subjective status-change which divorce entails is mapped onto the search for an appropriate 'masculine' identity at a time of heightened anxieties around the meaning and status of masculinity *per se* within western cultures (Hearn, 1996). Yet, crucially, this is a gendered project which is taking place at a time in which a particular figure of the child has itself come to assume an importance within a range of discourses concerned with the maintenance and security of the social bond. Indeed, the concept of the child within postmodern cultural configurations has been increasingly identified as the site for the relocation of a variety of discourses concerned with questions of stability, integration, and the maintenance of sociality.[12] In view of the demographic changes taking place in household structures at the end of the twentieth century it is perhaps unsurprising that an acceleration in the intensity, purchase and currency of emotions centred round the idea of the 'fragmenting' heterosexual family should have assumed a central significance in understandings of how women's and men's experiences of the 'social' are grounded in the first place.

In such a context the heightening of economic, cultural and sexual anxieties around 'gender roles' can be seen as doing more than reflecting the privileged position of the heterosexual family *per se* within modernity (Donzelot, 1980; Collier, 1995, pp.77-80; Jenks, 1996, p.14; Rose, 1996). What is *also* becoming apparent is that a complex range of diverse social, cultural and economic reconfigurations are connecting this 'fragmenting' family with a set of more general concerns around men, masculinity and heterosexuality in which a reconceptualisation of the child/childhood has become inextricably bound up with the discursive constitution of the 'family crisis' *as* a 'paternal masculine' crisis idea. As the relationship between adults and children becomes as contested a terrain as the breach of the social, what appear as contestations around childhood are thus reformed as questions about the (re)constitution of social. No wonder, perhaps, that 'father-absence' should then assume such an iconic status across a range of debates, be it in relation to child welfare, youth crime, family breakdown and the contours of social (dis)order more generally.

To return to the sexual politics of divorce, it is in the context of a reconceptualisation of childhood that changes within the ideology of 'care' implicit in the now dominant notion of gender-neutral parenting can be seen as playing out differently for men and women. Men and women have been positioned very differently in relation to both children and child care within the discourses of modernity, their experiences of 'inevitable dependencies' (Fineman, 1995) differentially constituted in terms of sexed embodiment and gendered lives. This is not to argue that the parenting practices of men and women may not significantly 'overlap' in terms of both form, function and emotionality.[13] It is to argue, however, that within the dominant gendering of this ideology of care what emerges is a masculine subject which is constituted in many ways as Other to children/child care, beyond the primary men/child nexus of economic provider and socialising role model. It is not 'adults' but primarily mothers who have been (and continue to be) routinely depicted as 'sacrificing everything' for their children, women who are judged, held responsible and who are seen as having 'failed' or 'succeeded' in the acting out of this duty of care. Men, in contrast, have been constituted 'as' familial in other ways and through reference to other discourses.

The reconfiguration of the meaning of the 'familial' has, alongside the social, cultural and economic realignments outlined in this chapter, rendered as problematic that which has hitherto been unspoken, natural, inviolable, and, in so many ways, unquestioned: *the relationship between men and children*. The values of autonomy, control and separateness through which cultural understandings of the 'masculine' continue to be made sit most uneasily with the qualities of 'everyday' nurturing and sacrifice implicit in the 'new fatherhood' ideology. The crisis of the family (equals) crisis of fatherhood association may have deep historical roots. Yet, at the present moment, both the concepts of the child and fatherhood are being transformed in the face of changing sexual subjectivities, employment structures and cultural formations which have disturbed a sexual division of labour which 'lubricated and legitimised the investment of economic and cultural capital in the "promise" of childhood' (Jenks, 1996, p.15). In a context in which 'the enhanced interest in men's relationship to children and of men in children' grows (Jenks, 1996, p.20), and where the construction of both fatherhood and (hetero) masculinities are subjected to increasing critical scrutiny, the iconic status of the (postmodern) child has become the disputed territory in which this more general assessment of the contribution of men to the social is taking place.

Concluding Remarks

In this chapter I have explored some of the contours of the reconfiguration of heterosexual social relations presently taking place within British family law policy. I have sought to counterpose readings which have privileged the idea of a 'crisis of the family' (equals) 'crisis of masculinity' association with an approach which has sought to problematise the mutual discursive constitution of heterosexuality, fatherhood and the familial. I have argued that a reconfiguration of the child has been central to the construction of the 'new' fatherhood implicit in this family law policy. In engaging with the discursive construction of the masculine heterosexual subject it becomes possible, I have argued, to identify some of the significant contradictions which exist within this family policy.

To conclude and summarise the main points of my argument. Firstly, far from seeing heterosexual relations designated as 'familial' as being in each and every case a site of (male) power and (female) submission (or vice versa), it is important to recognise that '...within broad cultural paradigms there are often localised situations where gendered attributes can be reversed' (Gutterman, 1994, p.221). To no longer presume that men or women unproblematically 'have' more or less 'power' in the family is to locate power itself, in a Foucauldian sense, as something which may be deployed in different ways, at different times and towards different ends. This approach does not simply 'write in' the agency of a psychologically complex subject (Henriques *et al*, 1984; Hollway, 1989; Jefferson, 1994). It presumes, importantly, a (hetero)sexed identity which is itself always partial, uncertain and fragmented, a subject constituted through reference to its dependency on that which is defined as Other in the processes of its constitution (Gutterman, 1994, p.221). If social 'identities' encoded as familial, far from being 'natural', are seen as grounded by a series of discursively produced oppositional binarisms which constitute the categories of the inside/outside of the 'family' (categories such as man/woman, husband/wife, mother/father, hetero/homosexual) what is rendered social and political is the question of how individual men and women come to take up particular discursive positions and how, importantly, these binaries are made to signify within particular discourses.

The analysis of the 'heterosexuality' of 'fatherhood' presented in this chapter reveals a male subject, encoded *as familial,* produced and sustained by interwoven discourses of sexuality and gender which are themselves rooted in the dualistic configurations pervading liberal legal thought. Thus, we have seen above something of the ways in which men and women have each been constituted within debates around divorce in relation to a guilt/innocence binary which has been 'sexed' in very different ways; compare the 'Casanovas', 'errant' and 'good' fathers with the 'innocent' abandoned spouses, the vindictive, mendacious and, more recently, 'implacably hostile' mothers. How does the *sexing* of these dualisms through which familial subjects are constituted - subjects which remain within a '... stranglehold grip of identity binarisms' (Murphy, 1996, p.59) - then relate to what research has suggested is the (sexed, as different) experience of divorce? The model of the 'new' fatherhood which has emerged during the 1980s and 1990s continues to embody normative presumptions about 'family', marriage and sexuality which only make sense in terms of the hierarchic binaries which have constituted (hetero)sexual difference in the first place. The new images of men and fatherhood in and through reference to which the meaning of divorce is being reconstituted continue to emerge *against, and in relation to* those of women and motherhood. Importantly, this 'fatherhood' in/of legal discourse actively participates in the construction of the category of 'men' more generally, involving a 'way of seeing' that is constructed hegemonically through the mobilisation and consolidation of various practices and the exclusion of others.

Secondly, the contemporary cognitive, ethical and aesthetic reconfiguration of the men/gender relation - indeed, the individual and collective experience of *being* a man in western society - increasingly appears to bespeak crisis, contestation and resistance. Refigurations of the 'family man' within recent debates around family policy are no exception in this regard. Yet some familiar and powerful imaginings of the past continue to resonate in these debates: the past of an unproblematic family, of unquestioned and unchallenged (hetero)sexuality, a past in which gender 'roles' were understood to be a function of ontology. It is no wonder that these changes should prove particularly disturbing for those men whose sense of self-identity has been enmeshed within a model of heterosexual relating which has itself become so radically unstable. Nor should it surprise that such tensions become particularly evident at the point of relationship breakdown; for, as the grievances of the fathers' rights movement illustrate, painful contradictions and ambivalences inhere in this masculine subject. What is increasingly clear in the performative project of men's negotiations of divorce are the all-too-evident emotional and psychological, material and corporeal costs of their (our) endeavours to 're-establish' and 'reassert' heterosexual masculine identities; in the vilification of mothers, and women in general, in the 'seizing' of children, in 'domestic sieges', and ultimately, in the increasing numbers of men who have killed their children as 'the ultimate act of revenge against their wives'.[14]

Thirdly, and finally, let us be clear. Underlying present family policy in Britain is not a concern to challenge existing social structures which continue to sustain and promote such separations. There continues, crucially, to be limited engagement with the conceptual basis of the 'private' family

(Fineman, 1995, p.205). Far from engaging in any 'deconstruction' of the idea of the family itself the aim is, as the provisions of the FLA 1996 make all too clear, to reproduce quite traditional norms of heterosexual monogamous marriage and the dominance of heterosexuality in public discourse and institutional arrangements through the use of, what is in effect, moral invective, individualist explanation and a pervasive pathologising of divorce. Yet the conflicts which arise in divorce and which the new law seeks to remove are, I have argued, not simply the consequence of an adversarial process. Nor can they be reduced to a manifestation of psychological dynamics (though these are significant and under explored: Sclater, 1998). They are, rather, an expression of tensions inherent in the reconfiguring of heterosexuality presently taking place.

Family law, social policy and legal studies remain places set apart from those forms of politics which would seek to break down the fixed boundaries which presently constitute the contours of the 'familial'. And yet it may well be that it is in looking 'outwith' these taken for granted understandings of the family, in allowing the 'undercurrents' of divorce to push us towards the boundaries of both 'law' and 'family', that it might ultimately be possible to seek to dissolve the oppressive categories which constitute ideas of 'the family' itself and, in so doing, to take analysis of family law - and the lived experiences of heterosexual relationships - into new and as yet uncharted territory.

Notes

1. The 1969 DRA was the product of a reassessment of both the procedural laws and societal attitudes towards divorce which had been underway for some years (see further Archbishop of Canterbury's Group, 1966; Law Commission 1966; McGregor, 1957; Morton, 1956). The DRA 1969 and subsequent MCA 1973 enacted what was seen at the time as a morality reflecting the 'new reality' of heterosexual relations whereby divorce was to henceforth be available on the sole ground of irretrievable breakdown. On the 1996 FLA see further below.
2. I do not wish to underestimate the importance of this, notably the introduction of the so-called 'special procedure' in 1977 under which all undefended divorces could be obtained without a court hearing. Since about 99% of divorce petitions are undefended (Law Commission 1990, para 2.2) this 'special' procedure was itself to become the rule rather than the exception: see further Dewar, 1992, pp.258-259.

3. Something of the policy background to the FLA can be found in the Law Commission (1990) and Lord Chancellor's Department (1995). On the passage of the Family Law Bill see further Smart and Neale (1997).
4. In 1956 the Morton Commission predicted that divorce reforms of the kind being proposed would lead to an increasing tension between the experiences and expectations of women and men, as wives' growing demand for greater equality in the home was contrasted with husbands' 'traditional notions of subservient wives'.
5. References to securing the 'responsibility and duty' of men abound in the Reports which have preceded divorce reform: e.g. Morton, 1956, para 8-11.
6. Law Commission (1966) at para 46.
7. *The Times*, 14 February 1980.
8. On aspects of this debate see further Deech (1977), O'Donovan (1978) and Smart (1984).
9. Though it is important to remember that this notion was from the outset contested notably, though not exclusively, by feminists, (see, for example, Smart, 1984).
10. Perhaps the clearest manifestation of this continues to be the way in which, within the welfare principle underscoring recent family policy, certain deleterious consequences attached to 'father-absence' continue to be invoked in the name of the well-being of children in some sex-specific ways.
11. To clarify: in the negotiation of or straining towards being a 'good father', and in seeking to establish and assert identities *as men* (following Arendell, 1995) the notion of gender performativity (Butler, 1990, 1993) can be seen as linking in some respects to Giddens (1991, 1992) suggestion that, within late modernity, a prerequisite of what he terms confluent love is an engagement with the 'project of the self'; that is, a making and re-making of the self at different stages of the life-course.
12. Note, in particular, the work of Beck, 1992; Beck and Beck Gernsheim, 1995; Qvortrup, 1995: see, more generally, James and Prout, 1990; Qvortrup *et. al.*, 1994; Brannen and O'Brien, 1995; Jenks, 1996; James *et al*, 1998).
13. See further, on the 'feminine' qualities of fatherhood, Lupton and Barclay, (1997).
14. There is some evidence that men involved in bitter family recriminations appear increasingly likely to seize their children and former partners as hostage thus provoking what have become known as 'domestic' sieges ('Angry fathers blamed for domestic sieges' *The Guardian* 16 June 1997). In the Netherlands concern has grown over the number of men who have killed their children 'as the ultimate act of revenge against their wives' (*The Sunday Times* 16 February 1997). See also, on suggestions that some men are using post-divorce contact with children as a way of harassing ex-partners, 'Big Bad Dad' *The Guardian* 25 June 1996.

References

Allan, D. (1982), *One Step From the Quagmire*, Campaign for Justice on Divorce, Aylesbury.

Archbishop of Canterbury's Group (1966), *Putting Asunder: A Divorce Law For Contemporary Society*, SPCK, London.

Arendell, T. (1995), *Fathers and Divorce*, Sage, London.

Beck, U. (1992), *Risk Society: Towards a New Modernity*, Sage, London.

Beck, U. and Beck Gernsheim, E. (1995), *The Normal Chaos of Love*, Polity, Cambridge.

Bell, D. and Valentine, G. (1995), 'The Sexed Self: Strategies of Performance, Sites of Resistance', in S. Pile and N. Thrift (eds), *Mapping the Subject: Geographies of Cultural Transformation*, Routledge, London .

Berotia, C. and Drakich, J. (1993), 'The Fathers' Rights Movement: Contradictions in Rhetoric and Practice', *Journal of Family Issues*, vol 14(4), pp.592-615.

Brannen, J. and O'Brien, M. (eds) (1995), *Childhood and Parenthood: Proceedings of the International Sociological Association Committee for Family Research Conference*, Institute of Education, London.

Butler, J. (1990), *Gender Trouble: Feminism and the Subversion of Identity*, Routledge, London.

Butler, J. (1993), *Bodies That Matter: On the Discursive Limits of Sex*, Routledge, London.

Callahan, S. (1997), 'Gays, Lesbians and the Use of Alternate Reproductive Technologies', in H.L. Nelson (ed), *Feminism and Families*, Routledge, London.

Collier, R. (forthcoming) 'Reconstructing the Good Father', in C. Wright and G. Jaggar (eds), *Changing Family Values*, Routledge, London.

Collier, R. (1996), '"Coming Together?": Post-Heterosexuality, Masculine Crisis and the New Men's Movement', *Feminist Legal Studies*, vol 4(1), pp.3-48.

Collier, R. (1995), *Masculinity, Law and the Family*, Routledge, London.

Deech, R. (1977), 'The Principles of Maintenance', *Family Law*, vol 7, pp.229-231.

Dewar, J. (1992), *Law and the Family*, (2nd ed), Butterworths, London.

Donzelot, J. (1980), *The Policing of Families*, Hutchinson, London.

Doyle, R.F. (1996), *The Men's/Fathers' Movement and Divorce Assistance Operation Manual: History, Philosophy, Operation*, Men's Defence Association, Poor Richard's Press, New York.

Fineman, M.A. (1995), *The Neutered Mother, The Sexual Family and Other Twentieth Century Tragedies*, Routledge, New York.

Giddens, A. (1992), *The Transformations of Intimacy*, Polity, Cambridge.

Giddens, A. (1991), *Modernity and Self-Identity*, Polity, Cambridge.

Griffiths, M. (1995), *Feminisms and the Self: The Web of Identity*, Routledge, London.

Gutterman, S. (1994), 'Postmodernism and the Interrogation of Masculinity' in M. Kimmell and M. Kaufman (eds), *Theorizing Masculinities*, Sage, London.

Hall, W. (1994), 'New Fatherhood: Myths and Realities', *Public Health Nursing*, vol 11(4), pp.219-228.

Hearn, J. (1996), 'Is Masculinity Dead? A Critique of the Concept of Masculinity', in M. Mac an Ghaill (ed), *Understanding Masculinities*, Open University Press, Buckingham.

Henriques, J., Hollway, W., Urwin, C., Venn, C. and Walkerdine, V. (1984), *Changing the Subject: Psychology, Social Regulation and Subjectivity*, Methuen, London.

Hollway, W. (1989), *Subjectivity and Method in Psychology: Gender, Meaning and Science*, Sage, London.

James, A., Jenks, C. and Prout, A. (1998), *Theorizing Childhood*, Polity, London.

James, A. and Prout, A. (eds) (1990), *Constructing and Reconstructing Childhood*, Falmer Press, London.

Jefferson, T. (1994), 'Theorizing Masculine Subjectivity' in T. Newburn and E. Stanko (eds), *Just Boys Doing Business? Men, Masculinities and Crime*, Routledge, London.

Jenks, C. (1996), *Childhood*, Routledge, London.

Law Commission (1990), *The Ground for Divorce*, Law Comm. No 192, HMSO, London.

Law Commission (1966), *Report on the Reform of the Grounds of Divorce: The Field of Choice*, No 6, HMSO, London.

Lord Chancellor's Department (1995), *Looking to the Future. Mediation and the Ground for Divorce, A Consultation Paper*, HMSO, London.

Lupton, D. and Barclay, L. (1997), *Constructing Fatherhood: Discourses and Experiences*, Sage, London.

Maynard, M. and Purvis, J. (1995), *(Hetero)Sexual Politics*, Taylor and Francis, London.

McGregor, O.R. (1957), *Divorce in England*, Heineman, London.

Midgley, M. and Hughes, J. (1997), 'Are Families Out of Date?', in H.L. Nelson (ed), *Feminism and Families*, Routledge, London.

Mort, F. (1996), *Cultures of Consumption: Masculinities and Social Space in Late Twentieth Century Britain*, Routledge, London.

Morton, Lord (1956), *Royal Commission on Marriage and Divorce 1951-1955 Report*, HMSO, London.

Murphy, T. (1996), 'Bursting Binary Bubbles: Law, Literature and the Sexed Body' in J. Morison and C. Bell (eds), *Tall Stories? Reading Law and Literature*, Dartmouth, Aldershot.

O'Donovan, K. (1993), *Family Law Matters*, Pluto, London.

O'Donovan, K. (1985), *Sexual Divisions in Law*, Weidenfeld and Nicolson, London.

O'Donovan, K. (1978), 'The Principles of Maintenance: An Alternative View', *Family Law*, vol 8, pp.18-24.

Probyn, E. (1993), *Sexing the Self: Gendered Positions in Cultural Studies*, Routledge, London.

Qvortrup, J. (1995), 'Childhood and Modern Society: A Paradoxical Relationship?' in J. Brannen and M. O'Brien (eds), *Childhood and Parenthood*, Institute of Education, London.

Qvortrup, J., Bardy, M., Sgritta, G. and Wintersberger, H. (eds) (1994), *Childhood Matters: Social Theory, Practices and Politics*, Avebury Press, London.

Richardson, D. (ed) (1996), *Theorising Heterosexuality: Telling it Straight*, Open University Press, Buckingham.

Rose, N. (1996), *Inventing Our Selves: Psychology, Power and Personhood*, Cambridge University Press, Cambridge.

Sclater, S.D. (1998), 'Divorce - Coping Strategies, Conflict and Dispute Resolution', *Family Law*, pp.150-152.

Sedgwick, E. (1994), *Epistemology of the Closet*, Harvester Wheatsheaf, Hemel Hempstead.

Smart, C. (1984), *The Ties That Bind*, London, Routledge and Kegan Paul.

Smart, C. (1996a), 'Collusion, Collaboration and Confession on Moving Beyond the Heterosexuality Debate', in D. Richardson (ed), *Theorising Heterosexuality: Telling it Straight*, Open University, Buckingham.

Smart, C. (1996b), 'Desperately Seeking Post-Heterosexual Woman', in J. Holland and L. Adkins (eds), *Sex, Sensibility and the Gendered Body*, Macmillan, London.

Smart, C. (1997), 'Wishful Thinking and Harmful; Tinkering? Sociological Reflections on Family Policy', *Journal of Social Policy*, vol 26(3), pp.301-321.

Smart, C. and Neale, B. (1997), 'Good Enough Morality? Divorce and Postmodernity', *Critical Social Policy*, vol 17(4), pp.3-27.

Smart, C. and Brophy, J. (1985), *Women in Law*, Routledge and Kegal Paul, London.

Stanworth, M. (ed) (1987), *Reproductive Technologies*, Polity Press, Cambridge.

Steinberg, D.L. (1997), 'Eugenic Reproductions Under Glass', in D.L. Steinberg, D. Epstein and R. Johnson (eds) (1997), *Border Patrols: Policing the Boundaries of Heterosexuality*, Cassell, London.

Steinberg, D.L., Epstein, D. and Johnson, R. (eds) (1997), *Border Patrols: Policing the Boundaries of Heterosexuality*, Cassell, London.

Stychin, C. (1996), *Law's Desire*, Routledge, London.

Warner, M. (ed) (1993), *Fear of a Queer Planet*, University of Minnesota Press, Minneapolis.

Wittig, M. (1992), *The Straight Mind and Other Essays*, Harvester Wheatsheaf, Brighton.

Wilkinson, S. and Kitzinger, C. (eds) (1993), *Heterosexuality: A Feminism and Psychology Reader*, Sage, London.

7 Divorce: A Psychodynamic Perspective

JOANNE BROWN AND SHELLEY DAY SCLATER

Introduction

In July 1996, the Family Law Act received the Royal Assent, after a turbulent passage through Parliament. The passionate nature of the debates in both Houses, and their extensive coverage by the media, bear testament to the deep feelings many of us have about issues concerning marriage and divorce, and to our emotional investments in intimate relationships and 'the family'. Yet, paradoxically perhaps, to remove the heated emotions from the divorce process is precisely what the new law seeks to do. In this chapter we explore intimacy and separation from a psychodynamic perspective and, in doing so, we hope to shed light on the myriad of reasons why divorce can evoke such passions, both in the reform debates and in the process itself. In the light of our arguments, we then consider to what extent the reforms are likely to be successful in removing the heat out of divorce, and we make some suggestions as to how the process might be made more humane and more suited to the emotional needs of divorcing people.

The Family Law Act, 1996

The Act received the Royal Assent in July 1996,[1] only after heated debates in both Houses, and only after a significant number of amendments had been incorporated in it. In 1988 the Law Commission in their Consultation Paper *Looking to the Future* (Law Commission, 1988) had taken the view that the retention of 'fault' in divorce was not helpful, particularly for children, in so far as it encouraged acrimony and recrimination between the adults involved, and they pointed to a need for 'calm and sensible' negotiations about the future needs of the parties and their children. Their report in 1990, *Family Law: The*

Grounds For Divorce (Law Commission 1990), which included a draft Bill, formed the basis of the last government's attempt to introduce more 'civilised' divorce. The 1993 Consultation Paper (Lord Chancellor's Department (LCD), 1993) on reform of the divorce law advocated a 'no fault' basis for divorce; divorce would follow a waiting period during which time the couple would be expected to consider the consequences of a decision to divorce, and to make plans for the future - plans about money, property and children. It was envisaged that couples would avail themselves of mediation services during this period, with the aim that the involvement of lawyers would be diminished, resulting in a reduction of the financial and the emotional costs of divorce and the Legal Aid bill to the public purse.

The Consultation Paper acknowledged that the emotional costs of divorce are often too high. However, it exhibited a marked tendency to attribute those high emotional costs to the operation of the adversarial system. It was said that the involvement of lawyers in divorce increases 'bitterness and conflict' and it was assumed that the increased involvement of mediators would instead promote harmony and co-operation. Recent evidence, however, suggests that this contrasting of mediation and the legal process may be over simple, because the legal process itself aims for avoidance of litigation, and in the vast majority of cases, this aim is achieved (Davis, Cretney and Collins, 1994). Further, many couples who mediate their divorces nevertheless engage solicitors at some stage in the process.

The White Paper which followed (LCD, 1995) embodied a number of assumptions concerning the psychological aspects of divorce which later became incorporated into the Act: the assumption that divorcing people generally are able to behave in a restrained and co-operative manner and the assumption that the abolition of 'fault' and the use of mediation would substantially reduce the 'conflict' which is commonly associated with divorce proceedings. These assumptions relate directly to the discourse of welfare as the underlying philosophy of the legislation:

> Research has shown that children suffer and are damaged as a result of *conflict* between their parents, whether the parents are living together or apart. Consultees considered that the current system encourages conflict, by providing an incentive to seek a quick divorce on the basis of allegations of fault (LCD, 1995, para 2.22, emphasis in original).

The Act envisages that the removal of fault and the introduction of mediation as a dispute resolution procedure would address these evils and provide the necessary protection for children's welfare.

In the House of Lords the Bill (HL Bill 1, 1995) met with fierce opposition from those peers who felt that its provisions undermined marriage and the family. At the same time, the *Daily Mail* launched a campaign against it on that basis. Many commentators of this persuasion saw that nothing less than 'civilisation' itself was at stake (see, for example, Morgan, 1996). These are strong sentiments, and were expressed repeatedly and with great passion. How should we explain this massive emotional investment which people make in matters concerning marriage and the family? The heated nature of the debates surely illustrates the naivety of thinking that emotion is separable from divorce. By the time that the Bill entered the Commons for the first time, a set of 'general principles' had been introduced, including that the institution of marriage is to be supported,[2] that couples are to be encouraged to do what they can to save their marriages, and that where divorce is inevitable, this should be done with the minimum of distress to all concerned. The principles are now set out in the Act, section 1. The introduction of these principles had the effect of allaying some of the anxieties about the undermining of marriage which had formed the main plank of opposition to the Bill. The fact that a divorce law has, as its general principle, that marriage is to be supported, is indicative of a profound social ambivalence about divorce, an ambivalence which parallels that in the feelings and experiences of each divorcing person.

What are the psychological roots of the ambivalence and of the hostility in divorce which the legislation addresses? Might hostile emotions serve a psychological function on the breakdown of an intimate relationship? If so, do people need to be given the chance to express these emotions? Will mediation be sufficient for this purpose? In what follows, we address these questions with reference to psychological and psychodynamic theories.

A Psychoanalytic Understanding of Separation and Loss

In this section, we introduce a psychoanalytic perspective on love and loss, which implicitly challenges the welfare discourse of co-operation enshrined in the 1996 Family Law Act. We have already seen how one of the premises of the new Act is to minimise conflict and introduce what is seen as a more civilised approach to divorce, but in psychoanalytic terms these developments in family law can be seen as resting upon an over-simplified and limited view of subjectivity where ideology operates to deny the existence of chaotic emotions or to carefully circumscribe passions which would otherwise be uncontrolled.

It is the psychoanalytic discovery of an unconscious area of the mind which alerts us to the fact that when two people begin a separation process, the 'agent' of rationality (the ego) may be weakened and have to contend with the power of irrational thoughts, feelings and phantasies which assail it (us) from within. The fully conscious, rational individual, is not, therefore, the psychoanalytic starting point as it is in traditional psychology and, indeed, the law. Indeed in psychoanalytic terms the existence of contradictory, conflicted emotions is not pathologised, but seen as intrinsic to our developmental 'fate'. From a psychoanalytic perspective, our relationships from infancy onwards are coloured by a strong vacillation between love and hate and ambivalent, contradictory feelings. The ambivalence between love and hate is particularly acute, according to this perspective, when we are faced with separation. Indeed it is individuation, that is, becoming one's own person, which is in developmental terms our emotional task; this necessarily involves learning to cope with our ambivalent feelings. Adolescence is typically seen as the life stage when separation is finally effected but, from a psychoanalytic perspective, we encounter what is called separation anxiety much earlier on in infancy and this anxiety is caused by feelings of helplessness, loss and abondonment. Hence it is separation which tests our ability to cope with conflict, as feelings of hate, jealousy, betrayal, and so on are potentially unleashed.

From a psychoanalytic perspective we can, therefore, understand why the psychology of divorce begins with the psychology of intimate relationships and of marriage. In 1964, Berger and Kellner published a paper which has become a classic text. In it they analysed marriage as a social arrangement which created for the individuals involved a vital means of experiencing their own lives as making sense, as having purpose and meaning. They saw marriage as a process in which meaningful reality was constructed, maintained and modified. More importantly, marriage enabled the two partners to redefine themselves and each other. Through intimacy, two strangers merge their views of the world, reconstructing the past, the present and the future, into a framework of new shared meanings. Images of the self and of the other are constructed, maintained and modified during intimacy, and self esteem becomes contingent on the regard of the other.

This complex psychological process whereby both the self and 'reality' are constructed occurs and reoccurs throughout the life of an intimate relationship, accompanied by a major emotional investment. Johnston and Campbell (1988) argue that separation and divorce involve a destruction of the shared reality of the marriage, a shattering of the self image, and a disintegration of the image of the other. Vaughan (1987) argues that recovery involves the creation of a new self; in this process the history of the marriage is fundamentally reinterpreted. This re-interpretation of personal history takes place from the standpoint of the present (Freeman, 1993); it begins with the fact of the failure of the intimate relationship, of the loss of the significant other. Herein, as we shall argue, lie many of the psychological problems of divorce.

Freudian Psychoanalysis: The Mind in Conflict

Sigmund Freud is the founder of psychoanalysis and the first perhaps to systematically question the dynamics of family life. Indeed it is Freud's models of mind and theories of infantile sexuality which disrupt the harmonious view of family life and childhood innocence. Although Freud's own normative assumptions about gender, homosexuality, monogamy and so on are evident in his work, it nevertheless provides a starting point from which to think about complex human subjectivities and problematic family dynamics.

Neither Freud nor, later, Melanie Klein questioned the social construction of the family and it is not our aim to deconstruct the discourse of the family in psychoanalysis. We are using a psychoanalytic perspective in order to highlight the complex and unconscious nature of our emotional life which is embedded in our own family of origin. That is, 'the family' continues to exert an emotional hold over us long after we have ceased to feel ourselves to be dependent upon it. We can surmise, therefore, that the passionate nature of the debates about family breakdown may partly have their roots in our unconscious memories of, and ambivalent feelings, about 'home'. These ambivalent feelings come from many sources according to Freudian theory. Freud's two models of the mind (Freud, 1900 and 1923) posit a mind in conflict, torn between the demands of an impulsive, instinctual emotional life and the dictates of reality and conscience. Furthermore, these impulses, which are sexually anarchic (Freud, 1905) and aggressive, form the vast seabed on which everything else rests and from which everything else grows. The fully conscious, waking self is therefore the tip of an iceberg, because our roots are buried deep in an instinctual, emotional life, with which we are born. We may not feel, therefore, as though we can always be in control of parts of our mind and may speak from a position of passivity or enslavement when emotions like rage, despair or panic overwhelm us.

Freud, therefore, analysed the extent to which our own emotional, unconscious life can alarm us, especially when it reveals our own capacity for destruction. In 1920 Freud (having by then witnessed the First World War) introduced the idea of a death instinct or destructive drive in human nature and the aim of psychotherapy thus became one of strengthening the ego (Freud, 1923) just as the aim of civilisation, according to Freud, was to institutionalise limits to our desires or instinctual freedom (see Freud, 1930). Marriage is obviously one such way to regulate sex, sexuality, sexual freedom and acts to naturalise what our expectations from home and family life are. To the extent that marriage is thus essentialised, divorce is simultaneously cast as an unnatural destructive act. The acrimonious divorce, in particular, then becomes a symbol of society's fears about that which destroys our foundations. Freud, however, maintained that aggression is intrinsic to emotional life, a fact which the rhetoric of harmony must, not therefore, aim to repress or deny.

In 1926 Freud explained why it is that our earliest relationships are conflicted, rather than harmonious. He pointed out that the human infant is born prematurely in relation to most other animals and is dependent on its carers for an incomparably long period of time. This protracted dependency on its carers, the awakening of the sexual and aggressive impulses, all bind the child to the parent in an intense and complex way. Thus our first and prototypic love is ambivalent. Consequently, according to Freud, there is an impossibility at the heart of our love for our parents which, like a faint memory trace, will colour later relationships. Freud, therefore, said that 'all finding is a refinding' (Freud, 1905) which means that later relationships catalyse, if not recreate, early experiences of love and loss; hence divorce may unleash emotions, memories and projections from childhood:

> If sex is the way out of the family, falling in love is the route back, the one way ticket that is always a return. From a psychoanalytic point of view these miracles of affinity are echoes of our first fascinations (Phillips, 1994, p.39).

Divorce may therefore recall ambivalent feelings regarding prior separations which may or may not have been mourned. According to Freud (1917) mourning is a normal reaction to object loss whereas melancholia is a psychic state in which we are not able to mourn or separate from our lost 'object' of love. What this means is that unresolved feelings of anger and dejection tie us to this person at an unconscious level. The resulting depression and self-denigration is, then, a veiled attack on those whom we feel have let us down. What Freud alerts us to, therefore, is the fact that separation is an internal as well as an external achievement - a process which is difficult and slow.

Freud said that living for us means the same as being loved, and that our greatest anxiety is caused by the fear of being deserted by protecting forces when we do not feel strong enough to cope alone. This, he says, recalls the infantile anxiety of longing and the fear of separation from a protecting mother (Freud, 1923). Experiencing separation as something other than a dismemberment (which Phillips (1996) maintains it is) is thus a developmental achievement and one which we have to continually negotiate throughout life. However, melancholia and the inability to mourn is, according to Melanie Klein (the first to practice child psychotherapy), a psychic state we have all experienced in our childhood and which can be catalysed at times of stress in our adult lives. Let us now consider Klein's theory in more detail, since we regard it as having such an important contribution to make to the psychology of divorce.

Kleinian Psychoanalysis: Loss, Mourning and Melancholia

It was Klein who most developed Freud's ideas about mourning; she saw mourning and melancholia as central to normal, healthy development. For her, loss and the fear of the loss of the loved person assume a central importance throughout life. Klein maintained that we all experience a melancholic reaction to loss in infancy and that we likewise experience a melancholic state when we learn to separate and reconcile our feelings of both love and hate towards the same person. The ability to mourn and repair this sense of loss is dependent upon how we reconcile both feelings of love and hate towards the same object which will inevitably disappoint us and which we will inevitably attack.

Klein agreed with Freud's idea that human nature has a share of destructiveness and she maintained that these death instincts are directed towards our first objects (significant others we are instinctually or libidinally bound to) and colour our relationships from infancy onwards. We can, therefore, experience disappointment from external reality (when we are weaned or left) and from our internal reality (our own aggressive feelings towards those we also love).

As we can see, from Freud onwards, it has been a fundamental premise of psychoanalytic thought that love is ambivalent, but the concept of ambivalence is most elaborated in Kleinian thought. According to Klein our earliest relationships as infants occur while we occupy what Klein called the 'paranoid-schizoid position' (Klein 1946), a term which she gave to a particular grouping of anxieties and defences, which although born in earliest infancy, recur throughout life. It is this state of mind - the paranoid-schizoid one - which is important for our discussion of loss.

The paranoid-schizoid position is characterised by conflictual impulses of love and hate, envy and gratitude. The infant perceives the mother as both the source of gratification and as a potential persecutor (someone who is capable of abandoning or withholding satisfaction). In order to be able to tolerate the anxieties associated with these contradictory and threatening feelings, the infant uses defences of 'splitting' whereby the source of satisfaction (the mother/breast) is perceived, not as a unified object, but as fragmented into good and bad. Splitting the object, however, also involves splitting one's own ego (one's anger, for example, is disowned and located in the other) and thus one's sense of self and reality is weakened. We may, therefore, withdraw (become schizoid) and feel suspicious (paranoid) of those around us. In this context, the 'bad' mother is the one responsible for everything that's wrong, and the infant is unable to acknowledge that the 'good' and 'bad' mother are one and the same person, both gratifying and frustrating. This splitting protects the infant from the knowledge that feelings of plenitude are also threatened by its own destructive feelings, which because of its immaturity it cannot yet manage and which are, therefore, projected out.

These unacceptable, bad parts of the self are expelled into the other and we cannot, therefore, protect the loved person from our own bad feelings. It is only as development proceeds and the infant becomes aware of its own incapacity to protect the loved person that the infant begins to feel genuine sorrow and concern. This is the transition into what Klein calls the 'depressive position'. Learning to acknowledge our own attacks (originally on mother) involves the unbearable pain of acknowledging the damage we can inflict and we, therefore, suffer from what Klein refers to as depressive anxiety, pining for the loved object, and a need to repair the damage. This is akin to a process of mourning. For example, the loss of a partner or relative may make us feel unconsciously guilty or responsible for their loss or death, because present loss revives fears that it is our own badness, envy or greed which has killed or destroyed a valuable object. Depressive anxieties, however, express concern for the damage we have done to others and the attempt at reparation, whereas paranoid-schizoid anxieties centre on fears for our own survival.

We could hypothesise then that, in times of stress in later life, someone who was unable to work through this state of mind in infancy would be prone to excessive splitting, paranoia and withdrawal, whereas someone who was capable of withstanding depressive anxiety might be better able to cope with ambivalent feelings. But, even in the latter case early paranoid-schizoid defences could be resorted to and once again necessitate the work of mourning. A transitory paranoid-schizoid state of mind is indeed to be expected. Klein maintains that early mourning is revived whenever grief is experienced in later life.

By using Kleinian theory, we can, therefore, argue that there is not, in fact, a panacea for the pain or complex unconscious dynamics which separation may provoke. This does not mean, however, that we are promoting the importance of adversarial disputes. It is our contention that the ideal of the harmonious divorce is more likely to emerge (if at all) when the emotional conflict that psychoanalysis alerts us to is somehow acknowledged if not contained. Containment is the model that Bion (see Symington, 1996) introduced for the mother-infant couple in which the infant projects undigestable raw elements of experience and then re-introjects (via mother's reverie and thinking capacity) these elements of experience in a more palatable 'thought-full' form. This is what the divorcing couple may also benefit from: the dispute resolution process acting as a container for some of their conflict and thus perhaps increasing their own trust in reparation, new beginnings, and a new sense of self. Crucially, however, our ability to mourn and to repair losses depends upon an acknowledgement of conflicted emotions consequent upon separation.

It is, therefore, necessary to acknowledge that divorce involves loss for both partners, and possible emotional (or physical) injury to one, if not both of them. The dismantling of a shared reality may, of course, be a necessary good, and the final acknowledgement of a relationship breakdown may bring relief, but the subtext here is loss, separation and endings, all of which have unconscious significance in psychoanalysis. Hence a present loss can stir up memories and feelings which belong to past relationships, and which may be difficult to recall, even if they have been worked through. The dispute resolution process needs to acknowledge, therefore, that phantasies of damage, death, failure, guilt, and so on are potentially very alive and possibly persecuting in divorce cases. Acrimonious divorce disputes are, therefore, perhaps unsurprising, and in this context it is important that the mediation process itself can take cognizance of the powerful infantile feelings which divorce itself may catalyse. Although we are not insisting that mediators should adopt an object relations approach in their work, or indeed try to analyse their clients' psyches, it is useful to think about the prevalence of acrimonious divorce disputes and the media's moral scare regarding the decline of the family, in the light of Klein's work on loss and the paranoid state of mind it may temporarily catalyse or recall.

Discussion

Although Klein's work posits love as a developmental achievement and the ability to love as the guarantor of mental health, the ideal of harmonious family relations are implicitly problematised as is the idea of a harmonious separation. The 'depressive position' is, therefore, introduced as representing a more mature relation between self and other, but one that is difficult to sustain. Thus Klein uses the notion of positions, rather than stages, because a stage implies that it is something we pass through, never to return. Consequently, although the current prevalance of divorce discourses which emphasise co-operation and which denigrate conflict may well have resonances with Klein's depressive position and its central notion of the desire for reparation, the former nevertheless deny the psychological realities of loss.

There are, of course, many dynamics which may inform exactly how a divorce dispute is resolved, and we do not wish to argue that they are all explicable by the same Kleinian theory. Indeed some Kleinian concepts, such as genuine concern for the other, might appear to be hard to reconcile with divorce disputes in which domestic violence occurs, for example. But it must be understood that Klein's concept of reparation refers to an internal world and internal object relationships. For Klein, it is reparation internally which may have the effect of protecting us from damage in the external world. However, the relation of internal to external reality is a complex issue which is pertinent in the case of divorce.

Divorce, for example, is not just an internal psychological process; it is also a legal event and a time of great change. Many divorcing people experience real material difficulties, concrete problems and obstacles to progress outside their control, alongside the emotional turmoil; and the material and the psychological interact in complex ways. In divorce, for example, it is not uncommon for reality to reiterate and confirm our worst phantasies, stirring up further feelings of frustration and hate. From cases where, for example, there is violence or other forms of bullying and abuse, to less extreme cases where there is differential command of or access to resources, the realities of vulnerability and powerlessness outside can resonate with powerful persecutory phantasies within, seemingly confirming that the world is set against us. Small wonder, perhaps, that so many divorcing people carry around such a profound and enduring sense of injustice which the legal system seems powerless to address. We cannot assume, therefore, that because the law moves away from allegations of fault and discourages litigation that divorcing people will easily be able to follow suit.

On the contrary they may continue to be preoccupied with questions of blame, responsibility and culpability. These preoccupations reflect psychological coping strategies and will not easily be disposed of simply by virtue of a change in the law. Most, if not all, divorcing people are likely to struggle to understand what went wrong with their marriage; making sense of the past is a necessary part of negotiating a new reality to replace the shared reality of the marriage (Day Sclater, 1997). In many cases the need to rewrite the story of the marriage is so important that couples compete for their own version to be accepted as the true and authentic one. This competition can easily turn into conflict which, as we have seen, has deep psychological roots; in some particularly litigious divorces it is expressed in a proliferation of affidavits, as each partner struggles to have his or her own story heard. But, as Day Sclater argues in the next chapter, this conflict is not wholly negative and it serves some positive and constructive purposes.

Telling stories is one of the ways in which people make sense of their experiences; in stories, people can organise both memory and self, laying claim to a particular past in order to project themselves into an uncertain future. The crucial importance of being able to tell one's story in divorce relates not only to the pychological imperatives of conflict, but also to the need to reconstruct a new self post-divorce (Day Sclater, 1997). The dismantling of the 'shared reality' of the marriage, discussed by Johnston and Campbell (1987), often results in stories of the marriage as having been destructive to the self; the past is narrated in negative terms but, simultaneously, positive reconstructions of the self can emerge (Day Sclater, 1997, 1999).

Thus a consideration of the psychodynamics of divorce, such as we have presented in this chapter, enables us to appreciate the extent to which the splitting processes, as theorised by Klein, represents a survival strategy which has both negative and positive aspects. In divorce stories, splitting processes manifest themselves as polarisations between self and other, past and present, marriage and independence (Day Sclater 1997). In stories, subjectivities are created and transformed, often in opposition to a denigrated other; the past of the marriage is constructed as destructive or detrimental to the self, in opposition to the present and the future in which an idealised goal of 'independence' is embraced. These, then, are stories which have a profound psychological significance.

Adopting a psychoanalytic perspective on divorce enables us to appreciate that divorce is not only a negative and traumatic experience, but one which also has a positive side. Importantly, too, it permits us to move beyond the traditional models which focus only on the trauma and which pathologise the emotions involved. The value of Klein's theory is that it enables us to acknowledge that divorce is emotionally traumatic without pathologising it, since the psychological processes which Klein describes are all part of ordinary human development and coping in adult life.

Conclusion

From a psychoanalytic perspective, we have argued that the welfare discourse of co-operation enshrined in the Family Law Act 1996 shows very little understanding of a psychologically complex subject. Indeed, the sociologist and group psychotherapist, Ian Craib (1994) thinks that our culture tends to increasingly deny the 'Importance of Disappointment' and thus promises a management of the emotions, which denies an unconscious, irrational area of the mind and disquieting view of subjectivity. He maintains that in some forms of popular culture, such as the proliferation of self-help books (of which there are many addressed to divorcing couples), and in contemporary sociology (such as the influential work of Giddens, 1992), there is the illusion of an all-powerful self, in which self-mastery and the management of messy emotions like hate, jealousy, envy has become the new ideology for living.

It is easy to see how this ideology is reflected in the new ideas about divorce dispute resolution; we have already seen how one of the premises of the new Act is to minimise conflict and introduce what is seen as a more civilised approach to divorce. In Craib's terms, these developments in family law could be seen as resting upon an over-simplified and limited view of subjectivity where ideology operates to deny the existence of chaotic emotions or to carefully circumscribe passions which would otherwise be uncontrolled. Craib, however, argues that it is absolutely necessary to accept that we cannot always be in control of ourselves or life (death and illness are cases in point) and that we should not, therefore, expect emotional satisfaction continuously. It is equally important, he alleges, to expect frustration, unmet desires and anger, alongside the ideal of harmonious family relationships. He uses and prefers psychoanalysis to other psychologies, because for him it is psychoanalysis that recognises the importance of the disappointment he discusses.

We have argued that the divorce dispute resolution process will benefit from the insights which psychoanalysis can offer on the importance of unconscious processes, the dynamic nature of the psyche and conflicted emotions consequent upon loss and separation. The value of this perspective, however, goes beyond the insights which it provides into individual experiences, as it also enables us perhaps to have some insights into the social significance of divorce for our society and the reasons for the passionate debates over reform of the divorce law. Psychoanalysis helps us to appreciate the significant emotional investment which we all make in notions of 'family'; when demographic and attitudinal changes seem to threaten what we regard as traditional and proper family forms, the unconscious foundations of the symbolic significance of 'family' are stirred and powerful phantasies come into play. We can see these reflected, for example, in the debates leading up to the passing of the Family Law Act.

It is tempting to conclude that the recent divorce reforms, with their emphasis on 'no fault' and co-operative dispute resolution, are addressed as much towards quieting our panic in relation to 'the family' as they are towards bringing the divorce law up to date. Looked at from a psychoanalytic perspective, the progress of the reform proposals and the premises of the Family

Law Act can be seen again to reflect the tendency towards splitting, this time as a social phenomenon. The adversarial system is denigrated and mediation, the alternative, is dangerously idealised. The desire underlying the Family Law Act to create the conditions for harmonious divorce can thus be seen as an attempt to deny the uncomfortable fact of family breakdown.

Crucially, however, the provisions of the new law, examined in the light of psychoanalytic understandings, look very much as though they are denying the psychological realities of loss and neglecting the psychological significance of the need to rebuild the self. We have, therefore, used psychoanalysis to show that that dispute resolution procedures, whether mediation, litigation or bi-partisan negotiation, would benefit from thinking about the inevitability of divorce conflict which cannot be legislated away or waved away by the magic wand of mediation. Whilst the introduction of therapeutic family mediation in Britain does not seem to be a likely or perhaps even a desirable development, it is nevertheless the case, we would argue, that dispute resolution procedures can, and do, serve psychological functions. Not only do dispute resolution procedures serve as forums for the production of divorce stories, but they also act as 'containers' for some of the unprocessed emotions and anxieties we have talked about, some of which might lose their destructive power as the work of mourning proceeds in a containing setting. The focus of dispute resolution and mediation should, therefore, be on containing conflict, which means creating structures which can metabolise and transform it, rather than thinking quantitatively in terms of a reduction or denial of it.

As Craib points out, rows, attacks, hurting and being hurt are part and parcel of intimacy and a society which denies the importance of this disappointment is one in which emotions are managed rather than contained. What this means for the dispute resolution process is that it can only act as a container for the powerful feelings divorce may catalyse, if it does not, because of a simplified view of co-operation, represent a denial of them. We conclude, therefore, that dispute resolution discourses need to be re-thought so that proper respect can be given to the feelings of adults and the needs of children, without pathologising either.

Notes

1. For a brief discussion of the background to the Act see, for example, Bird and Cretney (1996).

2. Insertion of the statement of general principles was moved at the Report stage by the then Lord Chancellor in the House of Lords (Hansard, 22 February 1996, col 1145).

References

Berger, P.L. and Kellner, H. (1964), 'Marriage and the Construction of Reality', reprinted in M. Anderson (ed) (1971), *Sociology of the Family*, Penguin, Hardmondsworth.

Bird, R. and Cretney, S. (1996), *Divorce: The New Law*, Family Law, Jordans, Bristol.

Craib, I. (1994), *The Importance of Disappointment*, Routledge, London.

Davis, G., Cretney, S. and Collins, J. (1994), *Simple Quarrels*, Clarendon Press, Oxford.

Day Sclater, S. (1997), 'Narratives of Divorce', *Journal of Social Welfare and Family Law*, vol 19(4), pp.432-441.

Day Sclater, S. (1999), 'The Bubble that Burst: Jane's Divorce Story', *Self, Agency and Society*, (in press).

Freeman (1993), *Rewriting the Self: History, Memory, Narrative*, Routledge, London.

Freud, S. (1900), *The Interpretation of Dreams*, Standard Edition (S.E.) 4 and S.E. 5.

Freud, S. (1905), *Three Essays on The Theory of Sexuality*, S.E. 7.

Freud, S. (1917), *Mourning and Melancholia*, S.E. 14.

Freud, S. (1920), *Beyond The Pleasure Principle*, S.E. 18.

Freud, S. (1923), *The Ego and The Id*, S.E. 19.

Freud, S. (1926), *Inhibitions, Symptoms and Anxiety*, S.E. 20.

Freud, S. (1930), *Civilisation and Its Discontents*, S.E. 21.

Giddens, A. (1992), *The Transformation of Intimacy*, Polity, Oxford.

Johnston, J. and Campbell, L. (1988), *Impasses of Divorce: The Dynamics and Resolution of Family Conflict*, Free Press, New York.

Klein, M. (1935, reprinted 1991), 'A Contribution to the Psycho-genesis of Manic-depressive States', in *Love, Guilt and Reparation*, Virago, London.

Klein, M. (1940, reprinted in 1991), ' Mourning and its Relation to Manic-depressive States', in *Love, Guilt and Reparation*, Virago, London.

Klein, M. (1946, reprinted in 1988), 'Notes on Some Schizoid Mechanisms' in *Envy and Gratitude*, Virago, London.

Law Commission (1988), *Looking to the Future*, Law Com. No. 170, HMSO, London.

Law Commission (1990), *Family Law: the Grounds for Divorce*, Law Com. No. 192, HMSO, London.

Lord Chancellor's Department (1993), *Looking to the Future. Mediation and the Ground for Divorce*, Law Com. No. 2424, HMSO, London.

Lord Chancellor's Department (1995), *Looking to the Future. Mediation and the Ground for Divorce*, Law Com. No. 2799, HMSO, London.

Morgan, P. (1996), 'Family Crisis Affects Us All', in C. Donellan (ed), *Marriage and Divorce: Issues for the Nineties*, Independence Educational Publishers, Cambridge.

Phillips, A. (1994), *On Flirtation*, Faber and Faber, London.

Phillips, A. (1996), *Monogamy*, Faber and Faber, London.

Symington, J. & N. (1996), *The Clinical Thinking of Wilfred Bion*, Routledge, London.
Vaughan, D. (1987), *Uncoupling: Turning Points in Intimate Relationship*, OUP, Oxford.

8 Experiences of Divorce

SHELLEY DAY SCLATER

Introduction

This chapter discusses some findings from a recent empirical study[1] whose central aim was to understand the ways in which psychological processes in divorce interact with those of dispute resolution. The research was conceived in the context of the Family Law Act 1996, which introduced a new scheme for divorce, *inter alia* abolishing matrimonial 'fault' and providing for the resolution of divorce disputes by mediation rather than bi-partisan negotiation or litigation. Part of the impetus behind the reform of the law was a recognition that the emotional costs of divorce are too high. As chapter 1 points out, the adversarial system was seen as encouraging 'bitterness and conflict' as well as the expenditure of excessive legal costs, and it was envisaged that more widespread use of mediation could assist in minimising both.

There is a well-established psychological and psychiatric literature which documents the emotional trauma suffered by many, if not most, divorcing people (see, for example, Kitson and Morgan, 1990). Little is known, however, about the ways in which the psychology of divorce interacts with dispute resolution (Vermont Law School, 1987; Day Sclater, 1995). There are some indications in the existing literature that the harmonious divorce, envisaged in the Act, may be difficult to achieve by virtue of the psychological processes that underlie separation. Vaughan (1987), for example, found that the adoption of an oppositional stance *vis a vis* the former partner was an integral part of the 'uncoupling' process and a pre-condition for the establishment of a new self outside of the relationship. Bailey-Harris *et al* (1998), in a study monitoring private law applications under the Children Act, show how the implementation of the Act has coincided with a significant increase in the numbers of disputes about children, despite the co-operative rhetoric of the Act and the widespread emphasis on settlement in the legal process. In our pilot study (Day Sclater, 1997) it emerged that a degree of opposition to the former partner was a central element in the stories people tell to make sense of divorce; they are often constructed around oppositions of self/other and before/after, as people reappraise the past from the vantage point of the present in order to be able to move forward to the future.

The question therefore arose as to the extent to which polarisation, opposition, even conflict, may be part and parcel of the psychology of divorce and not simply an artefact of the adversarial system (see Day Sclater and Richards, 1995). The central question which motivated the research discussed here was whether the new scheme for resolving divorce disputes would be effective in promoting the desired harmonious divorce, or whether the psychodynamics of divorce might militate against such an achievement.

As Brown and Day Sclater argue in the previous chapter, it may be that the conflict associated with divorce reflects deeper psychological processes. To summarise their argument based on psychoanalytic theory, the fundamental nature of love is ambivalent and, in marriage breakdown, the 'loss' involved is not only the loss of a once-loved person, but also the undermining of psychic equilibrium. This calls into play defensive manoeuvres as 'strategies for survival', the operation of which may explain the conflict which so often accompanies divorce. In traditional psychological research, particularly those studies that adopt only quantitative methodologies, the nuances and the complexities of personal experiences, and of their underlying emotional subtexts, are often submerged in the quest for categorisation and statistical correlation. By contrast, the psychosocial approach (Day Sclater, 1995) adopted in the study reported here relies upon a combination of quantitative measurement of psychological well-being and qualitative case studies; the research design permits something to be said about the range of psychological 'symptoms' reported by the participants, and to put those 'symptoms' in the context of each individual's account of their experience.

This approach draws upon recent advances in psychology and, in particular, the emergence of what can be called a 'critical' movement (Parker and Spears, 1996; Wilkinson, 1996; Fox and Prilleltensky, 1997; Ibanez and Iniguez, 1997; Henriques *et al*, 1998). In particular, it draws on work which points to the crucial role of narration in making sense of personal experience (Mishler, 1986; Sarbin, 1986; Denzin, 1989; Personal Narratives Group, 1989; Riessman, 1993). A further strand which informs the approach adopted here is that of the use of psychoanalytic concepts in social research (Hollway, 1989; Hunt, 1989). While this strand is, as yet, less well established, it represents an innovative approach that seems to hold great promise in challenging the old disciplinary barriers as well as the limited notions of subjectivity which inform psychology, sociology and law.

How do divorcing people make sense of the fact that the 'happy ever after' of fairy tales never happened for them? The ideology of romantic love continues to exert a strong hold over people's expectations of intimacy and marriage, despite the fact that divorce is now so commonplace. There is a sense in which divorce continues to be a 'hidden' experience; divorcing people find that others are reluctant, even embarrassed, to talk about it, in the way they are about death, possibly because it resonates with our deep-set fears about the fate of our own relationships. There seems to be something of a cultural hiatus where divorce is concerned; this is so despite the fact that statistics tell us how increasingly commonplace it is, and media reports remind us that it can affect anyone. But, when the experience is ours, we find an absence of culturally available scripts in which to construct our stories and to make sense of what has happened to us.

The problem here seems to be that such divorce story genres as exist in our culture are generally ones of chaos, disaster and pathology. Particularly where children are concerned, there is a vast literature and a pervasive rhetoric that constructs children as 'damaged' by divorce. Piper (1996), for example, has argued that an image of the child as 'victim' informs the Family Law Act 1996. The existence of such discourses renders it difficult for divorcing people to regard their experiences in anything other than negative terms.

We are the first generation of people who might expect to divorce but, at the same time as the divorce rate has risen, so too have we witnessed a reassertion of family ideology (Abbott and Wallace, 1992; Jones *et al*, 1995; Fox Harding, 1996). 'Family' is a powerful signifier; it continues to exert a profound emotional pull and, in this context, it is perhaps unsurprising that people struggle to contend with feelings of confusion when trying to make sense of their lives and to plan for, or even just imagine, a future. The need to make a psychological 'adjustment' to divorce, to come to terms with 'loss' in all its complexity, is rendered more difficult by the dominance of discourses which idealise the 'intact' family and pathologise family 'breakdown', problems which are compounded by the very real material privations, obstacles and changes which many divorcing people face. These external difficulties can interact in complex ways with the trauma of loss. The personal narratives of divorcing people can be used as a way to understand some of these complexities, and of looking into the extent to which people take up, negotiate or resist pathological positionings (Davies and Harre, 1990; Day Sclater, 1999).

Methods

Detailed case study material involving three types of data was collected from divorcing people over an eight-month period in 1996-97. First, each participant completed three self-administered General Health Questionnaires (GHQ-28) at two-monthly intervals. The GHQ has been extensively validated in general practice where it is used to identify probable 'cases' of psychiatric morbidity, which can then be either confirmed or disconfirmed by means of a clinical interview (Goldberg and Williams, 1988). In social scientific research, it is not used to assist in 'diagnosis' in this way, but simply as a means of providing a quantitative assessment of psychological well-being. The GHQ-28 consists of 4 sub-scales, each with 7 items (total 28 items): somatic symptoms (SS), anxiety and insomnia (A/I), social dysfunction (SD), and severe depression (D). Its purpose is to detect recent changes in affect, and subjects are asked to indicate which symptoms they have experienced in the last few weeks and also their severity. For example, one question asks 'Have you recently felt constantly under strain?' and participants may choose from the following range of replies: 'not at all' (score 0), 'no more than usual' (score 0), 'rather more than usual' (score 1), 'much more than usual' (score 1). Most studies suggest that a threshold score of 4/5 is an appropriate indicator of possible morbidity in the general population.

Secondly, qualitative data on subjective experiences of divorce was obtained by means of in-depth, unstructured, life-history interviews in which subjects were asked simply to tell the interviewer about their experiences of divorce and how disputes had arisen and been dealt with. Subjects were interviewed three times at two-monthly intervals. Interviews lasted on average one and a half hours and were tape recorded and transcribed in full. These interviews yielded lengthy personal narrative accounts of a range of divorce experiences, in which the feelings, meanings and concerns of the interviewee were expressed, rather than the pre-conceived categories of the research team. In the analysis, the focus was on both the form and the content of what people said, and the nature of the stories they told (Riessman, 1990, 1993). Whilst the data were not subjected to discourse analysis in any systematic way (Potter and

Wetherell, 1987; Parker, 1992; Parker and Berman, 1993), the discourses subjects invoked in telling their stories were important in the analysis.

Thirdly, we collected retrospective data by means of semi-structured interviews in the final stage of the project. At this stage, participants were asked specific questions concerning the 'symptoms' and feelings they had experienced, and the progress and outcome of divorce disputes.

The Participants

Participants were recruited to the study with the help of local mediators and solicitors over a wide area in the south of England. Several people also joined the project having read articles in local newspapers where the research was reported. The discussion presented here is based on 11 complete case studies where the full range of data is available. Material from 2 men and 9 women, aged between 40 and 59 years (average 45 years), married for between 4 and 26 years (average 17.8 years), and separated for between one month and 4 years (average 16.9 months) at the start of the study has been used in the analysis discussed here. All participants were separated but not divorced at the start of the study, and their divorces were finalised, with disputes resolved, by the end of the study. Their educational qualifications ranged between 'none' (4 people) and 'A Level or above' (4 people). Two participants were in full-time paid employment (both men), two women were unpaid homemakers, and the remainder worked part time. All participants were parents; all but two had dependent children living with them. Five had petitioned for divorce, and five were respondents to divorce proceedings. One was involved in judicial separation proceedings for religious reasons. Four participants had begun dispute resolution by mediation, but all went on to instruct solicitors to negotiate on their behalf. No participant was involved in contentious litigation about any aspect of the divorce.

This sub-sample is not a 'random' one and I do not make any claims about its representativeness of the sort which are appropriate in quantitative statistical studies where validity depends upon random sampling techniques. In qualitative, ethnographic work, 'theoretical' sampling is more appropriate. The case studies illustrate a range of divorce experiences, where individual narrators provide what can be thought of as windows of understanding into the worlds they occupy. This does not mean an abandonment of a commitment to generalisability as an important research aim, but the generalisability which derives from case studies is of a different order from that appropriate to large scale quantitative research. Individual case studies are, of course, unique to the case in question but, at the same time, they tell us something about a wider world. Rosenwald, for example, points out that psychologists have tended to neglect the detailed study of individual lives because it has not seemed to contribute to the formulation of general truths. He argues that individual cases, if brought into 'conversation' with one another, permit shared realities to be reconstructed out of individual perspectival images (Rosenwald, 1988). It is obvious, but perhaps still needs stating, that individuals can only reveal what they are placed to reveal, and it is for this reason that it is important to pay particular attention to the context, the particularities and the partialities of individuals' perspectives. It is precisely upon this range of unique experiences, and the common threads which join them despite their uniqueness, that the focus of this research has been. A case study approach illuminates the nuances and the complexities in the personal experience of divorce which are hidden from view in more traditional studies, at the same time as it allows us to say something about the social structuring of those experiences (Day Sclater, 1999).

Findings

Throughout the eight-month study period, participants reported very high levels of psychological distress. The prevalence of 'symptoms' commonly associated with psychiatric morbidity was evident from the GHQ scores. At the same time, however, the personal narrative accounts permit us to regard these symptoms in the context of individual lives, and whilst divorce stories often speak of pain and loss, they also speak of positive things, of relief, of freedom, of building a new independent self and of looking forward to the future. The picture which emerges of divorce from the narrative accounts is a complex one, which does not have any straightforward correspondence with that which emerges from the GHQ data; indeed, the narratives indicate the variety of ways in which divorcing people negotiate, or even resist, conceiving of themselves in terms of pathologies.

Symptoms

Table 1: GHQ Scores at Time 1, Time 2 and Time 3

Mediation	**Time 1**	**Time 2**	**Time 3**
James	12	19	19
Richard	2	17	0
Helen	18	12	24
Molly	18	16	25
Average score	12.5	16	17
Non-Mediation			
Fiona	10	10	9
Laura	5	1	0
Sheila	19	7	11
Alison	19	14	11
Gina	8	4	8
Jill	10	13	0
Alice	21	22	15
Average score	13.1	10.1	7.7
Overall Average	12.9	12.2	11

Table 1 shows the range of GHQ scores at Times 1, 2 and 3. The 'mediation' group consists of people who began divorce dispute resolution by mediation (although all went on to involve solicitors); the 'non-mediation' group consists of people who had not used mediation at all, and who had instructed solicitors throughout. A person free of symptoms would be expected to score 0, whilst someone who was experiencing trauma would be expected to score more. Goldberg and Hillier (1979) suggest a score of more than 4/5 as indicative of possible morbidity. Using this threshold, it can be seen that only one subject, Laura, obtained a score below the threshold at all three testing times. The average scores range from 12.9 at Time 1 to 11 at Time 3, indicating the severe drop in psychological well-being which the majority of our participants experienced.

Table 2 shows the GHQ scores broken down by sub-scale. For each sub-scale, the minimum score is 0 and the maximum is 7. Total scores on the 'anxiety' sub-scale are highest at all times, and those on the 'severe depression' sub-scale are lowest.

Table 2: GHQ Scores by Sub-scales at Time 1, Time 2 and Time 3

(SS: Somatic Symptoms; A/I: Anxiety/Insomnia; SD: Social Dysfunction; D: Severe Depression)

Mediation (n=4)

GHQ 1	**James**	**Richard**	**Helen**	**Molly**	**Totals**
SS	1	0	6	4	**11**
A/I	6	1	6	6	**19**
SD	0	1	3	4	**8**
D	5	0	3	4	**12**
Totals	12	2	18	18	50
GHQ 2					
SS	2	6	5	5	**18**
A/I	6	7	7	6	**26**
SD	6	4	0	3	**13**
D	5	0	0	2	**7**
Totals	19	17	12	16	64
GHQ 3					
SS	4	0	7	7	**18**
A/I	5	0	7	6	**18**
SD	5	0	5	6	**16**
D	5	0	5	6	**16**
Totals	19	0	24	25	68

Non-Mediation (n=7)

GHQ1	Fiona	Laura	Sheila	Alison	Gina	Jill	Alice	Total s
SS	4	0	5	3	0	2	4	**18**
A/I	4	1	7	7	6	3	7	**35**
SD	2	4	2	5	2	3	6	**24**
D	0	0	5	4	0	2	4	**15**
Totals	**10**	**5**	**19**	**19**	**8**	**10**	**21**	**92**
GHQ2								
SS	4	0	2	2	2	3	5	**18**
A/I	5	1	3	6	1	3	5	**24**
SD	1	0	0	4	1	3	7	**16**
D	0	0	2	2	0	4	5	**13**
Totals	**10**	**1**	**7**	**14**	**4**	**13**	**22**	**71**
GHQ3								
SS	4	0	4	2	4	0	1	**15**
A/I	5	0	5	5	3	0	6	**24**
SD	0	0	2	3	1	0	7	**13**
D	0	0	0	1	0	0	1	**2**
Totals	**9**	**0**	**11**	**11**	**8**	**0**	**15**	**54**

The GHQ data are supported by the retrospective semi-structured interview data collected at Time 4, eight months after the start of the study. Tension, irritability and anxiety were reported to be the 'symptoms' felt most strongly. In addition, some subjects attributed physical ill-health they had suffered to psychological trauma, and most subjects, looking back, judged that the period between separation and divorce was the most difficult.

The narratives collected during the unstructured interviews permit some insight into the personal meanings of these distressing symptoms. Thus, subjects talked about feeling as though they were 'cracking up', some told how they reached 'breaking point' whilst others said how they had lost confidence in their ability to 'carry on any more'. Some sought relief from this pain in fantasies about 'running away from it all'. Reports of depression, of an absence of energy and motivation, even a desire to 'give up and die' were not uncommon.

However, alongside these painful scenarios there exists, in most cases, a determination to survive, a determination not to give in to or be beaten by circumstances which, at times, manifests itself in the narratives as an angry resistance that reasserts the self and challenges the image of divorce as pathology. People 'explained' their 'symptoms' with reference to material and relational difficulties over which they felt they had little or no control. For example, for those subjects who were parents of children living with them, issues around the children's contact times were felt to be particularly problematic.

Laura, for example, (who, incidentally, had the lowest GHQ score) found the idea that her husband's girlfriend was forming a relationship with her children almost unbearable. She perceived herself as having become, at one point, suicidal: 'I literally went to pieces'. Laura felt that she had only been saved by the re-emergence of her 'fighting spirit' that her mother encouraged; she understood that it was acknowledging her anger which prevented her from reaching the depths of despair. Yet Laura, like others, had problems in accepting, let alone expressing her own anger: 'It just hurt the whole time. Angry, I was really, really angry but, on the other hand, I knew I couldn't do anything because of the children'. Laura's case was not the only one in which the discourse of welfare, which emphasises the need for parental harmony for the sake of the children, seemed to operate to de-legitimise the anger she felt. But in her case, as in others, acknowledging her anger was closely tied to the surfacing of her will to survive, and to her ability to repair and reconstruct her self.

Laura's case illustrates the complex relationship between the quantitative and the qualitative data; it is all the more potent because her GHQ score was comparatively low. It is possible, of course, that Laura (who had been separated for 20 months at Time 1) had grown accustomed to high levels of anxiety such that the GHQ items which specifically sought to identify changes 'in the last few weeks' had failed to pick up on her more chronic difficulties. But Laura's case also illustrates the way in which acknowledgement of how angry she felt served to ward off her symptoms of depression and despair, to provide a basis from which she could begin to move forward and to build a new self. This beginning came with the surfacing of her 'fighting spirit', giving her energy to carry on. Yet, the dominance of the welfare discourse posed a barrier to Laura's strategy for survival: 'If I see him, I hate him. My idea would be to have nothing more to do with him whatsoever. Then I could start getting on with my life. But I cannot do that because of the children'.

Feelings

Data about the range of feelings and emotions which subjects reported having experienced were collected at Time 4 in the semi-structured interviews. Loss, anger, upset and sadness are the feelings reported most strongly, but others such as low self-esteem, fear, loneliness and numbness also feature prominently. Others, such as guilt, hatred, viciousness, loss of trust, a desire for vengeance, self pity and a sense of injustice were also spontaneously mentioned.

The narratives, again, shed some light on the complexities of the feelings involved in divorce. Importantly, at the same time as subjects talked about coping with these negative emotions, they were also able to talk positively about themselves as they pursued desired goals and searched for a new place for themselves in the world. The narratives indicate that divorce is a difficult emotional experience, but it is one that has positive aspects too. At Time 4 when subjects were asked to reflect on whether anything positive had come out of the experience, only one was doubtful. Richard mentioned 'freedom, happy, content with myself, not living a lie any more, healthier, more relaxed'. Molly talked about 'having discovered reserves of an ability to cope and make my own decisions, discovered more of myself, a freer person. I have blossomed as a person, made new friends, started new interests. I am getting better at saying "no"'. Gina too said that the positive things included 'no more arguments, more peaceful at home, independence, developing my own friendship network, discovered more about myself, competence, liking myself more'. But reflecting on the positive did not mean that the pain had disappeared or been forgotten. Helen talked about feelings of 'relief and freedom' that the divorce initially brought her 'but they didn't last'. Fiona said she felt both 'frustrated and relieved'. Sheila mentioned, in the same breath, 'anger and anxiety over money, wanting to kill him, knowledge that I can survive'. Jill summed up these ambivalences in this way: 'I know it is a very painful process, but sometimes you do come out of it thinking, well, I have lost a lot, but I have gained a lot as well'.

The narratives thus illustrate the complexity and the contradictory nature of the feelings associated with divorce. Separation and loss are painful, and they invoke frightening feelings which are difficult to manage. But separation also signifies an exit from a marriage which is often perceived, in retrospect, as having been destructive to the self, and so it provides an opportunity to build a new self and to pursue a goal of independence.

Survival Strategies

Brown and Day Sclater, in the previous chapter, show how Kleinian psychoanalytic theory can be used to theorise the complex and contradictory psychology of divorce. Analysis of the personal narratives indicates that divorcing people do indeed deal with 'loss' in the way Klein describes; the use of 'splitting' is common as a coping strategy. In the narratives, this phenomenon can manifest itself as a polarisation between self and other, and between past and present/future. It intersects in complex ways with culturally available scripts and divorce discourses to produce what we have termed 'survival strategies' which people use to cope with loss, rebuild the self and imagine futures. We now go on to discuss these issues in more depth, drawing on the narrative material.

The Importance of the Past A consistent theme in the narratives of our participants was that of looking back over the marriage, of trying to make sense of what had gone wrong, trying to piece together a coherent and plausible account which would convince the listener that the subject's experience was comprehensible. As Freeman (1993) points out in relation to autobiography generally, the past is continually being reconstructed from the vantage point of the present; when a divorcing person tells their story, there is a sense in which the ending is already known; the 'happy ever after' was never realised. Through narration, our subjects confronted the ways and the reasons their own marriages had departed from the fairy-tale expectations but, importantly, they find no readily available alternative genre in which to construct their stories. As we have seen, divorce narratives are stories of loss, but they can also be stories of survival, of triumphing even, against the odds. Importantly, these stories can also be seen as the locus for the production of a new post-divorce self (Riessman, 1990; Hermans and Hermans-Jansen, 1995).

In divorce stories, 'splitting' defences can manifest themselves in a rigid division between past and present. Participants most commonly denigrated the past and the marriage, and idealised their present pursuit of independence. But some did the opposite and idealised the marriage and felt a sense of terrible despair about the impending divorce. Both are strategies for survival which assist in making sense and in the work of mourning. Both involve reinterpreting the past from the vantage point of the present. This revisiting and reinterpreting of the past involves engaging with discourses of romantic love; divorce accounts inevitably challenge romantic notions of marriage, and it is perhaps unsurprising to see these ideas turned on their heads in divorce stories. Crucially, though, there are no positive alternative genres and so divorce stories are ones that struggle for coherence amid a range of competing social discourses.

One such discourse which pervades divorce stories in a number of ways is that of gender. James, for example, had been married for 23 years, but the breakdown of his very traditional marriage led him to question whether he had ever really loved Pamela at all; was their relationship ever based on 'love', or was it merely a convenience of complementary gender roles? Whilst married, James felt that he had happily accepted the male breadwinner-female homemaker gendered division of labour, but when Pamela left, he felt very cynical about it, and saw it as having caused the breakdown of his marriage. Divorce dispute resolution was difficult for James with this background, because he found it difficult to accept that Pamela was entitled to assets to which she had not contributed in direct financial terms. Yet, James' understanding, in terms of gender relations, of what had gone wrong with the marriage, led him to feel a substantial share of guilt, producing a situation in which he was torn in two; the guilt he felt about his part in the marriage breakdown sat uneasily with his assumption that, because he had been the breadwinner, the assets belonged primarily to him. The problems were compounded by the difficulties James had in coming to terms with loss; Pamela's departure reactivated old unresolved losses for him, and he felt immobilised. Dispute resolution, in this case, although not acrimonious, was slow and painful, as James sought to deal with the complexities and contradictions of the situation by doing nothing, 'burying his head in the sand', as he put it.

James' case is only one example; other subjects, even if they did not 'blame' problems caused by gender-differentiated roles in marriage, at least saw such differentiation as having been problematic and as contributing to the breakdown. It may be that this reflects nothing more than a convenient way, at a time when gender relations are in flux, of accounting for what went wrong. But, interestingly, participants did not blame feminism, neither were they critical of developments which have provided opportunities for women to have a life outside the home, or for men to participate more in caring activities. Rather, participants were much more critical, as James was, of traditional gendered divisions.

There are those who argue that the disruptions brought about by feminism to traditional gendered ways of being is what has caused the 'decline' of the family, and it is often said that it is the influence of feminism which underlies the willingness of so many nowadays to divorce (see, for example, Morgan, 1995; Whelan, 1995). The findings from this study, however, do not support such a contention and, on the contrary, many participants expressed the view that, had they been able to organise their married lives in a more egalitarian manner, more free of gendered constraints, their marriages might have survived. Most participants were preoccupied with the problematics of gender, reflecting some of the contemporary concerns with transformations in intimacy, of the sort discussed by Giddens (1992). But what is interesting is that gender constitutes an important focus for the polarisations which occur in divorce.

It may be that this polarisation, as it appears in divorce accounts, reflects not only changing gender relations but also a deeper psychology of loss. Richard's case illustrates this point. Richard's narrative told only obliquely of the profound emotional pain the divorce had caused him. He saw Jennifer's preoccupation with their child as the main reason his marriage had failed. He blamed Jennifer for wanting and having the child, and for mothering her in the way she did. Blaming Jennifer in this way was accompanied by an intense feeling of injustice, and a profound anger and hatred, which was generalised beyond Jennifer to include all women. The effects of Richard's way of coping was to make him feel persecuted, first by Jennifer, then by women as a category, then by the whole edifice of social gender relations. In seeing things in this way, Richard became the victim of generalised social structures which were beyond his control. But underlying the blaming, the anger and the conflict was, as Richard put it, an intense cry of pain. Here is Richard talking about the biggest hurt he feels he is reacting against:

> The lies that society puts upon us. That tells your gender to play with dolls, go

> out and have little girls, and tells my gender that they have got to be macho and hard and not cry, all those things. And then puts us together and lets us loose. And it doesn't work like that, and we wind up hurting each other. And anything I do to my wife, to my child, to your gender, is simply a cry of pain. When I told my wife that if she didn't get it sorted, and she took everything away from me, I was going to clump my daughter with a sledgehammer one day, that was the loudest cry of pain she would ever hear from me. There were no tears involved, no shouting. And she will never know it. She will never know it.

Thus, it can be argued, that it is in the splitting and the psychological manoeuvres by which the past becomes the opposite of the present, by which the marriage is denigrated and by which part of our own badness and destructiveness comes to be located in the other, in the elisions which link the denigrated characteristics and behaviours of the other to wider manifestations of gender difference, that it is possible to detect the moorings of deeper strategies for psychological survival.

In divorce, as in many other aspects of social life, gender is a crucial organising category, and the site where the opposition between self and other is played out. Psychological coping strategies intersect in complex ways with existing social discourses and structures, and real material constraints. In Richard's case, dispute resolution was not acrimonious, although mediation was unsuccessful. Agreement was reached between solicitors giving Richard the lion's share of the assets, but he continued to feel a profound sense of injustice that was rooted in a deeper sense of the injustice of gender relations. James, too, talked about his worry that he had 'lost everything', despite the fact that he had remained in the former matrimonial home and had the children with him.

In summary, the divorce narratives show the profound emotional significance of revisiting and reinterpreting the past. Significantly, as this is done from the vantage point of the present, the past of the marriage is effectively reconstructed, probably by each partner differently, and it is not uncommon for the marriage to be seen in negative terms, as having been destructive or undermining of the self. In this way, the divorce can be seen more positively, as a route out of oppressive relations (often conceived in gendered terms) and as the way towards an idealised independence. It is argued that these polarisations, as they are reflected in divorce stories, are manifestations of psychological coping strategies, as 'splitting' is invoked to assist in coming to terms with loss.

Self and Other 'Splitting' also results in a polarisation between self and other, as bad and painful parts of the self are expelled or projected outwards, and are then perceived as belonging to the other. Sometimes, it is guilt which is projected, as the subject turns hostility inwards to attack the self, or adopts a victim status. Small wonder, perhaps, that so many divorcing people report an enduring sense of persecution and injustice (See, for example, Davis, Cretney and Collins, 1994).

These manoeuvres manifest themselves in the narratives in stories that tell of wrongs done to the subject, in which the ex-partner is blamed for the breakdown of the marriage, or for instigating divorce conflict. They appear in stories where survival depends on getting even or even on getting revenge. They manifest themselves in stories of struggles within the confines of a dispute resolution procedure that is seen as favouring the other. It seems likely that it is these psychological survival strategies which underlie the bitterness and conflict which is so often associated with divorce. Laura's case, mentioned earlier, however, alerts us to the possibility that such 'conflict' should not be seen in purely negative terms. It will be remembered that, for Laura, it was the resurgence of her 'fighting spirit' which overrode a suicidal depression; for her, it was a necessary aspect of rebuilding her self which she felt had been destroyed when Peter abandoned her. Richard also rebuilt himself in opposition to Jennifer; in his story, he positioned himself as everything she was not, he saw the divorce as her fault, and he experienced an intense anger and hatred towards her. At the same time, as we have seen, seeing things in such polarised terms was accompanied by Richard's recognition of his own underlying vulnerability. James, on the other hand, was not quite so ready to polarise; but he found himself stuck in an impasse, with his 'head in the sand', unable to move forward and feeling, instead, a profound sadness. The process of rebuilding the self had hardly begun for James, though he had been separated for 9 months at the time of the first interview. Jill, too, found it difficult to be angry and hostile with John, even though she felt that way inside. In her case, it was the welfare discourse which provided the obstacle. Here she is talking about how painful she finds the contact arrangements:

> Because I am finding this very difficult, you know, knowing that she has got to go over there, and that his girlfriend is going to be dealing with her at some point. And I am finding it very hard to cope with. You know, at the end of the day, I have got to put up with it, but I don't like it. I haven't got to like it. I will never like it.

Jill, in accordance with the welfare discourse, refrains from expressing anger to John, believing that it will be bad for her daughter:

> I don't think two wrongs make a right, you know, um (p), for the sake of my own - my daughter, you know, I just basically say to him, 'look, you talk to my solicitor, you know I don't want to argue with you'. But he knows he has got one over on me all the time. He knows that he upsets me. I am sure of that. But for the sake of my daughter, I don't say very much or raise my voice in front of him. It's not going to do her any good.

Jill's narrative illustrates the ways in which the welfare discourse operates to constrain expressions of hostile emotion. At the same time, however, the particular constructions of children's 'interests' embedded in the discourse are perceived as posing constraints upon the achievement of the valued 'independence'. We have already heard what Laura had to say about that. Here is Helen talking:

> I really don't want to have any contact with him any more. I don't want to have to consider his needs. It would be much better if we could move completely to the other end of the country or something like that, and never see him again.

The presence of children, and the prescriptions of the welfare discourse, makes the desired autonomy difficult to achieve, because of the necessity of continuing relations with the other parent, and because of the prohibition on the expression of hostile emotion.

Yet, there is also a sense in which the presence of children allows some of the ambivalences around attachment to be worked through. Both Laura and Jill, for example, invoked a welfare discourse in which they accepted that the children had a need for continued relations with their father, but they were quite clear in seeing that the children's interests were in conflict with their own needs for a final separation. The children's needs were given priority. Had this not been so, neither Laura nor Jill could have maintained an image of themselves as a 'good' mother. Within the welfare discourse, the child is positioned as vulnerable (Piper, 1996), as potentially damaged by divorce, and it is this positioning of children which perhaps serves a psychological function; the welfare discourse provides a space into which adults' own vulnerabilities may be shifted; they can be disowned and projected onto the children (Day Sclater, 1998).

Helen, for example, sought (through mediation) a 'painless divorce' which she justified in terms of the children's interests. She explained why she had chosen mediation in this way:

> I didn't want to go to a solicitor who would take it all over. Well, I think they just go for the kill at times, and I didn't want that, because I didn't want to antagonise my ex-husband because we don't want to have that sort of relationship as far as the children are concerned.

It is as though, by avoiding solicitors, some of the negative feelings associated with divorce can be avoided. Helen's choice to mediate was made partly because she regarded mediation positively and partly because she regarded solicitors negatively. These, of course, are the same sentiments which underlie the Family Law Act and which have crept into popular rhetoric in the wake of the Parliamentary debates. This fear of conflict, here expressed by Helen, and justified in the terms of the welfare discourse, was also felt by others in the study. The choice of mediation perhaps addresses these fears, but it does so at the price of denying the psychological roots of conflict. Helen did of course discover that her 'painless' divorce was a fantasy, but that, in itself, was a painful realisation.

Putting mediation and the adversarial process on opposite sides of a divide is yet another example of the splitting which goes on in divorce; this time, however, the splitting occurs at a broader social level and links with divorce discourses and popular rhetoric. The adversarial process is denigrated, as mediation is idealised, in a process in which destructive and hostile emotions are disowned and projected onto the legal process. Once dispute resolution begins, however, the idealisation of the harmonious divorce is unstable, as people are confronted with the realities of their hostile emotions, and they find that they cannot always be amicable. In Helen's case, her ideal of amicable co-operation had been put under severe strain by Time 2. She says:

> He wants to be a major part of the children's life, without being a major part of the children's life. So I don't know, you know in many ways, I just wish I could be sort of a lot less in contact with him and a bit nasty to him when I do see him.

By Time 3, Helen and Michael had stopped going to mediation, and their solicitors were in the process of re-negotiating the 'memorandum of understanding' to take account of Michael's pension. At this stage, Helen felt even more strongly that, ideally, she would never want to see Michael again, and she questioned whether a harmonious divorce really was best for the children:

> I think it is not really clear to the children why people, why the parents have spilt up and, um, you know we went to mediation thinking that it would be -, what we were doing would be best for the children, and to me the answers just aren't very clear, because the children seem to have got the confused message now about, um, you know we both tend to have quite a good relationship in their eyes, why can't we live together? They can't see it, and I don't feel any more satisfied than before I went to mediation. I think, you know, if we had had a stormy break up, and just left it at that, the children might have been affected slightly differently, but I don't think they would be quite as confused as they are now. You know, I don't think it's very clear to them why our relationship didn't work, and I don't think mediation has made that clearer, and I don't know if doing what is considered to be best for children is actually what is best for them. I think it's a very grey area.

Discussion

At an individual level, then, it may be that the idealisation of the harmonious divorce reflects a deeper psychological splitting as a strategy for survival; this idealisation serves to put dangerous and destructive emotions at one step removed. This 'splitting works at both an individual and a social level (see, for example, Rustin, 1991). But, once reality-testing comes into play, subjects find that harmony is very difficult to sustain in practice. At a social level, discourses of harmony also serve to contain fears about conflict and about the power of destructive feelings which can be unleashed. Discourses of harmony seem to promise that our emotions are manageable; in doing so, they effectively deny that ordinary human nature has its darker side.

In their chapter, Brown and Day-Sclater found it useful to refer to the work of Craib (1994) in this context. He maintains that our culture tends increasingly to deny 'the importance of disappointment'. Divorce is therefore experienced in the context of a society which promotes an ideology of rationality and self control, where emotions are not so much denied as recast as 'feelings' which are seen as manageable. By contrast, Craib takes the view that some emotions truly are very deep set and not amenable to easy management of any sort. Thus, in connection with loss, he argues that it is the very unbearability of the feelings of panic involved in grief which lead us, as a society, to imagine that grief is controllable, that it involves the expression of a pre-determined sequence of emotions which the 'experts' understand and can manage. The way in which we, as a society, choose to organise bereavement (which includes our psychological theories as well as our rituals) reflects our deep inability to accept our own ambivalences around loss as well as the uncomfortable fact of our own mortality. Craib's points have obvious relevance in relation to divorce. On this view, it is our inability to accept the emotional complexities of divorce which lead us either to trivialise it (as in booklets distributed to divorcing parents which tell them that they must 'put their feelings to one side for the children's sake'), or to pathologise it, as when 'conflict' is regarded as dangerous, abnormal and avoidable. In both cases, the dominance of the welfare discourse can be seen as an attempt to manage the emotions and thereby to deny the realities of family breakdown. What we have here is perhaps a manifestation of a Winnicottian 'false self' at a social level,[2] as discourses of co-operation deny the psychological impossibilities of compromise, and the ideal of the harmonious divorce sustains our fantasies both that human emotions are controllable and that all is well with 'the family'.

The Family Law Act explicitly addresses itself to attempting to minimise the messy and destructive emotions associated with divorce. Co-operative dispute resolution procedures cannot deal with the emotions of divorce any more than the old adversarial ones could, but they can be seen as a means, typical in late modernity, of imposing prescriptions for behaviour which foreground our rationality at the expense of our emotions. The welfare discourses serve to sever the chaotic and destructive parts of ourselves from the rational and 'civilised' parts, with the former being driven underground, into the realms of the pathological. In the process, the natural disappointments which attend loss become sanitised and only with difficulty can find means of expression. It is indeed ironic that the psychological hold which discourses of harmony have over us is rooted in a fantasy that our emotional lives can be rendered smooth and predictable, that the pain of divorce can be minimised, if not eliminated altogether; for as long as co-operation and harmony are idealised, it is unlikely that the destructive feelings which underlie conflict can be properly owned, or the conflicts truly resolved. An awareness and an acceptance of our own darker natures, paradoxically, might mitigate our compulsion to act out or to expel our bad parts into others, thus laying the essential foundation for achieving a truly civilised divorce.

Notes

1 The research reported here was funded by the ESRC, April 1996-June 1997 (Award number R000236323). I am grateful for their support. See S. Day Sclater (1998), *The Psychology of Divorce: A Research Report to the ESRC*, University of East London, 1998. I am grateful to those men and women who participated in the study. Thanks are also due to Julie Jessop, the research assistant on the project, and to those solicitors and mediators who helped in recruiting the sample. Friends and colleagues have helped along the way, with encouragement and criticisms; I would like to express particular gratitude to all the contributors to this book, and especially to Christine Piper.

2 I am grateful to Juliet Mitchell who suggested to me this reading of current discourses of co-operation in divorce.

References

Abbott, P. and Wallace, C. (1992), *The Family and the New Right*, Pluto Press, London.

Bailey-Harris, R., Davis, G., Barron, J. and Pearce, J. (1998), *Monitoring Private Law Applications Under the Children Act: A Research Report to the Nuffield Foundation*, Department of Law, University of Bristol.

Craib, I. (1994), *The Importance of Disappointment*, Routledge, London.

Davies, B. and Harre, R. (1990), 'Positioning: The Discursive Production of Selves', *Journal for the Theory of Social Behaviour*, vol 20, pp.43-63.

Davis, G., Cretney, S. and Collins, J. (1994), *Simple Quarrels*, Clarendon Press, Oxford.

Day Sclater, S. (1995), *Theory and Method for a Psychosocial Approach to Divorce*, East London Papers, No. 2, University of East London.

Day Sclater, S. (1997), 'Narratives of Divorce', *Journal of Social Welfare and Family Law*, vol 19(4), pp.423-441.

Day Sclater, S. (1998), 'Children and Divorce: Hidden Agendas?' Paper presented at the Children and Social Exclusion Conference, University of Hull, March 1998.

Day Sclater, S. (1999), 'The Bubble that Burst: Jane's Divorce Story', *Self, Agency and Society*, (in press).

Day Sclater, S. and Richards, M. (1995), 'How Adults Cope with Divorce: Strategies for Survival', *Family Law*, pp.143-147.

Denzin, N. (1989), *Interpretive Biography*, Sage, London.

Fox, D. and Prilleltensky, I. (eds) (1997), *Critical Psychology: An Introduction*, Sage, London.

Fox Harding, L. (1996), *Family, State and Social Policy*, Macmillan, London.

Freeman, M. (1993), *Rewriting the Self: History, Memory, Narrative*, Routledge, London.

Giddens, A. (1992), *The Transformation of Intimacy*, Polity, Cambridge.

Goldberg, D. and Hillier, V.F. (1979), 'A Scaled Version of the General Health Questionnaire', *Psychological Medicine*, vol 9, pp.139-145.

Goldberg, D. and Williams, P. (1988), *A User's Guide to the General Health Questionnaire*, NFER Nelson, Windsor.

Henriques, J., Hollway, W., Urwin, C., Venn, C. and Walkerdine, V. (1998), *Changing the Subject: Psychology, Social Regulation and Subjectivity*, 2nd ed, Routledge, London.

Hermans, H.J.M. and Hermans-Jansen, E. (1995), *Self-Narratives: The Construction of Meaning in Psychotherapy*, Guilford Press, London.

Hollway, W. (1989), *Subjectivity and Method in Psychology*, Sage, London.

Hunt, J.C. (1989), *Psychoanalytic Aspects of Fieldwork*, Sage, London.

Ibanez, T. and Iniguez, L. (eds) (1997), *Critical Social Psychology*, Sage, London.

Jones, C.L., Tepperman, L. and Wilson, S.J. (1995), *The Futures of the Family*, Prentice Hall, New Jersey.

Kitson, G.C. and Morgan, L.A. (1990), 'The Multiple Consequences of Divorce: A Decade Review', *Journal of Marriage and the Family*, vol 52, pp.913-924.

Morgan, P. (1995), *Farewell to the Family: Public Policy and Family Breakdown in Britain and the USA*, IEA Health and Welfare Unit, London.

Mishler, E. (1986), *Research Interviewing: Context and Narrative*, Harvard University Press, London.

Parker, I. (1992), *Discourse Dynamics*, Routledge, London..

Parker, I. and Berman, E. (eds) (1993), *Discourse Analytic Research*, Routledge, London.

Parker, I. and Spears, R. (eds) (1996), *Psychology and Society: Radical Theory and Practice*, Pluto Press, London.

Personal Narratives Group (eds) (1989), *Interpreting Women's Lives: Feminist Theory and Personal Narratives*, Indiana University Press, Bloomington, Ill.

Piper, C. (1996), 'Divorce Reform and the Image of the Child', *Journal of Law and Society*, vol 23, pp.364-382.

Potter, J. and Wetherell, M. (1987), *Discourse and Social Psychology*, Sage, London.

Riessman, C.K. (1990), *Divorce Talk: Men and Women Make Sense of Personal Relationships*, Rutgers University Press, London

Riessman, C.K. (1993), *Narrative Analysis*, Sage, London.

Rosenwald, G.C. (1988), 'A Theory of Multiple Case Research', *Journal of Personality*, vol 56, pp.239-264.

Rustin, M. (1991), *The Good Society and the Inner World*, Verso, London.

Sarbin, T. (ed) (1986), *Narrative Psychology: The Storied Nature of Human Conduct*, Praeger, New York.

Vaughan, D. (1987), *Uncoupling: Turning Points in Intimate Relationships*, Oxford University Press, Oxford.

Vermont Law School (eds) (1987), *The Role of Mediation in Divorce Proceedings: A Comparative Perspective*, Vermont Law School Dispute Resolution Project.

Whelan, R. (ed) (1995), *Just a Piece of Paper? Divorce Reform and the Undermining of Marriage*, IEA, Health and Welfare Unit, London.

Wilkinson, S. (ed) (1996), *Feminist Social Psychologies*, Open University Press, Buckingham.

9 Divorce and Domestic Violence

FELICITY KAGANAS AND CHRISTINE PIPER

This book is about the ways in which divorce and divorce law and procedure have been constructed as problems requiring a legislative response. In that process the central themes which emerged have been those of marriage saving and child saving, linked by particular ideas about the risk of harm to children as a result of parental divorce. This chapter focuses on the introduction into that agreed story about divorce of an issue which has the potential to disrupt the coherence of the story and to challenge the ideal of the consensual and conflict-free divorce. That issue is domestic violence.

Amendments incorporated into the Family Law Act 1996 signified official acknowledgement of the problem of domestic violence and its persistence even after separation and divorce. Yet, we will argue, within the dominant talk about divorce there is no clear and agreed picture of the prevalence, nature and effects of domestic violence when relationships break down. The changing and elusive picture of domestic violence reflected in debates in the political arena has resulted in legislation that, despite its acceptance of the principle of protection, is short on detail as to how this principle is to be upheld. It does not indicate how important the principle of protection is relative to the other, potentially contradictory, objectives of the statute. Nor, aside from Part IV orders, does it put in place mechanisms for detecting violence or dealing with it within the divorce process. Essentially, it is left to those implementing the legislation to devise ways of protecting those at risk. However, there is no agreed picture of domestic violence apparent in professional practice relating to divorce either; diversity of views and differing priorities characterise the professional world as well as the political one. This, we think, has worrying implications. Professionals dealing, in the front line, with divorcing clients may underestimate the likelihood that any particular client is or has been experiencing abuse and may misinterpret the information - verbal or otherwise - that a client gives. As a result, they may fail to adopt proactive strategies for detecting whether violence is an issue and to protect clients where it is.

This chapter seeks, first, to give some indication of the images of violence that the framers of the legislation were intending to address in the statute. We then consider the extent to which these images are sustained by the available research. Finally, we examine current professional practice in order to assess whether, in that sphere, there may be the potential to resolve the contradictions between the different stories about divorce told by politicians, and which underlie the statute, as well as the contradictions between the stories told by some politicians and those told by researchers.

Writing Domestic Violence into the Script

Domestic violence was written into the story about divorce via amendments to the Bill which eventually became sections 1(d), 7(12) and 9(7)(d) (read with paragraph 4 of schedule 1).[1] Section 1(d) states that all professionals involved in the process of divorce must 'have regard' to the principle that 'any risk to one of the parties to a marriage, and to any children, of violence from the other party should, so far as reasonably practicable be removed or diminished'.[2] Section 7(12)(a) supplies an exception to the extension of the nine month period of reflection and consideration by six months where there is a child of the family who is under 16. The exception applies if there is an occupation or molestation order in force in favour of the applicant, or a child of the family, against the other party to the divorce application. Paragraph 4 of schedule 1, read with section 9(7)(d) creates an exception to section 9(2) and enables the court to grant a divorce order even though financial arrangements have not been settled. Again this applies only to cases where a Part IV order is in force. It is also subject to the provisos that the applicant has made efforts to reach agreement which have been unsuccessful and that delay in making an order would be detrimental to the child or prejudicial to the applicant.

The debates, particularly around section 1(d), reveal a clear difference of opinion among parliamentarians as to whether protection from violence or the other aims of the legislation, notably marriage and child saving, should be given priority. The Government ultimately accepted that 'the potential for domestic violence will be present for some at a number of points in the divorce and separation process, and that it is right ... to take that into account' (Mr

Streeter, Hansard, HC 17 June 1996, col 601). Yet there was concern in Parliament that to focus on violence is, potentially, to jeopardise the marriage saving project or, at the very least, the conflict-reduction exercise thought to be so important for the children's welfare: 'An ouster order will effectively scotch the prospects for reconciliation or second thoughts'.[3]

Perhaps surprisingly, section 7(12) appears to have been relatively uncontentious and there is little clarification of the reasoning behind it to be gleaned from the parliamentary discussion. Mr Leigh, urging adoption of an amendment embodying an earlier version of section 7(12),[4] explained the need for an extended period in terms of the 'safeguards' provided in relation to children (Hansard, HC 24 April 1996, col 502). The extended period was, he said, designed to send the 'important message that, if there are children in a marriage, that should make a difference to the divorce process. In such circumstances, the parties should not think first of themselves but of the interests of the children' (ibid). He assured the Committee of the House that 'it could be shortened to one year[5] - but not less - if there is a clear case of domestic violence, with a court order' or if, in the view of the court, an extension would be detrimental to the children concerned (ibid). These, he said, 'are clearly special cases' but did not explain why an exception for domestic violence was appropriate. Nor did he explain why, if domestic violence justified dispensing with the extension to the minimum period, it did not justify an abridgement of it too.

It appears that the specified period for reflection and consideration was considered the minimum necessary to prevent 'quickie' divorces and to promote reconciliation or, failing that, to establish that the breakdown was irretrievable and to enable practical arrangements for the future to be made (see Hansard, HC 24 April, cols 504-505, 529; Law Commission, 1990, para 525). These objectives could not be compromised under any circumstances. Why the extended period in children cases was considered less sacrosanct is not entirely clear, nor is it clear whether the exemption for cases involving violence was for the benefit of women, children or both. However it is significant that mention was made of the detrimental effects on children of violence generally (Hansard, HC 24 April 1996, col 498), and in terms of diminution of parenting capacity (col 494) as well as the risk that violence may be transmitted from one generation to another (idem). Reference was also made to the need to avoid fomenting conflict (col 506). The aims of marriage saving and child saving, it seems, were foremost in the legislators' minds; aims that could not be displaced in cases of violence.[6] However the benefits to children of making their parents wait longer appear to be offset by the damage prolonged exposure to violence might cause, but only if there is evidence of violence sufficient to warrant a Part IV order.

The debates on amendments which were the precursors of section 1(d) reveal clearer but more polarised pictures of domestic violence. Those in favour of the provision that protection from violence should be a principle underlying the whole of the new divorce process clearly had a picture of the pervasive and dangerous influence of domestic violence: 'domestic violence is not just an issue of occupation of the family home and immediate protection from violence for families but one that should permeate the thinking of all those involved in the divorce process' (Ms Corston, Standing Committee E, 30 April 1996, cols 59-60; see also Mr Boateng, at col 55). It should not, said one member, be dealt with as 'an afterthought or appendage to the law' but should be 'integral' to deliberations about the legislation (Ms Hodge, Standing Committee E, 30 April 1996, col 77). In particular, attention was drawn in that sitting to the potential perils to victims of the information meeting, attendance at court, mediation and contact (Mr Boateng, cols 57-59; Ms Hodge, cols 76 and 78-79; Mr Tipping, cols 84-85).

However, not all those who contributed to the debates had such a picture of domestic violence, with a corresponding commitment to protection for abused women. Rather, the debates reveal an assumption on the part of some speakers that what is inimical about domestic violence is primarily the effect it might have - directly or indirectly - on children. Mr Brazier, for example, expressed his belief that the main form of domestic violence is child abuse and that is more likely to be perpetrated by stepfathers than by natural fathers, suggesting that children face greater dangers from their mothers' future relationships than from their natural fathers (Standing Committee E, 30 April, cols 72, 63 and 79-80, respectively). Accordingly, said another speaker, having asserted that women variously attract, provoke and perpetrate violence,[7] children might be no better off 'as a result of destroying such a household' because mothers move on to further abusive relationships (Mr Rowe, Standing Committee E, 30 April, cols 65-67). In the light of that, as Mr Brazier pointed out later, 'it is not helpful to encourage the raising of the issue of domestic violence if it has not already been raised' (col 106).

The disadvantages attendant upon such encouragement were, it seems, compounded by the assumed proclivity of those involved in divorce to fabricate allegations of violence (cols 94-95 and 104). In any event, the inclusion in the general principles of a provision dealing with domestic violence was regarded by some speakers as unnecessary (Mr Evans, Standing Committee E, 7 May 1996, col 115) and the amendment was at that stage rejected. What became section 1(d) was reintroduced at a later stage when attention was being focused on domestic violence in the context of other clauses in the Bill.[8]

The Research Picture of Domestic Violence

The different pictures of domestic violence which emerge from the parliamentary debates are in contrast to the increasingly clear picture presented by recent research. The evidence now available suggests that a significant proportion of women experience abuse from their spouses during marriage, that separation and divorce are particularly dangerous times for women and that those who experience such abuse find it very difficult to admit to that fact.

Divorce is Dangerous

> As many as 1 in 3 divorces may involve domestic violence and this can be the starting point for divorce proceedings. Last year [Legal Aid] certificates issued for domestic violence injunctions within divorce proceedings numbered over 6,000 (Legal Aid Board Research Unit, 1996, p.44).

The figure of '1 in 3' quoted above refers to research conducted in the UK around 20 years ago (Borkowski *et al*, 1983). However the finding in that study that 20% of wives' divorce petitions used evidence of domestic violence to satisfy the behaviour ground was confirmed in a later one, which reported a comparable figure of 22% (Law Commission, 1990, appendix C).[9] At a more general level it is also now well documented that a significant proportion of women experience domestic violence at some time in their lives - and that their ex-partners are one of the main categories of perpetrators.[10] In a study by Rights of Women (Anderson, 1997), for example, nearly one third of the cases involved some form of violence after proceedings began (p.32).[11] There is, in addition, voluminous research on the extent of marital and separation violence from the other side of the Atlantic which yields similar evidence.[12] The cumulative effect of these research findings present a relatively clear picture of domestic violence: many women - across race and class - experience some form of violence and control at the hands of their husbands during marriage, after separation, or both. There is little doubt that separation and divorce are especially risky times.

Reluctance to Tell

There is also research evidence showing that those who have been at the receiving end of abuse do not always readily volunteer this information. Victims as well as abusers tend to minimise or deny violence: voluntary disclosure is relatively unusual (Pagelow, 1990, p.355). Researchers have advanced a number of possible explanations for this. First, to acknowledge violence by disclosing it, is to acknowledge that the relationship in which so much has been invested cannot continue. Disclosure may therefore signify too much personal loss for it to be psychologically possible.[13] Moreover, while some victims may refrain from seeking help for fear of retaliation, others may still be emotionally bound to their partners; Ellis and DeKeseredy refer to the loyalty/love that victims often feel (1997, p.601).The possibility that victims do not disclose during the course of their relationships is significant on divorce: it means that there is no 'official' evidence in the form of court orders or criminal proceedings that abuse occurred. This, in turn, makes it less likely that the abuse will be discovered on divorce.

Secondly, even on divorce the victim/survivor may not expect to be believed or taken seriously (Astor, 1991, p.21). Thirdly, she may fear being labelled a failure - a misplaced sense of shame therefore inhibits disclosure (Mooney, 1993, p.60). Fourthly, she may have fears that she will lose her children (Morley, 1993). Fifthly, it may be difficult for her to redefine an intimate partner as an abuser, particularly if he is the father of her children (Mahoney, 1994, pp.74-75). Finally, she may not disclose because she does not conform to her own stereotypes of battered women (Fischer *et al,* 1993, pp.2140-2141; Kelly and Radford, 1990/1, p.40).

Power and Control

Many abusive relationships are characterised by a pattern of 'coercive control' involving 'an *ongoing* strategy of intimidation, isolation, and control that extends to all areas of a woman's life, including sexuality; material necessities; relations with family, children and friends; and work' (Stark,1995, p.986).[14] As a result, the abused partner may agree out of fear (Mahoney, 1991; Kurz, 1996, p.137) or fatigue, to demands made by the abusing partner which are financially detrimental or potentially oppressive for herself or her children. In relation to the making of arrangements on divorce this can mean that the partner who has experienced longstanding intimidation and control may be unable to participate as an equal in informal dispute resolution procedures.

This makes attendance at mediation problematic though it is argued[15] that as long as mediation is voluntary, victims of abuse are adequately protected. However, research shows that an abused partner may agree to mediation even if she knows that it is voluntary and that, if she attends, this may prove detrimental to her. Hester *et al* point out:

> It needs to be recognised that there are a number of different reasons why women who have experienced ongoing violence and abuse from male partners will agree to attend mediation. For instance, in their desperation to have services deal with the abusive man they will attend mediation; or they may feel they have to attend in order not to appear obstructive to the courts; or they feel it would be more beneficial to the children in the long term despite the dangers to themselves (1997, p.59).

Knowledge that domestic violence is not a rare phenomenon in the context of divorce, coupled with knowledge that spontaneous disclosure is not common and that the experience of violence can affect negotiating abilities, may provide the impetus for professionals to adopt procedures designed to facilitate disclosure. Failure to use such procedures can have far reaching consequences.

A Risky Process

Family Law Act 1996

Section 1(d) of the Act establishes the principle that professionals should seek to remove or reduce the risk of violence. There are a number of 'risky' stages of the divorce process embodied in the Act 1996 which professionals will have to manage .

The most obvious of the risks to victims of abuse[16] is that their physical safety might be endangered during, as well as immediately before or after, appointments with professionals (for legal advice, for the preparation of welfare reports or for mediation). As a few highly publicised cases have revealed, a failure to protect clients from perpetrators of violence in these situations can have tragic consequences.[17] Another opportunity for violence or intimidation may be created pursuant to the application of section 13 of the Act. This gives the court the power to direct parties, once a statement has been filed, to attend a meeting to be told the benefits of mediation. Research conducted in 1995-6 showed that, despite National Standards directing otherwise,[18] court welfare officers usually saw couples together at directions hearings, only 4% of officers always seeing parties separately (Hester *et al*, 1997, p.18).

In any event, the risks to victims of abuse are not confined to physical harm during or around encounters with professionals. The divorce process may prejudice the interests of abused spouses in a number of other ways. There is a risk that contact arrangements might jeopardise their safety,[19] that continued communication will perpetuate dominance and emotional abuse and that 'agreed' financial and property settlements would be detrimental to their interests. The practices of solicitors, mediators and family court welfare officers, both in report writing and mediation, can contribute to, or make less likely, such outcomes.

Participating in Mediation

The major concern in relation to divorce and domestic violence has been the anticipated greater use of mediation within the new legal framework for divorce. Parties are to be encouraged to attend mediation during information meetings, as well as during section 13 directions hearings and through the criteria for the award of Legal Aid. The benefits of mediation are widely extolled:

> [Mediation] is seen by proponents and practitioners alike as more than a sensible strategy for settling disputed cases. It is said to be a civilised and civilising procedure, a process which returns to, or keeps control in, the couple, and a way of ensuring reliable arrangements for the future. As such it cannot be fully appreciated without consideration of such concepts as civility, friendship, trust and the pursuit of mutual interests (Walker *et al*, 1994, p.1).

Yet where violence or abuse has been a feature of the relationship between the couple, where the equality of power and control within that relationship is, as a result, doubtful and where trust may be non-existent, the benefits of mediation for the abused partner (and her children) are clearly thrown into question. As Shaffer puts it, 'mediation rests on the notion of two equally competent and effective negotiators, an idea which feminists point out does not conform to the reality of many male/female relationships' (1988, p.166). In cases of abuse, the divergence between the idea and the reality may be extreme.

Mediation services may be able to mitigate the effects of power imbalances by employing screening, coupled, in the cases they do take on, with support for the weaker party to enable her to bargain more effectively, and with constant monitoring for abusive behaviour (Ellis and Stuckless, 1996, pp.77-80). Mediation may even, provided it is voluntary, play a part in the reduction of 'postprocessing abuse' (Ellis and Stuckless, 1996, p.58).[20] However, research suggests that mediation is inappropriate and even dangerous and abusive in cases where mediators do not ask about violence, do not have knowledge about the impact of violence, or lack the skill to deal with these issues (Young, 1996, in Hester *et al*, 1997, p.60).

Leaving it to the Professionals

We have observed that, while the Family Law Act 1996 contains provisions intended to reduce risks to victims of domestic violence, it also creates a divorce process that, with its marriage saving and child saving agendas, may increase their exposure to risk. Moreover, reflecting the dissent and the ambivalence expressed within the parliamentary debates, the statute contains no unambiguous message about the relative importance of protection. Dewar has recently argued that this 'chaos' in legislation impacting on the family is normal:

> To put it another way, law more and more becomes the context in which those contradictions or oppositions that cannot be resolved politically are worked through. ... legislators have in fact created a set of inconsistent principles and commitments ... while at the same time using law to give the appearance of having created shared values; and then have off-loaded the detailed working out of those contradictions to the legal system (Dewar, 1998, p.484).

The contradictions and conflicting aims do not pose a threat to the functioning of family law, 'because [chaos] is held at bay by the practices of legal and other professionals associated with its day-to-day interpretation, application and administration' (Dewar, 1998, p.485). The task, therefore, of reconciling in practice the demands of child saving, marriage saving and spousal protection has, therefore, been left to the divorce professionals who may or may not, as the next section of this chapter is intended to reveal, have a clearer picture of domestic violence - individually or as a profession - than did the legislators.

Professional Practice

Mediators

Mediators may be accredited by various bodies. National Family Mediation (NFM), is the umbrella organisation for voluntary sector mediation which, together with the Family Mediators Association (FMA) and Family Mediation Scotland, now comprises the UK College of Mediators[21] which has issued a Code of Practice including guidelines in relation to domestic violence.[22]

Hester *et al* conducted a major survey of mediators working in the 59 NFM affiliated services in 1995. Few of their respondents said that their service had a screening policy (1997, p.43) and some were unsure whether they did or not. Moreover, only half of those who said their services did not have a policy thought it would be useful to have one. Hester *et al* categorised the practices of these mediators into 'safety oriented', 'an emphasis on always mediating' and 'non-specific' approaches. Only 11% of the responses could be categorised solely as 'safety oriented', the biggest category using the mixed, non-specific approach (1997, p.36 *et seq*).[23] The respondents who followed the safety-oriented approach would, for example, generally have separate initial meetings to screen for violence but only a handful of them believed that where domestic violence was known there should never be mediation. At the other end of the spectrum were those who took the view that mediation should always be tried and made little connection between issues of power and domestic violence (p.38). The 'non-specific' approach revealed a combination of elements from the other two.

The research also showed that, whilst 74% of respondents believed that violence would affect the balance of power in mediation and that techniques to address imbalance were necessary (p.47), these techniques did not always protect the abused spouse. Indeed, mediators sometimes exacerbated the victim's plight:

> In their attempts to appear 'fair' respondents were indeed likely to create dangerous situations for women. For instance, in their concern to 'equalise power' in domestic violence situations, a number of respondents, in effect, placed greater power and control in the hands of the male abuser, whom they saw as the 'real victim' or 'loser' in the situation ... One interviewee explained that once women leave violent men they are elated and feel empowered ... The men, on the other hand, are deflated, depressed ... (Hester *et al*, 1997, p.48).

These findings are cause for concern but they have been widely disseminated in order to promote change. Nevertheless it would be easy for individual mediators to slip through the training net: there is, after all, no legal requirement that mediators - unless working for services franchised by the Legal Aid Board - are either accredited by one of the major organisations or trained in specific issues.

Family Court Welfare Officers

The picture of court welfare service practice revealed by Hester *et al* - in relation to mediation and the preparation of welfare reports - is more encouraging: there is evidence that it is more informed by an awareness of domestic violence, perhaps because court welfare officers are more likely to deal with difficult and conflicted cases.[24] Yet, of the 319 individual court welfare officers who returned a completed questionnaire, only 16% could be said to be adopting the 'safety-oriented' approach, with a further 7% of respondents fulfilling some of the 'safety-oriented' criteria (pp.12-13). The 'non-specific' approach was again the largest single group (26%).

Court welfare officers who used a 'safety-oriented' approach were those who, for instance, took allegations of violence 'at face value ... acting as if such allegations were established fact', and reported accordingly (p.13). Those following the 'impartial report writing' approach, by contrast, took domestic violence into consideration in relation to safety but not necessarily in regard to outcomes. Those using an 'agreement-focused' approach mostly worked within a family therapy framework (p.14)[25] which might downgrade the factor of domestic violence.

Again service policies were not always known by individual officers (p.16) and screening was by no means routine,[26] mainly being used once a welfare report was underway (p.15). The three main approaches used were inspecting files and court records, asking clients or relying on clients or other professionals to disclose abuse (p.15). As with the mediators, the belief of all court welfare officers that violence would increase the possibility of a power imbalance in mediation did not necessarily lead to a safety first approach: only a very small minority commented on the unsuitability of joint meetings in these circumstances (p.25). Nevertheless, 85% of respondents said they would challenge 'intimidating, controlling or undermining behaviour' to counteract the power disparity and 65% would ensure women received legal advice.

Again, practice may have changed since this research was carried out. In November 1996, the Association of Chief Probation Officers circulated national guidance designed to provide a starting point for the creation of more detailed local policies. It recommends that family court welfare officers use a 'screening schedule' and notes that it is generally inappropriate to see parties together or to refer them to mediation in cases of violence (paras 6.1 and 8.4).

Solicitors

Solicitors have not been subjected to a similar large scale survey in relation to domestic violence. We therefore draw on the small study conducted by researchers at Brunel University (see Piper and Kaganas, 1997). This used an interview sample of 36 solicitors selected from firms (in two geographical areas) with at least three partners and which claimed a family law specialism in the Law Society regional directories.[27] In addition, we ensured there were equal numbers of male and female solicitors, with just over half of them working in firms franchised by the Legal Aid Board for family law work.

The research aimed to illuminate solicitor practice in relation to divorce clients with children. We gave our interviewees a list of topics about which they might wish to seek information, and asked them to tell us, for each item, how routinely they sought such information. Twice as many solicitors said they 'sometimes' asked 'whether domestic violence was used or threatened' as said they 'always' asked. Furthermore, the use of transaction criteria did not ensure that franchised solicitors 'always' asked.

Although a relatively high proportion of solicitors in this study routinely enquired about domestic violence, we are concerned that many of these solicitors found knowledge about domestic violence only to be 'useful' in relation to establishing 'grounds' for divorce. In other words, their enquiries related to the completion of the divorce petition - a procedure which will become unnecessary under the new 'no fault' divorce law. Fourteen solicitors (almost 40%) said they needed to know about violence if their client would have to rely on the 'unreasonable behaviour' fact[28] and half of these mentioned no other reason for asking about domestic violence.

> [I]f one is saying 'what are the grounds for divorce?' and one's looking at preparing a schedule of unreasonable behaviour one would of course say 'What's the problem? Wouldn't he wash his socks or did he beat you up everyday' [laughs] or something like that.

> Not only does it arise when I go through the checklist but also it's brought out when I say 'Well, what's the reason for the breakup of the marriage? Is it another person or is it violence?'

On the other hand, half of the solicitors said or implied that information about domestic violence was useful for the purpose of protecting the client or the client's child. Of these 18 solicitors, 10[29] referred explicitly to protection,[30] while the remaining eight referred to it implicitly by mentioning, for example, 'the possibility of injunctions'. However, comments made by some of these solicitors when mentioning contact suggest that they might be thinking less in terms of the client's safety or freedom from intimidation and more in terms of domestic violence as an issue that compounds contact difficulties:

> [O]ne parent might not want to have contact at all with the other - it's going to have repercussions for the fetching and carrying of children.

> [P]eople are reluctant to have contact where the husband who's used physical violence in the past comes and collects the child from the home.

Moreover, almost half of the interviewees gave reasons that did not relate at all to their clients' welfare and just over half made no reference to children's welfare.[31]

Professional Pictures of Domestic Violence

'They Will Tell Us'

It emerges from these studies that a significant proportion of solicitors, mediators and court welfare officers had not, by 1995-6, modified their procedures to take account of what is now known about domestic violence. One reason common to the three groups was the belief that clients who had experienced domestic violence would '"screen" themselves out' (Hester *et al*, 1997, p.58) or that 'domestic violence would always be raised by clients or their representatives if important' (p.17): 'they normally ring up and say "we want to have an appointment about domestic violence"' (a solicitor).

One in six of the solicitors we interviewed accounted for their reluctance to screen/ask all clients by stating that they were confident they could identify those clients who had suffered domestic violence: 'I don't ask the questions unless I start getting a smell'; 'You tend to gauge there's a situation when there might have been [domestic violence]'. For these solicitors, screening was a mental procedure based on instinct and experience rather than on explicit criteria.

A proportion of all three professional groups researched, therefore, had faith that they could sense whether clients were victims of domestic violence or that clients - or another professional - would tell them. No group had taken on the responsibility of finding out and none had routinised practice to do so. Two solicitors even appeared to think that routine questioning about domestic violence might be positively offensive because it would constitute 'a huge invasion of somebody's privacy'.[32]

'It Encourages Allegations'

Comments made by mediators and court welfare officers echo fears expressed in the parliamentary debates and in the preceding consultation documents about encouraging false allegations of domestic violence. Hester *et al* report that court welfare officers were of the opinion that 'any emphasis on screening would only "invite" unnecessary and malicious allegations' (1997, p.17) and quote a mediator as saying: 'I would not like to see unsubstantiated allegations of domestic violence used as a way of distorting the process and sabotaging agreements' (1997, p.40). Despite the fact that Parliament has acknowledged the importance of taking account of domestic violence in the divorce process, professional thinking is often still influenced more by the pre-Act discourse, in evidence, for example, in the Consultation Paper:

> [T]he objective here would be to separate the divorce process ... from other

> matters such as violence and molestation by removing the jurisdiction to grant injunctions for molestation and violence ancillary to divorce proceedings ... [otherwise] some separating partners might seek to exploit allegations of molestation and violence in order to avoid considering the merits of mediation (LCD, 1993, para 10.2).[33]

Protection from violence - though 'of vital importance'- should be a 'separate process' (para 10.3). Indeed, that document also gives the impression that petitioners may rely on the 'unreasonable behaviour' without any real substance: 'It is not difficult to obtain a divorce on intolerable behaviour' (para 5.2.); 'A finding of adultery or behaviour certainly need not mean the respondent is any more to blame than the petitioner for the breakdown of the marriage' (para 5.13); 'It is argued that the behaviour fact is particularly misleading. The behaviour need be neither unreasonable nor blameworthy' (para 5.18). The earlier Law Commission proposals included the same message: 'In most divorces the spouses will both be "at fault" in varying degrees and it will be impossible to apportion responsibility for the breakdown' (Law Commission, 1988, para 3.16).

Of course, behaviour 'facts' cannot be equated with violence and, no doubt, there are cases where allegations are fabricated. But statements like the above help construct a story about divorce in which unfounded allegations are very common and in which parties are generally equally to blame. To some extent this divorce story deprives the victim's voice of legitimacy. In addition, it contributes to the ambivalence of those who have incorporated that tale into their knowledge base, and explains in part the shortcomings in professional practice in responding to domestic violence.

Mediators, in their future-oriented approach, also translate into practice the belief expressed in the Consultation Paper that the past should be left alone: 'Allegations of behaviour require the recollection of incidents which would best be forgotten ... A beginning of this kind is not constructive to the divorce process' (LCD, 1993, para 5.6). Hester *et al* refer to mediators who did not support routine screening for domestic violence for this reason:

> They emphasised that they should have *no* knowledge about clients prior to the first mediation session, arguing that such knowledge would skew their perception of the individuals concerned and would compromise the 'neutrality' of their approach (1997, p.58).

Irrelevant Violence

It appears that some professionals do not accord significance to violence or to violence of certain kinds. Where violence is judged mutual, for example, there is little need to protect one of the parties over and above the other. Similarly, it is assumed that violence ends on separation and that there is no risk to the victim afterwards. Hester *et al* report conflicting views about the mutuality or otherwise of inter-spousal violence and the effect on violence of separation. Twice the proportion of mediators as family court welfare officers believed that all domestic violence was mutual or 'as likely to be from women to men as from men to women' (Hester *et al*, 1997, p.41).[34] Whilst this view was evident in the parliamentary debates,[35] it does not accord with the generality of research findings and contributes to a 'normalisation' of violence which diminishes professional motivation to implement pro-active policies in regard to domestic violence.

Some court welfare officers appeared to assume that violence ceases on separation: 'A few respondents did not consider screening for domestic violence relevant as it was no longer felt to be a problem once the partners had parted' (p.17). This view is clearly at odds with the picture from research and is one which feeds into the tendency to ignore the past.

Other reasons provided by court welfare officers reflect the dominance of the child saving strand in the divorce reform debates. If the violence 'concerned the adults and not the children'[36] then screening was not important. What is more, it 'might prevent the possibility of agreement between the parties by precluding any joint meetings' (p.17). Here the aim of protection for abused spouses is subordinated - as it often was in Parliament - to the aims of marriage saving and conflict reduction (for the sake of the children and the Exchequer).

Knowledge and Practice

In the study by Hester *et al* there appears to be a correlation between wider definitions of violence given by court welfare officers and mediators and more safety-oriented practice (1997, pp.41-42 and 56-57). Similarly, in the Brunel study, the explanations of those solicitors who said they 'always' asked about domestic violence revealed the influence on their practice of knowledge about the prevalence of domestic violence and reluctance to disclose. Some solicitors appreciated that a client might 'feel awkward about coming out with it':

> And it's amazing - if you just, rather subtly, leave the question there then you'll get an answer - sometimes 'don't be stupid - we don't come from that part of town'. But amazingly it's sometimes quite surprising what does pop out [later you mean?] I'd always leave it ... just leave, give them an opportunity to say 'and I'm frightened of him' - for some reason or other. I always do that.

On the other hand, knowledge about prevalence did not automatically determine practice. As a solicitor commented: 'I wouldn't raise it unless they did ... Um - then *I know they are frightening statistics with domestic violence* but - um - it's either relevant to the process or it's not, in my view' [emphasis added]. Professional imperatives can override concern. In the case of solicitors the need is to complete a divorce petition within the time available, in the case of court welfare officers the need is to give priority to the 'client' (the child), and, in relation to mediation, the need is to be seen as neutral and settlement oriented. It remains to be seen whether these professional imperatives will change or be outweighed as a result of the implementation of the Family Law Act 1996.

Implications for the Implementation of a New Divorce Process

The Consequences of a No-Fault Law

By removing the fault principle, the new law aims to eliminate the unfairness and resentment that is said often to accompany the public denunciation of one spouse by the other. Instead of exacerbating hostility, it is said, the divorce process should minimise it and reduce the trauma inflicted on children. This could be achieved by increased use of mediation (see LCD, 1993 and 1995).

The new law, then, is based on an assumption that divorcing couples are, generally speaking, able to behave reasonably and responsibly, to negotiate fairly and to co-operate in reaching satisfactory arrangements for the future. It was presumed that all that is needed is that couples be given the opportunity to do this and that mediation provides the key. However, the proposition that amicable resolution of disputes is unlikely where there is a history of violence or abuse was introduced into the story during the parliamentary debates. In Standing Committee, Mr Llwyd expressed his concern that there was 'precious little reference to violence in the Bill' (30 April 1996, col 92). 'There seems', he went on, 'to be more references to the word "amicably" than to domestic violence. In my experience, very few divorces are amicable ... By contrast, divorces that have come about through violence are prevalent' (idem). This alternative picture underpins the concern - within the higher echelons of professional bodies at least - to ensure the implementation of practices to remove the risk of abused spouses taking part in mediation or, alternatively, to diminish the risks attendant on doing so. Whether professionals of all 'ranks' will adopt such measures depends to a significant extent on which picture they have of domestic violence. It also depends on the message given to professionals about how the new legal provisions 'should' be used. Even if the picture of violence they hold changes to take account of issues such as separation violence and power imbalance, there are other factors that may continue to inhibit their adoption of more protection-oriented practice. These are the philosophy of conflict reduction and agreement that pervades divorce policy and practice as well as the prevailing images of 'good' parents and also 'good' lawyers.

'Good' and 'Bad'[37] *Solicitors*

There is a consensus within the family justice system that legal remedies should be used as a last resort; the dominant welfare discourse precludes an adversarial, rights-based approach (see the final chapter in this volume). In addition, the original divorce reform proposals aimed to separate[38] domestic violence and the divorce process: it is difficult to sustain images of the good absent parent and of the child as victim of non-co-operative parents if violence is allowed to intrude (Piper, 1996). The prioritisation of mediation, the non-intervention principle in the Children Act 1989 and the stress on parental responsibility and co-operative parenting after divorce lead to two relevant outcomes. First, they place pressure on divorcing parents, particularly on mothers, to keep in contact with, talk to and co-operate with, a perpetrator of violence. Secondly, they constrain solicitors from activating legal provisions which might cause conflict. The strength or otherwise of these pressures and constraints will be a significant determinant of the successful implementation of section 1(d).

As we have pointed out, many solicitors ask about domestic violence only to ascertain information necessary for the preparation of a divorce petition. With the removal of fault from the grounds for divorce a major impetus to seek out domestic violence is also removed[39] and the impact of section 1(d) on solicitor practice could be negligible.[40] It might also be negligible at other stages of the process. For example, there is no statutory requirement (as there is to be on mediators franchised by the Legal Aid Board) to screen for domestic violence at section 13 directions hearings and neither are there any statutory duties imposed on privately funded mediators. Solicitors, mediators and court welfare officers would need to routinise screening if abused spouses are not to fall through the net at that point. They also need clearer guidance to the effect that protection from violence should take precedence over other aims. Even Mr Boateng, in supporting the amendments concerned with protection, went only so far as to state that, while it was right for Parliament to send a message about the value of the institution of marriage, it was '*equally right* that Parliament should send out a message about the value and importance of maintaining a home environment free from violence' [emphasis added] (Standing Committee E, 7 May, col 117).

Indeed, it may be that parliamentarians did not anticipate that section 1(d) would have a significant impact on practice; doubts were expressed as to whether it would 'materially affect the operation of the legislation' (Standing Committee E, 7 May, col 101). There are, however, other provisions relating to domestic violence which could furnish an impetus for change, provided that a professional consensus emerges that the need to protect from violence and its effects trumps the current professional imperative to avoid conflict and the use of courts. One solicitor involved in the Brunel research felt unable to ask about domestic violence unless 'legally' he had to do so.[41] Section 1(d), if 'promoted' by the LCD and by professional bodies could provide such a catalyst but it is more likely that role will be played by sections 7(12) and 9(7)(d), read with schedule 1, para 4. If solicitors assume that it is in their client's interests to keep the period for reflection and consideration to the minimum, they may routinely enquire about domestic violence to see if there are grounds for the non-molestation or occupation order which preclude the extension of that period. Similarly, solicitors may ask about violence if they consider it important to ensure that their clients will be able to get an order even if the financial arrangements are not settled. The use of these provisions could lead to more, not less, litigation, but could uncover more domestic violence and protect more family members.

Whether they will do so, as we have pointed out, will depend on a complex web of factors: the way the professional picture of domestic violence now evolves, the strength of guidance about priorities and aims for those operating the new divorce process, the amount and type of legal advice to be state funded and the influence of particular ideas about the welfare of the child and the family. In this area at least, there is room for optimism that the legislative 'chaos' - which to some extent became apparent during the passage of the Family Law Act 1996 - will be resolved in a way that provides greater protection for those subject to domestic violence.

Notes

1. See also section 4(5)(a).
2. The duty to do this is placed on 'the court and any person, in exercising functions under or in consequence of Parts II and III', in other words all lawyers, probation officers, social workers, mediators and Legal Aid administrators, *inter alia*.
3. Ruth Deech, *The Times* 22 March 1996, quoted in Hansard, Standing Committee E, HC 7 May 1996, col 95).
4. See also Hansard, HL 27 June 1996, cols 1069, 1092.
5. The 12 month period is now made up of the 9 month period of reflection and consideration and the 3 month period between attendance at an information meeting and the making of a statement of marital breakdown. See Hansard, HC 17 June 1996, col 604ff. See, for a review of the history of section 7, Cretney and Masson (1997) p.349, n.15.
6. Some concerns were expressed about the effects of delay on wives who are victims of domestic violence. However, these did not appear to extend to the minimum period (see Hansard, HC 17 June 1996, cols 608-609; HL 27 June 1996, col 1066).
7. Giving, as an example of such behaviour, a woman making great play of the sexual impotence of her partner.
8. See Hansard, HC 17 June 1996, col 600.
9. See also Ingleby (1992).
10. See Mayhew *et al* (1993, p.98); Mirrlees-Black *et al* (1996); Mooney (1994); Polk (1994); Stanko *et al* (1998).
11. See also Polk (1994) on separation violence.
12. See Kaganas and Piper (1994) p.268; Ellis and DeKeseredy (1997); DeKeseredy and Macleod (1997); Sev'er (1997).
13. See, for example, the *Guardian* article by Beatrix Campbell (1996).
14. See also Hester *et al* (1997, p.9). Ellis and Stuckless identify three types of violence: conflict- instigated, control-instigated and anger-instigated. While all three types may be intermingled behaviourally, it appears that men are more likely to engage in both control-instigated violence and in serious conflict-instigated violence (1996, pp.42-46).
15. As the White Paper does (LCD, 1995 para 5.29).
16. The safety of professionals too might be endangered when dealing with violent clients. Examples of such cases are provided by Wardle (1994, pp.743-744).

17. One such incident is referred to by a mediator in Hester *et al*'s research (1997 pp.46-47).
18. See the *National Standards for Probation Service Family Court Welfare Work* (Home Office, 1994, para 4.13).
19. See Hester and Radford, 1996.
20. Ellis and Stuckless suggest that mediation makes a greater contribution to reducing abuse than lawyer negotiation because of the use made by lawyers of affidavits containing hurtful allegations (1996, p.58).
21. There are other mediation trainers in existence or proposed, for example BALM (British Association of Lawyer Mediators) and the Law Society.
22. See Hester *et al* (1997, Appendix D) which reproduces the most recent guidance for screening for abuse, for deciding whether to terminate or proceed with mediation if abuse is discovered (sections A3 and A4) and for practice where mediation does take place despite knowledge of abuse (section A5).
23. 29% 'always mediated', while sixty percent of respondents adopted the mixed approach.
24. Hester *et al* note that 'court welfare officers talked of up to 90% of their case load as involving violence' (1997, p.7).
25. It is not entirely clear what this entails but, if a therapeutic approach based on family systems theory is used, and violence is attributed to intra-family interaction, welfare officers might be failing to take account of control-instigated abuse (see Ellis and Stuckless, 1996, pp.30-34).
26. Only 14% of respondents screened their clients at whatever stage of the process they were dealing with them (p.17) though half of the remainder thought the use of screening should be extended.
27. Half the interviewees worked in a court area which had a high rate of section 8 private law applications and half in an area with a low rate of applications. (See Children Act Advisory Committee Annual Report 1992/93 (Lord Chancellor's Department, 1993, pp.94-95), based on the period June 1992 - June 1993). The 'high' area had around 30 applications per 10,000 of the population compared with around 10 in the 'low' area and an average of 21.3 for England and Wales as whole. Because of their geographical locations these are referred to as the Northern (high rate) and Southern (low rate) samples.
28. Questioning in relation to the use of the unreasonable behaviour fact is significant for disclosing abuse given that, in England and Wales in 1994, 54% of all decrees granted to wives rely on unreasonable behaviour as the fact proven (and 71% of all decrees granted to one party - that is, excluding divorces awarded in response to joint petitions - were granted to wives): Haskey, 1996.
29. All of whom worked in franchised firms and seven of whom said they always asked about domestic violence.
30. One solicitor referred specifically to its relevance to advice on attendance at mediation: 'For example, if I suggested mediation and she said "There's no way I'm going to mediation" then I would ask about the possibility of domestic violence'.
31. 15 and 19 solicitors respectively.

32. Solicitors who participated in the research were invited to seminars (in 1997-8) to discuss the results. Individual solicitors in both areas still expressed their inability to ask questions about domestic violence unless they 'needed' to.
33. Those who responded to the Consultation Paper were also 'particularly concerned about the possibility of petitioners making allegations of fault that were exaggerated or uncorroborated' (LCD, 1995 para 2.28).
34. This is a stance which gains support from research using the Conflict Tactics Scale (CTS) which, in its more simplistic versions, ignores the reason for violence (see Kurz, 1996, p.72). The notion that domestic violence is a contest between equals is often criticised as being based on a failure to distinguish between acts of aggression and self-defence; a failure to discriminate adequately between different types of violence; and a failure to take account of the effects of an act or the severity of any injuries caused. It ignores issues of dominance and control and renders disparities in power and vulnerability invisible. See, for example, for critiques of the 'family violence' approach to research on domestic violence, Dobash and Dobash, 1992a; Dobash and Dobash, 1992b; Kurz, 1993.
35. As a Conservative MP expressed it: 'perhaps as part of the movement towards greater equality ... there has been a considerable increase in the amount of violence perpetrated by women as well' (quoted in ROW, 1996, p.9).
36. Increasingly, links are being made between the abuse of mothers and harm to children (Mullender and Morley, 1994; Hester and Radford, 1996). However, as Behrens says, 'a woman should not have to argue for her safety based solely on the best interests of the child' (1996, p.43). See also Graycar (1995, p.69).
37. See Neale and Smart, 1997.
38. As Smart has recently pointed out (1997, p.312), even the important sociological work of Giddens on 'confluent love' contributes to perpetuating the invisibility of 'violence, bullying, economic deprivation and various forms of cruelty ... [because] these grimmer elements of married life and intimate relationships do not occupy much of the analysis'.
39. This should not be read as a plea for the resurrection of the old fault-based system. Nor should it be read as affording any support to the arguments recently put forward by Wardle (1994) to the effect that no-fault divorce culture fosters violence. For a text which is in contrast to the official discourse of divorce see Whelan (1995).
40. Some members of parliament had anticipated this outcome: doubts were expressed as to whether it would 'materially affect the operation of the legislation' (Standing Committee E, 7 May col 1010).
41. Participant at the follow-up seminar held in the northern area on 15 July 1998.

References

Anderson, L. (1997), 'Contact Between Children and Violent Fathers - In Whose Best Interests?' Rights of Women, *Bulletin*, Summer.

Association of Chief Officers of Probation (1996), *Guidance to Area Probation Services on Family Court Welfare Service and Domestic Violence*, ACOP, London.

Astor, H. (1991), *Position Paper on Mediation*, Prepared for the National Committee on Violence Against Women, Commonwealth of Australia.

Barron, J. (1990), *Not Worth the Paper..? The Effectiveness of Legal Protection for Women and Children Experiencing Domestic Violence*, WAFE Ltd, London.

Behrens, J. (1996), 'Ending the Silence, But ... Family Violence under the Family Law Reform Act 1995',*Australian Journal of Family Law*, vol 10, pp.35-47.

Borkowski, M., Murch, M. and Walker, V. (1983), *Marital Violence: The Community Response*, Tavistock, London.

Campbell, B. (1996), 'Big Bad Dad', *Guardian* 25 June.

DeKeseredy, W. and Macleod, L. (1997), *Woman Abuse: A Sociological Story*, Harcourt Brace, Toronto.

Dewar, J. (1998) 'The Normal Chaos of Family Law', *Modern Law Review*, vol 61(4), pp.467-485.

Dobash, R.E. and Dobash, R.P. (1992a), *Women, Violence and Social Change*, Routledge, London.

Dobash, R.E. and Dobash R.P. (1992b), 'The Myth of Sexual Symmetry in Marital Violence', *Social Problems*, vol 39, p.71.

Ellis, D. and DeKeseredy, W. (1997), 'Rethinking Estrangement, Interventions and Intimate Femicide', *Violence Against Women*, vol 3, pp.590-609.

Ellis, D. and Stuckless, N. (1996), *Mediating and Negotiating Marital Conflicts*, Sage, London.

Fischer, K., Vidmar, N. and Ellis, R. (1993), 'The Culture of Battering and the Role of Mediation in Domestic Violence Cases', *SMU Law Review*, vol 46(5), pp.2117-2174.

Graycar, R. (1995),'The Relevance of Violence in Family Law Decision Making', *Australian Journal of Family Law*, pp.58-69.

Haskey, J. (1996), 'Divorce Statistics', *Family Law*, p.301.

Hester, M. and Radford, L. (1996), *Domestic Violence and Child Contact Arrangements in England and Denmark*, Policy Press, Bristol.

Hester, M., Pearson, C. and Radford, L. (1997), *Domestic Violence, A National Survey of Court Welfare and Voluntary Sector Mediation Practice,* Policy Press, Bristol.

Home Office (1994), *National Standards for Probation Service and Family Court Welfare Work,* Home Office, London.

Hooper, C. (1996), 'Men's Violence and Relationship Breakdown: Can Violence be Dealt with as an Exception to the Rule?', in *Women & Social Policy. An Introduction*, C. Hallett (ed), Harvester Wheatsheaf, Hemel Hempstead.

Ingleby, R. (1992), *Solicitors and Divorce*, Clarendon Press, Oxford.

JRF (Joseph Rowntree Fund) (1997), *Findings: Social Policy Research 117*, JRF, York.

Kelly and Radford (1990/1), 'Nothing Really Happened: The Invalidation of London Women's Experiences of Sexual Violence', *Critical Social Policy*, vol 10(3), pp. 39-53.

Kurz, D. (1993), 'Social Science Perspectives on Wife Abuse: Current Debates and Future Directions' in P. Bart and E. Morgan (eds), *Violence Against Women: The Bloody Footprints*, Sage, London.

The Law Commission (1988), *Facing the Future. A Discussion Paper on the Ground For Divorce*, Law Com. No. 170, HMSO, London.

Legal Aid Board Annual Reports 1995-6 (1996), HMSO, London.

LCD (Lord Chancellor's Department) (1993), *Looking to the Future, Mediation and the Ground for Divorce*, Consultation Paper, Cm 2424, HMSO, London.

LCD (Lord Chancellor's Department) (1995), *Looking to the Future, Mediation and the Ground for Divorce*, Cm 2799, HMSO, London.

Mahoney, M. (1991), 'Legal Images of Battered Women: Redefining the Issue of Separation', *Michigan Law Review*, vol 90, pp.1-94.

Mahoney, M. (1994), 'Victimization or Oppression? Women's Lives, Violence and Agency', in M. Fineman and R. Myktiuk (eds), *The Public Nature of Private Violence. The Discovery of Domestic Abuse*, Routledge, New York, London.

Mayhew, P., Maung, N. and Mirrlees-Black, C. (1993), *The 1992 British Crime Survey*, HMSO, London.

Mirrlees-Black, C., Mayhew, P. and Percy, A. (1996), *The 1996 British Crime Survey, England and Wales*, HMSO, London.

Mooney, J. (1993), *The Hidden Figure: Domestic Violence in North London*, Centre for Criminology, Middlesex University.

Morley, R. (1993), 'Recent Responses to "Domestic Violence" Against Women: A Feminist Critique', *Social Policy Review*, vol. 5, p.177.

Mullender, A. and Morley, R. (eds) (1994), *Children Living with Domestic Violence: Putting Men's Abuse of Women on the Child Care Agenda*, Whiting and Birch Ltd, London.

Office of National Statistics (1997), *Marriage and Divorce Statistics, England and Wales 1994*, Series FM2, No. 22, HMSO, London.

O'Leary, K., Neidig, P. and Heyman, R. (1995), 'Assessment and Treatment of Partner Abuse: A Synopsis for the Legal Profession', *Albany Law Review*, vol 58, pp.1215-1233.

Pagelow, M. (1990), 'Effects of Domestic Violence on Children and Their Consequences for Custody and Visitation Agreements', *Mediation Quarterly*, vol 7(4), pp.347-363.

Piper, C. and Kaganas, F. (1997), 'The Family Law Act 1996 s1(d): How Will "They" Know There is a Risk of Violence?', *Child and Family law Quarterly*, vol 9(3), pp.279-89.

Piper, C. (1996), 'Divorce Reform and the Image of the Child', *Journal of Law and Society*, vol. 23(3), pp.363-382.

Polk, K. (1994), *When Men Kill. Scenarios of Masculine Violence*, Cambridge University Press, Cambridge.

Rights of Women (ROW) (1996) *Bulletin*, Summer.

Sev'er, A. (1997), 'Recent or Imminent Separation and Intimate Violence Against Women', *Violence Against Women*, vol 3, pp.566-589.

Shaffer, M. (1988), 'Divorce Mediation: A Feminist Perspective', *University of Toronto Faculty of Law Review*, vol. 46(1), pp.163-200.

Smart, C. (1997), 'Wishful Thinking or Harmful Tinkering? Sociological Reflections on Family Policy', *Journal of Social Policy*, vol. 26(3), pp.301-321.

Stark, E. (1995), 'Re-Presenting Woman Battering: From Battered Woman Syndrome to Coercive Control', *Albany Law Review*, vol 8, pp.973-1026.

Stanko, E., Crisp, D., Hale, C. and Lucraft, H. (1998), *Counting the Costs: Estimating the Impact of Domestic Violence in the Borough of Hackney*, Crime Concern, London.

Walker, J. McCarthy, P. and Timms, N. (1994), *Mediation: The Making and Re-making of Cooperative Relationships*, Relate Centre for Family Studies, Newcastle University.

Wardle, LD. (1994), 'Divorce Violence and the No-Fault Divorce Culture', *Utah Law Review*, pp.741-775.

Whelan, R. (ed) (1995), *Just a Piece of Paper? Divorce Reform and the Undermining of Marriage*, Institute of Economic Affairs, London.

Young, K. (1996), *Research Evaluation of Family Mediation Practice and the Issue of Violence*, Attorney-General's Department, Australia.

10 Dividing the Family Assets

ALISON DIDUCK

Introduction

There have been dramatic reforms in the past decade in the area of public and private child law, child support, domestic violence and divorce, incorporating new non-adversarial and co-operative values into legislation (Bainham, 1998). The one area of family law as yet untouched by the reformers' pen, however, is that of family finances and property. Although this area is currently under review, (Ancillary Relief Advisory Group, 1998) the law remains much as it was in the 1970s and 1980s, arguably expressing the older values of protecting legal property interests, clean break between the spouses and preserving judicial discretion. The Matrimonial Causes Act 1973 (MCA) has been amended in minor ways by the Family Law Act 1996 (FLA), but its basic objectives, principles and substance in relation to finance and property remain intact. It is curious that such radical change in other areas of family law, particularly in divorce, should not have been accompanied by changes in the law of ancillary relief, and indeed should have predated any review of that law. In fact, the FLA debates concentrated on matters other than finances and property, which were included only incidentally notwithstanding the government's acknowledgement at the time that the law on financial provision after divorce should be reviewed (Lord Chancellor's Department (LCD), 1995, para 9.4).

Of all the exhortations within the FLA debates, perhaps the strongest was the plea for the co-operative or 'civilised' (Walker *et al*, 1994) divorce. If the marriage could not be saved, it was to be the responsibility of the parties to ensure at least that they would create and maintain a harmonious post-divorce relationship for the sake of the children. Little discussion focused upon the procedure for or necessity of the parties arriving at a co-operative or 'civilised' post-divorce financial arrangement, although a pilot scheme incorporating case management for a quick resolution of litigated disputes was welcomed in the 1995 White Paper on divorce reform (LCD, 1995, para 9.7). It seemed that financial arrangements were to be subsumed within procedural changes made primarily to attempt 'marriage saving', to 'protect' children and to reduce cost; if private ordering - notably mediation - worked for those concerns, the assumption was that it would also work for financial matters.

The FLA itself makes little reference to financial matters. The parties ought to receive information about finances and property at the information meeting, they should use the period of 'reflection and consideration' to consider their arrangements for the future, and presumably the court may direct them to mediation to focus this consideration, but decisions about finances and property are then left to be decided in the light of, or the shadow of, the MCA 1973. All financial and property arrangements must be made before the divorce may be granted. Where matters of ancillary relief are to be litigated, diversion from the adversarial process to a Financial Dispute Resolution scheme (to be treated as a meeting for conciliation, FPR 1997, r.2.75) is proposed and currently being piloted. The lack of debate on this scheme is disappointing; it seems to have been promoted primarily in order to deal with rising costs in family litigation (Thorpe, LJ, 1998).

The law concerning ancillary financial matters seemed, by the mid-nineties, and after the initial upheaval created by the Child Support Acts 1991 and 1995 (CSA), to have become relatively clear insofar as solicitors could advise their clients of general trends in the substantive law. They could advise that property and financial provision was at the courts' discretion, and was not about legal entitlements *per se*, and that that discretion primarily was concerned to meet the wife's (and children's) housing needs first, usually in the light of the husband's means (Family Law Committee, 1998, para 8.5(a); Solicitors' Family Law Association (SFLA), 1998, para 23; Association of District Judges, 1998, p.2).

In most middle income families, then, the law had settled into a situation whereby the wife would usually remain in occupation of the marital home (because she usually had care of the children), and she often would receive a larger share of the equity, sometimes to be realised at a later date, in exchange for any claim she may have for ongoing support from the husband.[1] Any liability or potential liability under the CSA would be taken into consideration in making such a property adjustment. For these families, as for lower income families, the reliance of the wife and children upon state benefits was also taken into consideration. For high income families, any support and property distribution would also be based on the court's assessment of the non-earning party's, again usually the wife's, needs or 'reasonable requirements' (for example, *Dart v. Dart* [1996] 2 FLR 286) and the clean break principle. The dominant discourse in the discretion-based ancillary relief scheme tended to eschew spouse support in favour of property adjustments (Eekelaar 1991), and the values of the adjustments were calculated primarily according to needs criteria.[2] The parties were in this way thought best to be able to get on with their separate lives (for example, as in *Mawson v Mawson* [1994] 2 FLR 985).

However, the particulars of how the court's discretion would be exercised in a given case often could not be predicted by solicitors. Eekelaar (1998) points to evidence which demonstrates the difficulty solicitors face in assessing the likely outcomes of individual cases, highlighting that the discretionary nature of MCA section 25 allows for more than one 'correct' outcome in any given case (p.470). So, while solicitors may be able to see a broad trend in the law toward meeting needs,[3] details of the way in which needs or reasonable requirements would be assessed and met remain variable and indeterminate (see also Ancillary Relief Advisory Group, 1998).

The weight attached to meeting the dependant's 'needs' is itself curious. Arguably the weight is disproportionate,[4] given that MCA s.25 lists eight factors for the court to consider in making support and property allocation decisions (nine, if the welfare of the child is included).[5] From those factors, together with the admonition in section 25A to consider a clean break, and the law of trusts which has developed so as to accord value only to certain types of contributions to assets (*Lloyds Bank v Rosset and Rosset* [1991] 1 AC 107; [1990] 2 FLR 155), can be distilled at least three different models of financial and property adjustment. Subsections 25(2)(a), (b) (c), (d) and (e), for example, seem to further a needs-based income security or insurance model of financial adjustment; subsections (f), (g) and (h), along with the law of trusts, appear to prefer a compensatory model; and section 25A favours a pure clean break model.[6] No one factor is given legislative weight over the others and indeed, judges are not bound even to make financial or property orders at all. Virtually all respondents to the Lord Chancellor's Advisory Group favoured this situation continuing, saying the flexibility enabled courts to do justice in every case. Rogerson described a comparable Canadian situation with regard to spouse support as follows:

> [E]xisting [...] legislation is unclear, confusing and often contains conflicting directives. Its interpretation requires the exercise of judicial discretion and

> requires that judges articulate a philosophy of spousal support which will bring some coherence to the legislation and adapt it to its social context (1989, p.103).

The courts' focus upon meeting needs and achieving a clean break (Priest, 1997) between the parties appears to be the 'coherence and adaptation' to which Rogerson refers. Needs, or income security seem to be the theoretical framework in which orders and agreements are made, even while the decision to pursue this goal at the expense of others has not been explicitly articulated, reasoned, or debated. Whether orders or agreements achieve justice in every case is a matter of interpretation. What is interesting from the perspective of the FLA, is how the continued influence of this dominant discourse will affect the promotion of justice in a system of private ordering. For the dominant discourse is just that - it is only one of many possible interpretations of the legislative provisions, but one which emerged as dominant in the context of the perceived 'crises' of family breakdown and liberated women in the 1970s and 1980s, and the reaction to these 'crises': back to basics and clean break.

Complicating the matter further is the role that 'conduct' plays in assessments of entitlement and justice, and its paradoxical place within a (soon to be) no-fault divorce system. Courts have a difficult enough time assessing the role of conduct in ancillary relief, so that expecting parties and mediators (or judge-conciliators) to do as well or better is problematic. In the name of saving marriages, minimising conflict and achieving the co-operative or civilised divorce, what happens to justice when the parties' conduct is to be considered relevant as part of a discretionary package?

In the light of research which shows that generally women may do less well in mediated settlements (Axon and Hann, 1994; Freeman, 1997) and the difficulty in later overturning agreements either before or after they are made into consent orders (*Edgar v Edgar* [1980] 1 WLR 1410; ss.31, 33, 33A, 34 and 35 MCA 1973), we must look closely at the consequences for both parties of informal justice. This chapter will focus upon the possible inequities which may arise as a result of using informal private ordering of financial and property matters in a discretion based ancillary relief system. Mediating ancillary agreements on divorce when the legal 'rules' of distribution lack a principled foundation or clear objectives means that neither party can enter or leave mediation with a clear idea of entitlement, but rather must have recourse only to the discourse which emerges as dominant from competing legislative 'factors' for consideration (MCA, section 25) and their own, often conflicting, senses of 'justice'. The legal context in which the 'civilised' divorce is to be achieved, then, is a mixed one which incorporates anti-adversarialism coupled with unclear rights to entitlement.

Informal Justice and Gender

Postulating gender differences is always a difficult exercise. Not only must one first determine whether men and women are, indeed, situated in family, relationships, work and the world differently, one is then faced with the problem of deciding that if they are, what, if anything, law ought to do about it. If law ignores any identifiable differences in the name of formal equality, it runs the risk of creating substantive inequality, yet if it acknowledges and attempts to compensate for differences, it runs the risk of instantiating them further, perpetuating any disadvantage they create. Further, feminists do not agree on whether any identifiable differences are the results of social, economic and political forces, or whether there are more subtly sex-related male and female 'voices' (Gilligan, 1982; Gray and Merrick, 1996). I shall take the position that gender differences do exist in the negotiation of familial relationships, and that those differences can be attributed to social and economic forces which influence the ways in which women and men approach their familial and employment responsibilities.

It is still the case, for example, that women's role in families is perceived to be primarily as carer, such that even when they are engaged in paid employment outside the home, that employment tends to be part-time or work which can accommodate domestic responsibilities (Family Policy Studies Centre, 1995). It tends, therefore, to be lower paying than men's work and to have fewer benefits attached to it (Morris and Nott, 1995). Women, even employed women, still bear primary responsibility for housework (Brannen *et al*, 1994) and women's paid work is still viewed as secondary or marginal to the household income (Pahl, 1989). Men, on the other hand, find their familial roles constrained differently. Men still tend to be viewed as breadwinner rather than carer: they participate in housework to lesser extent than their female partners (Brannen *et al*, 1994) and their role as husband or father tends to be secondary to their role as worker[7] because the work world assumes a worker with little or no familial responsibility. Finally, law, while professing a disinterest in the sex of its subjects, serves to perpetuate these gender differences by discouraging workers from having identities also as family members. There is little state subsidised child care and no legal requirement for employers to provide it; while providing only moderately generous maternity leave, law provides for no paternity leave for fathers or general parental leave. Law and state policy thus create an economic advantage for men and single women to the disadvantage of wives and mothers.

The Breadwinner/Homemaker Ideology

Whilst the marriage subsists, these differences may or may not be problematic to the spouses.[8] Any material implications of a wife's lower income or earning capacity are masked by her interrelationship with her husband's wealth. On divorce, however, she often becomes acutely aware of her unequal wealth and this may place her in a subordinated bargaining position when she is negotiating the end of her marriage. She may be forced to accept less than she feels entitled to in the interests of short term gain and in order to avoid prolonging the bargaining process. There is a further and more insidious consequence of gender differences in wealth, however. Pahl's (1989) interviews with married couples enabled her to confirm the existence of 'his' marriage and 'her' marriage (pp.4-6; p.169). The following passage illustrates this difference in the context of household incomes:

> Husbands typically earned more than wives and had more fringe benefits from their employment. They usually saw themselves as breadwinners for the family, even when they retained substantial sums for their own use; wives' earnings were seen as more marginal to the budget, even though most women spent their wages on the family. Husbands were less likely to have to justify the money they spent and they tended to spend more on their own leisure. In general, husbands were likely to perceive a greater degree of sharing in marriage than wives, who were more aware of conflicts of opinion and of interest (Pahl, 1989, p.171).

Further, even where couples wished their relationship to be based upon equality, Pahl (1989) found that the husband's greater earning power was associated with greater decision-making power. More importantly, this classically patriarchal ideology of husband breadwinner/decision-maker and wife/dependent continued to legitimate his power, even where wives earned more than their husbands.

When the parties to these 'different' marriages separate, they bring with them to negotiations not only their different material circumstances, but also their different and often irreconcilable perceptions of the marriage and the roles and power relationships they assumed during the marriage. For men who were used to seeing themselves as the primary decision-makers in the family, that role may be difficult to reconcile with a mediation or court conciliation session which gives voice to their wives' views of the marriage and finances. This may be particularly important where husbands perceived a degree of sharing in the marriage that their wives did not perceive. Thus, Davis *et al* (1994) note that many men negotiating ancillary matters on divorce felt that it was 'their' money that was being dealt with (p.49). As Day Sclater points out in Chapter 8, it is a reasonable assumption that this affected the process of negotiation in which these men saw themselves as being asked to 'share' their wealth with someone who had no legal entitlement to it.

This ideology does not only affect husbands, however. Pahl states:

> A woman may contribute a higher proportion of her earnings to housekeeping than her husband but her income is still likely to be regarded as marginal; a man may contribute a lower proportion of his earnings but he still feels justified in spending more than his wife on leisure *because both define him as the breadwinner* (Pahl, 1989, p.170 emphasis added and references omitted).

Pahl's conclusions mean that bargaining on divorce is coloured by an ideology held by both parties, not only the husband. If this ideology informs both sexes' senses of the marriage, law reformers should be sensitive to the degree to which the process and results of the bargaining may also be affected. Research from the United States, for example, expands upon Davis *et al*'s finding about men's views: in divorce 'men discuss with their attorneys ways to "keep" their property or assets, and women discuss ways to "get" assets' (Gray and Merrick, 1996, p.243). When parties are encouraged to arrive at their 'own' agreements and where legal norms are disregarded in favour of the parties' own senses of fairness, a context is created in which the breadwinner/homemaker ideology is left to flourish. Where the wife is successful in 'getting' something from her husband, he can be left to feel 'robbed' of his money and his house (UK Men's Movement, 1997) and the wife left to feel that she succeeded in establishing not an entitlement to share family assets, but in establishing only either her 'wiles' or her dependence upon her husband's wealth and goodwill. That the parties sometimes do view such a settlement as vaguely 'fair' is, therefore, not the point. That which may seem 'fair' to a supplicant and a provider is almost certainly different from that which seems fair to equal partners.

Fairness and Justice

'The "flexibility" of the informal setting', along with the imprecision of the legal rules or norms, 'compels' the 'intrusion of nonlegal considerations into what are ostensibly legal decisions' (Ingleby, 1992, p.144). The informality envisaged by the FLA does not deny the legality of financial decisions on divorce, it merely removes much of the recourse parties have to legal rules in reaching those decisions. In this way, 'nonlegal considerations' such as the breadwinner/homemaker ideology are allowed freer reign and contribute to the parties' belief in the justice of their agreement.

Parties may also bring to private ordering their interpretations of the justice arising from other aspects of their relationship; more destructive nonlegal considerations such as power, intimidation, or guilt may inform, or intrude upon perceptions of justice. Mediators are aware of the intimidatory effect of histories of domestic violence but nevertheless tend to operate with a presumption of formal equality between the parties which may preclude consideration of gender differences in how the parties interpret the justice of their situations.

Divorcing parties are more concerned with attributing blame and responsibility for the marriage breakdown than are either law or mediators (Ingleby, 1992; Davis *et al*, 1994; Walker *et al*, 1994) and, as Brown and Day Sclater point out in chapter 7, a psychodynamic perspective provides an explanation for this 'need'. Clients also tend to believe that 'fairness' or justice dictates recognition of this 'culpability' through financial rewards and punishments. Perhaps the most extreme example of this belief is that felt by the UK Men's Movement (UKMM). The movement interprets statistics which show that almost 75% of all decrees of divorce are granted to wives (Social Trends, 1998) and states that '80% of divorces' are sought by and granted to women on their 'unilateral demand' so that the husband's 'commitment to the marriage is arbitrarily swept aside' (UKMM, 1997, p.2). It speaks of the 'divorce racket' in which the innocent 'respondent victim is robbed of his home, his money and his children' (UKMM, 1997, p.1). Less strident, but echoing similar sentiments, is Barry (1995) who writes of the 'moral duty' to comply with the expectations of marriage, and the adverse consequences which ought to accompany breaches of those expectations (p.51). To him, in the name of justice, the FLA ought to reflect this. In his view:

> Nothing in the [Family Law Act 1996] would prevent the unilateral repudiation of a marriage ... However, any spouse who so acts would forego any claim to (personal) maintenance, and the right to a share of the common property of the marriage would be qualified (p.52).

There is evidence that many husbands' views of justice correspond with this sentiment. Women do initiate divorce more frequently than men. Husbands in many of these cases feel that they are therefore the wronged or abandoned parties and that this consideration should be the determining factor in financial adjustment on divorce: 'My feelings on this is that my wife abandoned the house - which, in my opinion, she should lose all rights to the property - because she just walked out and left it' (Davis *et al*, 1994, p.52). As Davis *et al* (1994) then point out, however, this man's wife 'did not regard herself as having "abandoned the house" and nor did she see this as a factor to be weighed in the settlement. She claimed that she left the home for her own protection' (pp.52-53).

Mediators and lawyers tend to minimise the role fault or conduct plays in financial determinations; denying the relevance of conduct to financial matters is now a routine part of a solicitor's job (Davis *et al*, 1994), and mediators refuse to discuss questions of fault in mediation sessions (Walker *et al*, 1994). Thus, while perceptions of fault and justice remain largely irrelevant for law, and unresolved in informal sessions, they are left to 'intrude' in the negotiation or mediation process, and may leave many - especially propertied men - (Davis *et al*, 1994) dissatisfied and resentful of the process and the outcome. The FLA amendment to section 25(2)(g) of the MCA to make conduct relevant to the exercise of judicial discretion, whatever the nature of the conduct or whether it occurred during the marriage or after the separation, increases the likelihood of fault forming a part of the parties' perceptions of the justice of their situations. The difficulties with this are summarised by Ellman:

> The rule [of considering fault in financial division] does not buy justice but rather the injustice of unpredictable or arbitrary results, and at a price of heightened transaction costs. The loser will often be the financially dependent spouse who feels compelled to settle for a thinner financial package than she would get under a less discretionary no-fault system, for fear that the judge will

be sympathetic to her husband's (or his wife's) story (1997, pp.227-228).

Perceptions of justice, which include conduct or fault affect women as well. In the study by Walker *et al* women tended more frequently than men to speak of their guilt at deciding to end the marriage (Walker *et al*, 1994); for them, a certain justice may be served by their settling for less than any 'legal entitlement'. Law's focus upon meeting the applicant's needs and mediators' focus upon the parties' view of fairness, therefore, offer an 'out' for her in informal settings so that her conscience is salved if she reaches a settlement which falls short of any actual entitlement but still allows her to make ends meet. Her view of fairness or justice in this situation lies in contrast to the 'traditional' legal approach to justice. When mediating parties referred their agreements to a (partisan) solicitor, they ran the risk of being told that they were settling for too little. 'What might be viewed by the parties as "fair" within mediation may be considered "unfair" by a solicitor acting purely and properly in one client's best interest' (Walker *et al*, 1994, p.134). Solicitors are seen to 'change the focus of mediation towards entitlement rather than focusing on mutual needs and mutual fairness' (Walker *et al*, 1994, p.135). Even in a discretion-based system, then, recourse to law may change the parties' perceptions of justice.

The Legal (and Non-Legal) Subject

A further gender difference may be identified in how the parties 'fit' into the rhetoric of law and into the legal subject it assumes. Ingleby touches on a part of this difference, when he notes that the 'rhetoric of the law constructs its subjects as individuals who are to be treated as equals, and ignores the reality of substantive inequalities between them' (1992, pp.7-8). He mentions three such substantive inequalities: emotional, physical and financial. While these inequalities may not always be gender-linked, the research discussed above in relation to emotional and financial factors, and other research indicating the prevalence of domestic violence in divorcing couples' histories (Ingleby, 1992; Davis *et al*, 1994; Walker *et al*, 1994), point to a substantive inequality which tends to favour men over women. Those involved in private ordering of the consequences of divorce try to be sensitive to this by being aware of whether guilt, the need for retribution or physical or financial superiority influences the process (Walker *et al*, 1994). The legal and ideological context, however, in which dispute resolution is carried out includes an assumption of the formal equality of individual self-interested subjects, reinforced by '"supporting ideologies" of property, liberty, the minimal state, and the rule of law' (Cotterrell, 1988, in Ingleby, 1992, p.146). In the informal resolution of financial disputes, then, it is difficult to escape the legal and political context which privileges the preservation of individual possessive property interests at the expense of ideas of community or shared interests. In many contemporary families, that privilege tends to favour men over women and children.

Ingleby goes on: 'Trubeck also makes the point that "Legal discourse also includes subtle methods of valuing certain kinds of behaviour, such as instrumental striving for material goods, and disvaluing others"' (1992, p.146, reference omitted). Thus, even though the MCA section 25(2)(f) makes relevant non-financial contributions to the marriage or to property, it exists in a broader legal context that is antagonistic to such an idea. That antagonism is made manifest by trust law which usually disregards such contributions in determining property interests (*Lloyds Bank v Rosset and Rosset* [1991] 1 AC 107), by the relatively little weight attributed to section 25(2)(f) by judges (George, 1997; *Dart v Dart* [1996] 2 FLR 286; cf. *Conran v Conran* [1997] 2 FLR 615), and by the actual value attributed to those contributions when they are taken into account (Eekelaar 1991). In *White v White* [1998] 2 FLR 1, for example, the Court of Appeal seemed to confirm that non-financial contributions to the marriage are only relevant in some cases (per Thorpe LJ, p.9), and even then, only some non-financial contributions would be considered (per Thorpe LJ, p.8 and Butler-Sloss LJ, pp.15-16). Once again, mediators and judge conciliators must be aware of how this ideology may subtly empower men at the expense of women in private ordering.

Ingleby's work leads to a further examination of the presumptively equal subjects of law. The liberal philosophy upon which law is based assumes a subject who is universal, autonomous and abstracted at the expense of a subject who is particular, connected and concrete (Naffine, 1990). While we must be cautious in over-determining the sexes of these subjects, we cannot ignore the material and social manifestations of associations of the feminine with caring and context and the masculine with autonomy and abstract individualism. The material and social manifestations to which I refer are illustrated by Pahl's research referred to above, for example, on husbands' and wives' spending patterns, and by Smart's (1991) research on the moral and legal ordering of child custody. While we also cannot assume that women's subjectivity is always at odds with the assumed legal (masculine) subjectivity, the unspoken and unacknowledged 'sex' of the legal subject underlies both the bargaining process and the exercise of judicial discretion.

In suggesting that mediators and judge-conciliators remain sensitive to the particularities of the people with whom they are working, including their sexed and gendered identities and realities, I do not mean to reinforce stereotypes of women as disempowered or as victims of dominating men. Rather, I seek to subvert the material disadvantage that may result from formal gender blindness in the form of formal equality. As Lacey says:

> Much work, practical and theoretical, analytical and imaginative, needs to be done if the notions of neutrality, rights, equality and justice are to be understood in their racially, sexually and otherwise oppressively patterned reality, and if they are to be reconstructed in a way which promises the genuine accommodation of different forms of life, different subjectivities. ... [I]t may be that in seeking to imagine difference, in pursuit of its ultimate inclusion or recognition, we may not so much make a difference, as reproduce, as it were, the same difference. In doing so, we inevitably lend weight to its misinterpretation as fixed. Only if we are constantly aware of this double pitfall will we have any hope of developing strategies for stepping around it (Lacey, 1998, p.219).

Crucial are these differences which remain unacknowledged as part of divorce; they have not been sufficiently addressed by either reformers or commentators, and remain as undercurrents in the process and in the substantive law.

The Family Law Act

The Ancillary Relief Procedure

Ancillary Relief Pilot schemes were established first in 1996 and then in 1997 (Fam Proc (Amendment No. 2) Rules 1997, S.I. 1997/1056) the new procedure was incorporated formally into the Family Proceedings Rules 1991. As is stated in the President's Direction 16 June 1997, 'a key element in the procedure is the Financial Dispute Resolution appointment' ([1997] 2 FLR 304). The FDR is to be treated as an appointment for conciliation, and in this respect it is more than merely a case management scheme. Parties are expected to provide complete disclosure of financial information, of their offers and their proposals to resolve outstanding issues. Their disclosures are not later admissible in evidence (Practice Direction [1997] 2 FLR 304). Similarly, the judge in the FDR should openly consider the court's reasoning process should the matter proceed to litigation (Frenkel, 1997) and in this way give the parties norms with which to work as well as incentives for settlement. It is hoped that this process will reduce both costs and conflict in family proceedings. Once again, though, in the pursuit of these aims, it is important to bear in mind the undercurrents of the procedures.

In the light of the preceding discussion of gender, a number of difficulties can be identified with this scheme and its driving aims to reduce conflict and cost. First, the assumption that all conflict is to be avoided must be questioned. Conflict in family disputes may be the result of gendered perceptions of 'his' and 'her' marriages and the expectations these create. By submerging conflict, the material differences created by those different perceptions are buried as well and the result can easily be a homogenisation of the marriage on the dominant terms and unjust formal equality (Ingleby, 1992).

The second difficulty relates to procedure. The applicant for ancillary relief, usually the lower earning or non-earning wife, must file her application first. Bearing in mind that the courts are increasingly seeing the purpose of ancillary relief as being to meet the applicant's needs (or 'reasonable requirements', *Dart v Dart*), she must establish some case for these at the outset. As the matter progresses, including at the FDR, the onus is always upon her to justify her claim 'because the underlying assumption is that it is "his money"' (George, 1997, p.730). Thus, the process as well as the discretion-based law places her in the position of supplicant.

Thirdly, both parties must exchange and file with the court a completed Form E which details not only present and anticipated future income and expenses, but also their standards of living, contributions to the marriage, and personal details. The first thing to note about this detailed financial disclosure is Pahl's observation that of those who refused to take part in her study, it was men who tended to be more reluctant than women to disclose details about their income and finances (1989). The second point is that one district judge at least has found Form E to be overcomplicated in many cases (Frenkel, 1997). Finally, the onus upon the applicant to establish her reasonable needs in the future places her at a disadvantage relative to the respondent in anticipating the many details required for the form. Much legal effort is then spent in scrutinising her claims. As one practitioner has stated,

> with the emphasis on reasonable requirements the scrutiny of the budget has developed an increasingly important role in these cases. ... Are budgets to be tested against 'what we used to spend' or 'what he can afford' or 'what I think I need'? ... Understandably a lot of wives say 'why do I have to go through all this and not him?' (George 1997, p.730).

Finally, the role of the judge in the FDR remains unclear and is still 'in a state of development' (Frenkel, 1997, p.727). He or she is not to act as a mediator, but rather is there to make findings of fact and to facilitate settlements by canvassing possible outcomes or objectives of any court order (Frenkel, 1997). Once again, however, problems arise. The discretionary nature of section 25 and the indeterminacy with which courts can treat the section 25 criteria make any 'narrowing of the issues' or closing down of 'hopeless' arguments (Frenkel, 1997, p.728) at the FDR extremely problematic. On the one hand, a particular judge's reasoning process, objectives or assessment of the criteria carry the weight of judicial authority and are thus, as they are intended to be, powerful settlement incentives. On the other hand, if negotiation is unsuccessful, it is too easy to assume that another judge - the ultimate trial judge - can take a completely different view of the strength of an argument or the statutory criteria. The SFLA has found that the uncertainty engendered by section 25 means that some District Judges are 'less vigorous' than others in stating a view of a potential final outcome, and that some parties are therefore reluctant to settle (SFLA, 1998, p.6).

Further, judicial case management is still controversial in England and Wales (Zander 1997), and it therefore makes sense to pilot it before implementing it fully. While I do not adhere to all of Zander's criticisms of judicial case management, I do sympathise with his view of the importance, yet difficulty, of training judges for the role. It is particularly important that training should include an awareness of gender issues, power and relationship dynamics. Given the authority of FDR judge-conciliators, it is not sufficient to rely upon either the principles of formal equality which legal training has taught them, or the skills of the parties' solicitors to redress any fundamental imbalance which may be missed or instantiated by the judge's comments at the FDR.

Comprehensive Mediation

There is little reason to expect that these difficulties can be surmounted completely where the parties attend mediation sessions rather than FDRs. Mediation's focus on needs, even though they are said to be upon 'mutual needs', still places the wife in the position of having to justify her request for 'assistance' and her actual financial needs. Mediators spend a good deal of time going over budgets with their clients, and the detail required has been identified as a cause for concern by parties and mediators alike (Walker *et al*, 1994). Walker *et al* (1994) found evidence to support Pahl's (1989) research which suggests, for example, that the value placed upon leisure activities differs between men and women. Mediators had to encourage women to include expenditures for leisure, even though these were not within their actual means. 'Like he put down forty pounds a month entertaining, for going out basically. I put nothing and thought "Oh sod that" so I put forty quid in too ...', 'He claimed "golf", so I claimed "golf", even though I don't play!' (Walker *et al*, 1994, p.67). Walker *et al* summarise the difficulty as follows:

> For many women the basic problem was having enough money to feed and clothe the children. They were more inclined to focus on necessities than luxuries. On the other hand, men with more time on their hands were more likely to attribute importance to leisure pursuits (1994, pp.67-68).

The point is that a focus on mutual needs and mutual fairness may not end up 'balancing' the calculations out (Walker *et al*, 1994, p.68), so long as luxuries are viewed by husbands as 'needs', and by wives as 'wants' (Walker *et al*, 1994, p.67).

Section 8 of the FLA makes attendance at an Information Meeting mandatory before a statement of marriage breakdown and/or application relating to financial and property matters can be made. There, each party will be given information (not advice) about, among other things, the 'nature of financial questions that may arise on divorce or separation'. The content of this information is crucial to determining how husbands and wives will perceive their relative positions when it comes to choosing whether to negotiate, mediate or litigate their financial issues, and then in how they proceed in their chosen procedure. Legal information directed at presumptively equal parties and which appears to be neutral, remains subject to Cotterrell's and Trubeck's 'supporting ideologies', which may have the effect of psychologically empowering the property owning and earning partner at the expense of the non-earning, non-owning partner.

Further, if, as is expected, more couples will act in person on their divorces (SFLA, 1998), the importance of the information meetings cannot be overstated. Many of these couples will reach settlements after attending mediation and the 'dramatic swathe of discretion' (SFLA, 1998, p.6) offered by section 25 compounds the difficulties those without legal advice will face.

Legal Aid

Gender based difficulties may also exist in funding divorces. The FLA makes changes to the Legal Aid Act 1988. In particular, section 29 (which is not yet in force) requires the Legal Aid Board (LAB) to deny representation until the applicant has attended an initial meeting with a mediator to determine whether mediation is 'suitable'. Thus, mediation will play a more significant role in the divorces of the less wealthy than it will in those of the better-off who would not require legal aid. Further, Mossman (1994) has persuasively argued that legal aid is a gender issue, not least because in most family proceedings, women users overwhelmingly outnumber men users. Any changes made to the legal aid rules should take account of the fact that women are disproportionately affected by them relative to men.

Guidance issued to LAB caseworkers states that it is likely that a legal aid certificate will be refused if mediation is 'suitable', but offers no assistance on how 'suitability' is to be assessed. While NFM has maintained that mediation is unsuitable where either party feels coerced to attend, it is unclear whether the legal aid board will take this position (King 1998). Further, while mediation itself may be funded from legal aid funds, legal advice during mediation will be restricted to either 'green form' advice or 'family mediation linked legal services' (King 1998), neither of which provides services equivalent to those under a full legal aid certificate or to those paying privately for legal advice. Given that 'success' at mediation is measured by the fact of an agreement being reached, rather than by longer-term satisfaction with that agreement (Walker *et al*, 1994), that any delay in reaching agreement tends to favour the economically stronger party, and that the divorce may not be granted until the parties reach agreement, the wife-applicant may again find herself disadvantaged, this time by her dependence upon public funding.

Future Reform?

The Lord Chancellor's Department is currently considering possible reforms to financial and property allocation on divorce. It has referred to an Advisory Group the questions of legislating a presumption of a 50-50 split of property and accepting prenuptial agreements as legally valid. It has also produced a draft pension reform act based on a notion of compensation (Pension Sharing Bill).[9] Taken together, these possible reforms would seem to share a goal of introducing into ancillary relief law the notion of entitlement at the expense of judicial discretion, where entitlement is based upon some notion of compensation. Such a reform may go some way to ensuring that parties do not enter into dispute resolution with the assumption that the weaker party is seeking the other's benevolence, but rather proceed on the assumption that he or she is seeking a legal entitlement. The legal norm created by such a reform would be to deem as equally important different types of contribution to the family wealth.

There are some who believe many wives would get less under the proposed reform than they currently do under the discretionary system in which judges often give them a larger than 50% share of the property in order to meet their greater needs arising from their care of the children. They say equality would, therefore, not do justice. The Advisory Group on Ancillary Relief takes this position (para 7). The individual submissions to the Group detail different reasons, but reflect the unanimous view that retaining judicial discretion is necessary to do justice in individual cases. Judges of the Family Division point, for example, to the potential conflict between a presumption of equality and the principle of primacy for the children (Family Division Judges, 1998, para 6), and state their unanimity in 'opposing any introduction of equality in division of assets as a governing principle even subject to departures' (para 11). District Judges state that a 50-50 presumption would 'undoubtedly encourage false expectations among the public and would lead to unmeritorious litigation' (Association of District Judges, 1998, para 3.4). They suggest instead adding a list of 'aims and objects' to MCA s.25, with housing the children and the parties and meeting the reasonable requirements of the parties as priorities one to three, clean break as priority four and equality, subject to retention of separate property, at the end (para 2.3). The Family Law Bar Association agrees with the Family Division Judges (Family Law Bar Association, 1998, para 1.B), and the Family Law Committee of the Law Society believes that

50-50 splits should be avoided because :

(a) They will impact unfairly across the whole social spectrum;
(b) They will do nothing to counter the poverty experienced by women and children on divorce;
(c) The rule would be too rigid leading to unfairness and hardship;
(d) Non-financial contributions would cause a problem - it would be unfair not to value them, yet attempts to do so would inevitably fail (1998, para 2.9).

Finally, the SFLA is 'wholly opposed to a system of deferred community of property with equal division of capital as a starting point, or similar' (SFLA, 1998, p.2).

It is my view that the potential for injustice identified by the individual submissions to the Advisory Group is real. My difficulty lies with their unwillingness to see anything other than judicial discretion as a way of dealing with that potential. To me, they undervalue the role which can be played in these cases by support law. So, for example, where 'one spouse has given up her career, or at least prejudiced it, to spend time raising children, acting as home carer and similar whilst the other spouse has furthered his career' (SFLA, 1998, para 63), her disadvantage can be redressed through either on-going or lump sum maintenance rather than a discretionary property division. Reforms to ancillary relief, therefore, should also include reform of support law.

There is no currently theoretical basis for support in English law. Why an ex-husband, as opposed to the state, children, parents or anyone else should meet an ex-wife's 'needs' (however these are defined) is nowhere made clear. Arguably, it remains simply as a remnant of the common law duty of a husband to support his wife for life. As such, it immediately puts the parties in an unequal bargaining position, encourages wives into a role of dependency and leads to resentment on the part of husbands. Perhaps the answer lies with the principle of compensation. As I have argued elsewhere (Diduck and Orton, 1994), this model of spouse support allows for compensation of the economic consequences related to the division of responsibilities in a marriage:

> That is to say, the purpose of spousal support on marriage breakdown is to compensate for economic advantages and disadvantages which result form the functions performed or roles assumed in marriages. ... It means that the fact of the marriage itself does not justify an award of support, but rather, entitlement

> is based upon an 'examination of the events and actual roles played by the parties in the marriage'. Unlike the income security model, then, support does not redress all needs under this philosophy, only those related to or created by the marriage (Diduck and Orton, 1994, pp.690-691, references omitted).

The compensation model supports the view that 'support on divorce is not a gift bestowed through the discretion of the courts [or the payer], but rather is a just and equitable redistribution of resources, and [...] reflects a new valuing of caregiving and household work' (Diduck and Orton, 1994, p.700) that is usually performed by women, but also potentially by men. Support would therefore be seen as a right, earned by the recipient spouse, and not liable to be terminated automatically upon remarriage or once basic 'needs' are met. If pension reform can accommodate idea of compensation, there is no reason why support reform cannot. Indeed, it is one of the models which can be distilled from the MCA 1973, but which the dominant discourse has subordinated.

It is important that all of these reforms be made together. A presumption of equal sharing of family property without a renewed legal vision of support may result in formal equality leading to substantive inequality for women, just as the Advisory Group recognises. In that case, the law would presume a 50-50 split of the property, but support would remain discretionary and therefore discouraged. Although both parties would be operating under a stronger norm of equality, requests for and agreements for support would be deterred by that norm, regardless of whether economic advantages and disadvantages had been compensated by the equal property division.

Rather than being dealt with in one 'ancillary relief package', then, support and property adjustment should be determined separately, each with its own set of principles: equality for property and compensation for support. Under this system, and by using lump sums, many of the same types of financial arrangements could be made for non-earning spouses as are made now, but they would be based upon principles other than dependency, discretion or 'need'. The greater degree of certainty these reforms would bring to divorce matters would not only make litigation and negotiation less difficult and less adversarial, thus assisting toward the goal of the conflict-free divorce, but parties could mediate or negotiate the details of their entitlements based upon principles which assume equality in the value of marriage roles and therefore in bargaining power. Fairness to them, then, would encompass this new legal norm. Some idea of legal norms, in fact, seems to be what mediating couples want – they want some idea of 'what usually happens' to guide them in their perceptions of the fairness of their negotiations (Walker *et al*, 1994). Rather than mediators simply saying to them, 'it only matters what seems fair to you' (which often only perpetuates women's subordinated self esteem and economic dependence), they can state presumptions of substantive equality and the legal entitlements based upon that equality.

Notes

1. See generally, cases and discussion in Cretney and Masson, 1997, pp.408-497.
2. Eekelaar (1991) found that if one 'teases out' a common approach taken by the Registrars in his study to apportion property and finances on divorce, it would be an individualistic model based upon compensation principles. 'It would be possible to generalise their goal as the common one that the parties should take out of the marriage what they put in or at least some equivalent' (p.76). Two difficulties remain with this conclusion, however. The first is the valuation made of 'what they put in'. Only some of the registrars were prepared to value domestic contributions equally with financial ones, and many were prepared to do so only in longer marriages. The second difficulty is the Registrars apparent desire to qualify their compensation approach with the overriding influence of the 'circumstances of the case' and the needs of the parties (pp.75-76). Cretney and Masson (1997) also note that any 'starting points', including those of equality, must yield to the 'circumstances of the case', and that 'in practice, great emphasis is given to assessing the reasonable needs of the parties' (p.482).
3. Recently, in 'big money' cases, courts have begun to use the language of 'entitlement' based upon contributions to the family economy. Even in these cases, though, the courts have assessed the wife's 'reasonable needs' in the light of her contributions and equal or equitable 'entitlement' (see *White v White* [1998] 2 FLR 1; *Conran v Conran* [1997] 2 FLR 615).
4. See also *Dart v Dart* [1996] 2 FLR 286 per Butler-Sloss LJ.
5. See on this, *Conran v Conran*, above, and George, (1997).
6. This type of analysis is used in the Canadian context of spouse support awards on divorce; see Diduck (1992) and Rogerson (1989). See also Eekelaar (1991) where, in the English context, the author attempts to construct a theoretical framework for the basis of Registrars' decisions in financial and property matters on divorce.
7. British men average 48 hours per week at work (Family Policy Studies Centre, 1995, p.10).
8. Backett (1982) provides interesting research on how women 'explain' inequities while their marriages persist.
9. For an argument against basing pension reform upon the principle of compensation, see Hallam and Salter (1997).

References

Ancillary Relief Advisory Group (1998), *Report to the Lord Chancellor by the Ancillary Relief Advisory Group*, London.

Association of District Judges (1998), Submission of Association of District Judges, Appendix 8 to the *Report to the Lord Chancellor by the Ancillary Relief Advisory Group*, London.

Axon, L and Hann, R. (1994), *Working Document: Court Dispute Resolution Processes: The Application of Alternative Dispute Resolution in the Courts*, Research, Statistics and Evaluation Directorate, Department of Justice Canada, Ottawa.

Backett, K. (1982), *Mothers and Fathers*, Macmillan, London.

Bainham, A. (1998), 'Changing Families and Changing Concepts - Reforming the Language of Family Law', *Child and Family Law Quarterly*, vol 10(1), p.1.

Barry, N. (1995), 'Justice and Liberty in Marriage and Divorce', in R.Whelan (ed.), *Just a Piece of Paper?*, Institute of Economic Affairs Health and Welfare Unit, London.

Brannen, J., Meszaros, G., Moss; P. and Poland, G. (1994), *Employment and Family Life: A Review of Research in the UK (1980 - 1994)*, Department of Employment Research Series No. 41, University of London, London.

Cotterrell, R. (1988), 'Feasible Regulation for Democracy and Social Justice', *Journal of Law and Society*, vol 15, p.5.

Cretney, S.M. and Masson, J.M. (1997), *Principles of Family Law* (6th ed), Sweet and Maxwell, London.

Davis, G., Cretney, S and Collins, J. (1994), *Simple Quarrels*, Clarendon Press, Oxford.

Diduck, A. (1992), 'Spousal Support', in *Family Law Update*, Law Society of Manitoba Continuing Legal Education Series, VI - 1.

Diduck, A. and Orton, H. (1994), 'Equality and Support for Spouses', *Modern Law Review*, vol 57(5), p.681.

Eekelaar, J. (1991), *Regulating Divorce*, Clarendon Press, Oxford.

Eekelaar, J. (1998), 'Should Section 25 be Reformed?', *Family Law*, p.469.

Ellman, I. M. (1997), 'The Misguided Movement to Revive Fault Divorce, and Why Reformers Should Look Instead to the American Law Institute', *International Journal of Law, Policy and the Family*, vol 11, p.216.

Family Division Judges (1998), Submission of Family Division Judges, Appendix 7 to *Report to the Lord Chancellor by the Ancillary Relief Advisory Group*, London.

Family Law Committee of the Law Society, (1998), Maintenance and Capital Provision on Divorce, The Family Law Committee's Submission to the Ancillary Relief Advisory Group, The Law Society, Appendix 10 to *Report to the Lord Chancellor by the Ancillary Relief Advisory Group*, London.

Family Law Bar Association (1998), Submission of Family Law Bar Association, Appendix 9 to *Report to the Lord Chancellor by the Ancillary Relief Advisory Committee*, London.

Family Policy Studies Centre (1995), *Families in Britain, Family Report 3.*

Freeman, M.D.A. (1997), 'Divorce Gospel Style', *Family Law*, p.413.

Frenkel, J., District Judge (1997), 'Ancillary Relief Pilot Scheme in Operation', *Family Law*, p.726

George, P. (1997), 'In all the Circumstances - Section 25', *Family Law*, p.729.

Gilligan, C. (1982), *In A Different Voice*, Harvard University Press, Cambridge, Mass. and London.

Gray, C. and Merrick S.B. (1996), 'Voice Alterations. Why Women Have More Difficulty Than Men With the Legal Process of Divorce', *Family and Conciliation Courts Review*, vol 34(2), p.240.

Hallam, C. and Salter, D. (1997), 'Pensions on Divorce - Compensation or Needs?', *Family Law*, p.608.

Ingleby, R. (1992), *Solicitors and Divorce*, Clarendon Press, Oxford.

King, A. (1998), 'No Legal Aid Without Mediation - Section 29', *Family Law*, p.331.

Lacey, N. (1998), 'Feminist Legal Theory Beyond Neutrality' in *Unspeakable Subjects*, Hart Publishing, Oxford.

Lord Chancellor's Department (1995), *Looking to the Future Mediation and the Ground for Divorce*, Cm 2799, HMSO.

Morris, A. and Nott, S. (1995), *All My Worldly Goods: A Feminist Perspective on the Legal Regulation of Wealth*, Dartmouth, Aldershot.

Mossman, M.J. (1994), 'Gender Equality, Family Law and Access to Justice', *International Journal of Law and The Family*, vol 8, p.357.

Naffine, N. (1990), *Law and the Sexes*, Allen and Unwin, Sydney.

Pahl, J. (1989), *Money and Marriage*, Macmillian, Basingstoke and London.

Priest, J. (1997), 'Capital Settlements and the CSA - Part I', *Family Law*, p.115.

Rogerson, C. (1989), 'The Causal Connection Test in Spousal Support Law', *Canadian Journal of Family Law*, vol 8, p.95.

Smart, C. (1991), 'The Legal and Moral Ordering of Child Custody', *Journal of Law and Society*, vol 18, p.485.

Solicitors Family Law Association (1998), Proposals for Reform of Ancillary Relief Law, Orpington, SFLA, Appendix 11 to the *Report to the Lord Chancellor by the Ancillary Relief Advisory Group*, London.

Social Trends 28 (1998), Office for National Statistics, The Stationery Office, London.

Thorpe, L.J. (1998), 'The English System of Ancillary Relief', paper presented at SPTL Seminar, 'Dividing the Assets on Family Breakdown: The Strengths and Weaknesses of the Law', 21 March 1998, King's College, London.

United Kingdom Men's Movement (1997), 'The United Kingdom Divorce Racket', http://www.zynet.co.uk/gold/lymtel/ukmm/racket.htm.

Walker, J., McCarthy, P. and Timms, N. (1994), *Mediation: the Making and Remaking of Co-operative Relationships*, The Relate Centre for Family Studies, Newcastle.

Zander, M. (1997), 'The Woolf Report: Forwards or Backwards for the New Lord Chancellor?' *Civil Justice Quarterly*, vol 16, p.208.

PART IV
CONCLUSIONS

11 Changing Divorce

CHRISTINE PIPER AND SHELLEY DAY SCLATER

Introduction

The period in which this book has been produced could well be characterised as one which has seen a 'phoney war'. During the debates which led up to the passing of the Family Law Act 1996 (FLA) battle lines were drawn and 'real' battles took place in both Houses of Parliament. On one side were those who wished to 'protect' marriage and 'the family'; on the other, those who argued that irreversible changes have taken place in those institutions and that the best law can do is to provide procedures for organising and managing the ending of failed relationships in ways that are least detrimental to all. There were battles between those who wished to further the best interest of children in one way and those in another; and between those who argued for widening 'support' for separating people and those for whom reducing public expenditure was the main priority. These hostilities apparently ended via the acceptance of various amendments to the Bill, enabling it to become law.

But, we would argue, the war is not ended. Those skirmishes in Parliament, though influenced by pressure groups and various swathes of public opinion, have simply defined and consolidated the boundaries for the next offensive which will be conducted over questions relating to the implementation of the Act's provisions. Within those boundaries there is still much to say and much to fight for: the disputed territory of the meanings and significance of marriage, the family and the welfare of children has been circumscribed by a range of dominant discourses, with the result that much is left unsaid. The contributors to this book have each identified important undercurrents which have been hidden in these public debates. These undercurrents have included knowledge about the psychological effects of separation on the spouses involved, about risks to children other than those explicitly used to legitimate reform, and about neglected issues in relation to dividing the family assets. At another level, the undercurrents discussed have been those which have implicitly informed rhetorical strategies and legislative outcomes; for example, the construction of new ideas of what constitutes a 'good' post-divorce family and the emergence of particular notions surrounding heterosexuality. Thirdly, these undercurrents include those ambivalences which persist within the dominant discourses, notably about the autonomy of children and about the nature and relative importance of domestic violence.

Since the FLA was given the Royal Assent in 1996 pilot projects have been set up, researched and discussed. The particular formats for information sessions, the detail in Legal Aid Board working guidelines, the preferred structures for state-funded mediation provision and the timing and type of state-funded legal advice have all yet to be decided. Decisions will be made on the basis of the outcomes of the pilot schemes, in the context of available resources. Such decisions will determine not only the nature of divorce law and procedure for the future, but will also set the limits within which the protection of the more vulnerable family members will be possible within the legal framework of Parts I-III of the Act. These decisions about the precise implementation of the Act are also likely to have at least as much impact as the letter of the Act. One could reasonably anticipate real battles over those decisions.

These battles are already taking place, but not fully in the public arena. The pilot projects are being assessed and discussed in relative secrecy; the Lord Chancellor's Department has issued only minimal information, and discussion, so far, has been of particular issues with particular audiences. It seems that large scale engagements are carefully being avoided. At the conclusion of the phoney war, there may or may not be a public battle over the implementation of the Act; further hostilities may be precluded by a range of small scale peace treaties with the various parties to the engagement. This is an unsatisfactory state of affairs if it means that neglected issues remain hidden.

Anecdotal evidence would suggest that there is some confusion in the minds of the general public as to what the current attitude to divorce and divorce reform now is. We know that divorce procedures are changing, but neither the extent nor the nature of that change is yet clear. Contributors to this volume have been at pains to identify the dominant messages framing the divorce debate, but there is also a sense in which there is currently no message, at least not one that can easily be grasped. If there is any message at all, it is that the public debate ended in July 1996, and all that remains to be done is for the Lord Chancellor to make a range of procedural rules based on the outcome of the pilots and the authority of scientific research. Yet, the ideas which have framed the debate persist, with their unacknowledged undercurrents.

It seems to us that this period of phoney war, together with the early years of implementation of the FLA, constitute a crucial time in which to make explicit, and to debate, these ideas and assumptions. In that process those undercurrents of divorce which are currently inadequately known or understood, should be made visible, for they have a real bearing on how the provisions of the Act should be put into operation. All the contributors to this book have had that aim in mind, and the ambiguous title of this chapter reflects that aim: our book offers a contribution to the divorce debate which we hope will broaden its scope and so influence the nature and direction of change.

In our introductory chapter we outlined four themes which have characterised the dominant discourses surrounding divorce and with which contributors have engaged. We have also referred above to the range of undercurrents which contributors have identified. In addition, issues of practice have emerged which cross chapter boundaries and which have implications for future policy and practice. It is on these, and also on those issues which space has forced us to neglect, that we focus in this final chapter.

The Divorce Professionals

Not surprisingly, several chapters in this book have focused on the ways in which legal and social work trained professionals operating within the current divorce process respond to legal criteria and workload pressures. There has been discussion of the role of solicitors, divorce court welfare officers and the judiciary in relation to issues of domestic violence, ascertaining the child's wishes and feelings, 'mediating' conflict and setting norms for post-divorce family life. These professionals have been, and will remain, influential in determining the nature and outcome of divorce for individuals with whom they come into contact though that influence has changed and will change over the years. However, the dominant messages about divorce - for example those communicated in the Consultation and White Papers (Lord Chancellor's Department (LCD), 1993 and 1995, respectively) preceding the Family Law Act - have attributed particular roles to these professionals, roles necessary for the construction of a particular story about the 'old' divorce procedure. The courts are portrayed as places of last resort: as places where an impersonal judge decides and as places that are bad for children because they are adversarial and conflict ridden. Solicitors are portrayed as litigious and likely to foment conflict by their methods of working; divorce court welfare officers are perceived as conduits for the views and welfare of children and mediators as facilitators of harmony.

> The present system of divorce law is based on the adversarial model for litigating disputes through the civil courts. .... in a large number of cases the separating couple and their lawyers act, at least initially, as if the divorce petition will be defended (LCD, 1993, p.49).
>
> Mediation is an alternative to negotiating matters at arm's length through two separate lawyers and to litigating through the courts' (LCD, 1995, p.39).

In contrast to these negative images of legal professionals, mediation is presented as offering 'a constructive framework ... for consideration and reflection' (LCD, 1993, p.51). The succeeding White Paper accepted that there might be some 'good family lawyers ... who do their best for their clients' (LCD, 1995, p.41) but noted that the 'backdrop of allegation and counter-allegation' exists '[e]ven in circumstances where the parties and their solicitors approach negotiations in a constructive manner' (LCD, 1995, p.9) and there was no movement from the idea that solicitors can only work 'at arm's length' with other solicitors (pp.41 and 71). Mediation, on the other hand, continued to be presented as able to deal with 'issues' and not be concerned with allegations (LCD, 1995, p.39).

Solicitors

Research referred to in this book reveals professional approaches and attitudes which do not tally with that dominant picture of how the divorce system operates. The research on solicitors conducted at the Universities of Bristol (Bailey-Harris *et al*, 1998), Brunel (Piper, 1998; King, 1999) and Leeds (Neale and Smart, 1997) shows solicitors who very rarely operate within a strictly legal discourse in relation to disputes about the children of the marriage. Their working practices and notions of client care are related to the welfare of the child and to the welfare of 'the family' as a whole. They have reconstructed the interests of their clients in ways which downgrade the client's legal rights - and the use of an adversarial system to pursue them - but upgrades the welfare needs of his or her child and family. As a result, the normative framework within which they work is one which goes beyond general principles of law but is very influential in settling disputes (King, 1999):

> Disputes about children are referred, in growing numbers, to lawyers and courts. What then happens to them is rather curious. In the absence of legal rules, other than procedural rules, disputes tend to be settled by reference to norms. These are not in essence legal norms other than in the limited sense that they are employed within a legal context. Legal knowledge is hardly relevant. It is essentially 'welfare' discourse expressed as legal principle (Bailey-Harris *et al*, 1998, p.27).

In this normative framework certain parents are constructed as acting with common sense and taking the sensible approach to divorce. It is these parents who are co-operating with the other parent and are able to 'sort out' their family problems who are seen to be acting in the best interests of the child: those parents who refuse to co-operate and wish to use the courts are unreasonable (King 1999). Lawyers convey to their clients that they should agree outcomes with their spouse, that they should not make applications to court and that they should allow contact to the other parent. This elision of the needs and interests of the different family members means that a dominant discourse - in which contact between the child and the non-residential parent and increased co-operation within families are given top priority - goes unchallenged by solicitors. A comment of a solicitor, acting for the mother, from the research of Smart and Neale illuminates this development:

> The only time I lay down the law and I'm heavy handed is if I've got a mother who's not allowing contact ... I try to beat everybody into submission. ... In those circumstances I am prepared to overstep the line a bit and upset clients sometimes. ... The prospect of a court ever backing [a contact order] up with [committal proceedings] is very unlikely, but I would never tell the mum that. ... What you hope is that the judge will be strong enough to frighten the socks off mum ... I've got a particularly difficult case at the moment where the mother has ... been subject to what seems to be some nasty incidences of violence and fled the area specifically to get away. ... Now persuading her to get contact up and running again is very, very difficult. And in fact we [the two lawyers] were able to arrange that. ... It's a question of building up mutual trust again. (S.H. Male, SFLA [solicitor]) (Smart and Neale, 1997, p.392).

It is not, therefore, surprising that a mediator should quote 'My solicitor won't try to see my case' as a typical comment of clients who want professionals to uphold their point of view (Richards, 1998, p.488) or that an observer should gain 'an impression of solicitors acting in concert in the face of one (or two) difficult parents' (Bailey-Harris *et al*, 1998, p.29).

Solicitors depend on retaining clients and so, while explaining to parents that the law should not be used, must successfully give the impression that they, as lawyers, are the ones who know when to move from the non-use of law to the use of law (King, 1999). Solicitors then present themselves as good managers of the divorce process. What all three research projects therefore conclude - despite the different geographical locations and the different methodologies for data collection - is that being a family lawyer is 'primarily about client handling' (Bailey-Harris, 1998, p.33).

In order to do this, solicitors have reconstructed ideas of justice and fairness in relation to family law (Neale and Smart, 1997). And yet, as we have seen in Kaganas' chapter, their use of the welfare discourse in order to encourage settlement is a selective one in line with the dominant discourse about divorce: the Brunel interviews revealed solicitors who used their knowledge of what was good for children in order to persuade the implacably hostile mother to allow the non-residential father contact, but only one professed to encourage the non-residential father to maintain contact. Clearly there are legal reasons why they should do one and not the other, because section 8 of the Children Act gives parents a right to apply for contact but does not give parents a right to force the other parent to have contact. Yet this should not preclude solicitor pressure on fathers to sustain contact because, as we have seen, solicitors do not normally operate within a 'pure' legal discourse and often eschew an instrumental role for law. Bailey-Harris *et al* also found courts unprepared 'to intervene in cases where the parent with care is seeking to have the absent parent play a more prominent part in the child's life' despite this appearing to be in keeping with the welfare principle (1998, p.24). It would seem that particular welfare norms are harnessed to settle a dispute which might ultimately be the court's responsibility, but not to do so if no legal 'trigger' exists as, for example, when there is denial of contact by the non-residential parent against the wishes of the other parent. The dominant welfare discourse may not, therefore, deliver even on those desired outcomes which it promotes.

Judges

Just as the divorce debate utilised out-dated images of family law solicitors, so we find similar distorted images of the judiciary. In the White Paper, the place where judges operate - the court - is the site of 'battle' (LCD, 1995, p.62) and in popular ideas of the judiciary they are presented as the final arbiter, the people who make decisions about children and who ultimately decide the fate of families. Of course this is what judges do in the last resort but, what is not at all clear from popular debate about divorce, is that very rarely do judges decide. They, like their solicitor colleagues, are in the business of encouraging settlement. And, just as solicitors divide clients into the sensible and the unreasonable, so do judges appraise the solicitors appearing before them:

> District judges become familiar with solicitors appearing in their courts: ... Judges assume that proposals made by certain solicitors will be sensible. They are less likely to accept proposals advanced by solicitors whom they ... consider to be inexperienced or lacking sound judgement. Judges expect solicitors to control their clients' (Bailey-Harris *et al*, 1998, p.29).

The Bristol researchers refer to the 'family days' at the courts they observed - when the courts dealt with first and subsequent appointments in relation to section 8 applications - as '*negotiating opportunities*' [emphasis in original] (Bailey Harris *et al,* 1998, p.23) and note the continuing reluctance of courts to proceed to formal adjudication. 'The analogy that comes to mind is that of the butcher's shop which won't sell meat; district judges tend to be convinced vegetarians. ... Typically, scheduled "final hearings" turn out to be no such thing' (Bailey Harris *et al,* 1998, p.24). Even the anti-delay principle within the Children Act 1989 'conflicts with, and so inevitably gives way to, the much more powerful principle - powerful within legal proceedings - that cases should be settled rather than adjudicated' (p.26).

Barristers have rarely been the subject of research[1] and there has been little reference to their role in this volume, but the above research on section 8 applications suggests that in practice family law barristers also adhere to this principle. Within the judicial setting, 'barristers' advocacy skill is seldom required and the other functions come to the fore', their functions as negotiators and 'in supplying reinforcement' of 'unpalatable advice'. Because of their distance from the client they can, more so than the solicitor, be 'dismissive of the client's particular preoccupations' (Bailey-Harris *et al*, 1998, p.30). Barristers, in other words, add further weight to the welfare discourse espoused by judges and solicitors.

All the above legal professionals, who have been presented in talk about the current divorce process as adversarial, as upholding or adjudicating on the interests and legal rights of clients, seek, therefore, to be non-adversarial and to instill the dominant messages about the welfare of children. Yet their publicised 'shortcomings' have been used to justify reform in order to produce a new non-adversarial, settlement-orientated and welfare based divorce process. Even accepting a political need to justify reduced expenditure on courts and legal services, this is bizarre. It is also dangerous. People cannot make real choices about 'their' divorce process unless they are provided with knowledge which is not filtered by these misleading images of professional practice. It is also of concern that a settlement-seeking, homogeneous family justice system is being produced without clearer discussion of the interdisciplinarity which is being promoted - a theme we will return to.

Court Welfare Officers

Lastly, talk about the divorce process rests on a distorted view of the work of divorce court welfare officers. Their role is to draw attention to those aspects of the childrens' welfare that the court needs to take into account, in view of the checklist in section 1(3) of the Children Act 1989 and, when implemented, that in the FLA section 11(4). Nevertheless, the chapter on the wishes of children shows that court welfare officers do not always see children, talk to children alone and attempt to ascertain what those children would like to happen to them. What is determining the practice of solicitors, court welfare officers and the judiciary is the dominant attitude - drawing on legal, social and welfare concepts - to the responsibility of parents. What is seen as in the best interests of the child above all else is that the parents are co-operating and that they, not the court and not the child, make the decisions. This allows for professional approval of an outcome which may not be in the optimum interests of the child but which upholds the importance of the idea of parental responsibility - an importance perceived as not just being for the children of the marriage but also for their children and for society:

> If the children of today's divorcing parents are to develop into well balanced adults, capable ... of being responsible parents, then it will be desirable to ensure that their development is not weakened by the way in which the divorce process works. This is a crucial factor in ensuring the stability of the family and family life after divorce (Lord Chancellor's Department, 1993, p.16).

Therefore, as several chapters have shown, the apparent focus on children in the debates, and in the sections of the FLA, does not necessarily mean that in practice the traditional divorce professionals place the needs of the 'real' children very high up the list of priorities. Yet pressure for change in this respect has been muted because the divorce debate has placed the solution elsewhere. As chapter 4 pointed out, the hope of legislators, mediators and many divorce professionals is that mediation can, and increasingly will, provide the site where children's wishes can be ascertained and their needs adequately addressed. Whether that hope is realised depends on several developments, one of which is the nature of the process which becomes accepted as 'real' mediation.

Mediation

Talk about the new divorce process has usually presented mediation as something established, known and defined and as the 'way forward'. The Consultation Paper, for example included the following apparently unproblematic description of the mediation process as one which 'aims at encouraging parties to come to terms with the past, look to the future, meet each other on equal terms and, with the assistance of a neutral third party, reach decisions' (LCD, 1993, p.41). The debate has, therefore, been framed as a choice between a process which relies on the involvement of traditional divorce professionals and one which uses mediators.

Only a decade ago 'mediation was a peripheral pastime practised in church halls, voluntary centres and the occasional solicitor's office' (Walsh, 1997) and mediation is still supply, rather than demand, led. Worldwide, mediation is not yet a unitary entity: it is accepted in various forms in different jurisdictions. Even North America, with a longer history of mediation provision than the UK, exhibits a wide range of forms. A recent review of Canadian research concludes that 'family mediation is far from a monolithic field of professional practice: the process of family mediation comprises a wide spectrum of variations, and a plethora of practice models are being applied with mediation clientele' (Kruk, 1998, p.195).[2] There are are currently tensions amongst UK mediation providers, arising from different approaches and concerns (Pigott, 1996; Roberts, 1997, pp.30-38 and 64-66). Chapters in this volume have revealed a range of approaches in practice, specifically in relation to issues of domestic violence, the involvement of the child and the division of family assets. There is no compulsory registration of mediators in the UK and, as a recent article points out, 'It seems that the area of mediation is open to all those who fancy themselves as mediators' (Black-Branch, 1998, p.39) though the Legal Aid Board will set out standards for those services to be publicly funded.[3]

One undercurrent of divorce is, then, the existence of diverse views on what mediation can and should achieve and what techniques and knowledges can legitimately be used in the process of mediation. In order to secure government funding for mediation these differences have had to be played down. But there are still battles to be won in relation to these often conflicting ideas as to what mediation 'is'. The outcome of these battles will determine the mediation experience for clients and so will influence outcomes and protections for family members.

Professionalisation

The continuing undercurrent of debate about the nature of mediation is linked to a more public project on the part of mediation organisations - that of establishing mediation as a profession. 'Today, the degree of professionalism amongst mediators is perceived as being very ad hoc' (Black-Branch, 1998, p.40) and mediators believe that the acknowledgement of professional status is necessary to establish mediators as having equal status to the 'old' divorce professionals.[4] As Dame Margaret Booth said, before divorce reform proposals had been enacted, of the possible amalgamation of National Family Mediation (NFM) and the Family Mediators' Association (FMA),

> Such a body should in no way obstruct flexibility in working methods or prevent each couple receiving help in the way best suited to their needs. It would, however, achieve for the service a professional status at a national level which is essential if it is to undertake the work envisaged for it in the Green Paper. Without that status there is always the danger that mediation will be left on the sidelines ... (Booth, 1994, p.661).

As part of this, as yet, unresolved struggle to establish mediation as a profession in its own right, NFM (operating in England and Wales), the FMA and also Family Mediation Scotland did form the body envisaged by Dame Margaret Booth. The resulting UK College of Mediators has developed rules to govern entry to the mediation 'profession' and to control the conduct of its members. Their hope is that the College's system of accreditation and Code of Practice are accepted by those who need to fund and to use mediation so that one traditional aspect of a profession - self-regulation - is established.

The recent book by Marian Roberts (1997) is also part of this process of bidding for professional status by providing a clear - and particular - knowledge base for mediation, with academic credentials and self-awareness of limitations.

Definition and Practice

In the 1980s strong claims were made for a form of mediation which used techniques from a family systems approach and acknowledged a therapeutic focus (see Parkinson, 1986). Several passages in Roberts' book (1997, pp.14-19) specifically discredit approaches using particular counselling and social work techniques: 'it is not for mediators to decide that a quarrel over children is really a quarrel about finance or vice versa or an excuse to act out inter-personal emotional issues' (Roberts, 1997, p.84). Mediation - as taught by NFM - is specifically delineated from social work and from family therapy (pp.10-19) and Roberts argues against interventions by mediators which are too directive or based on systems theory (pp.124-125).

A perhaps more fundamental split in the history of mediation has been that between court-based and out-of-court services. Indeed, a major research project on mediation decided on samples and categorised its data in terms of the 'distance' or otherwise of mediation from the court (Conciliation Project Unit, 1989). In the 1980s, researchers as well as mediators in 'independent' services fiercely criticised 'mediation' on court premises as being no such thing (Davis and Bader, 1985). That criticism is still being made:

> Mediation tied to the court is inevitably infected with the court's settlement-seeking values. There is nothing 'alternative' about it: mediation becomes almost indistinguishable - other than in form - from bilateral negotiation conducted by lawyers. ....
> What is one to make of the re-invention of mediation within court proceedings? ... If the intention is primarily to divert and deflect, then it seems hard to justify the subversion of the core values of mediation in order to serve the courts' rationing strategies (Bailey-Harris *et al*, 1998, p.26).

This would suggest there is, therefore, no agreement over 'core values': whilst some commentators and mediators refer to 'core values' as an agreed entity, others are practising what they refer to as mediation but which clearly does not subscribe to these particular values.

Marian Roberts has been responsible for training within National Family Mediation and her book reflects the views about mediation which have been disseminated by that body - the longest running independent mediation organisation in the UK. Those views may be challenged by a new breed of lawyer-mediator - already numerous in North America - and evidenced in the UK in the establishment of BALM (British Association of Lawyer Mediators) and by the Law Society's publication of its own rules relating to the practice of mediation in 1993.[5] More specifically, the Law Society is planning to establish schemes by which lawyers who are members of the Law Society can become mediators through a Law Society accredited course, which will be separate from, and not necessarily totally in line with, the views and wishes of the UK College (see Roberts, 1997, p.66). The SFLA is also organising training for its solicitor members. This division of opinion as to whether a 'solicitor-mediator' is a valid practitioner of mediation is linked to the vexed question of how and to what extent comprehensive or all-issues mediation (AIM) should include legal input and advice. Various structures for making legal advice available to the clients of mediation have been set up and researched (Walker *et al*, 1994)[6] and are still under review. Currently, all issues mediation is experienced by very few divorcing couples. The decision as to which particular roles for solicitors in and around mediation will be publicly funded may well be the biggest influence on whether the solicitor-mediator becomes ubiquitous. It is agreed by all concerned that legal advice is necessary in relation to participation in mediation: the blurring of these distinctions between mediating and acting as a source of legal advice and representation is, we argue, not a helpful development.

Roberts' book is, therefore, a timely argument in favour of a particular form of mediation as 'true' mediation. The form described is conceptually more coherent as a result of nearly two decades of arguments within the mediation movement about practise issues, often fuelled by academic criticism from outside. Roberts is well aware of the dangers stemming from power inequalities, the existence of domestic violence, the power of the dominant welfare discourse and the possibility that mediators can manipulate those engaging in mediation. We would, therefore, prefer that this narrowly defined form of mediation - which sets out exceptions to the rule that mediation is suitable and a beneficial process for all couples - should become the basis for standard practice. Many of the concerns of feminists in particular might be abated. With wider or different definitions of mediation those concerns will not go away: identifying relevant undercurrents of divorce becomes crucial if forms of mediation which are less rigorous in their approach to practice boundaries in general and to screening procedures in particular are to be allowed to develop in the UK.

Interdisciplinarity

Despite the images of solicitors, judges and court welfare officers constructed through the dominant discourse of divorce we have seen that in practice there is a fudging of the lines between professional activities and boundaries. This practice is, paradoxically, in line with a professional discourse - backed by the messages from government enquiries in the child protection field[7] - that stresses interdisciplinarity. It is taken for granted in all training materials and comments on the operation of what is now called the family justice system (see Murch and Hooper, 1992; Walsh, 1998), that those working within it should take a multidisciplinary approach to problems and cases and that, therefore, the system should exhibit interdisciplinarity at all levels. Practice that has been pioneered in juvenile justice and child protection is now extended to divorce:

> In the course of our observations we witnessed many instances of bi-partite or tri-partite discussions between lawyers, welfare officers, and district judges. We were struck by the degree to which these discussions resembled 'case conferences' ... To the uninformed observer it might have been difficult to identify the status of each performer; there seemed to be no difference in the nature of their contribution or in the language employed ... These were, it seemed to us, almost hybrid practitioners' (Bailey-Harris *et al*, 1998, pp.32-33).

What is meant by interdisciplinarity is not entirely clear. Murch and Hooper, reporting their research on the family justice system (1992), use the term 'cross-disciplinary' in relation to professional training and collaboration. Their focus is the implications for training of the 'urgent need to ensure that practitioners .... understand more fully the functions, roles, techniques, assumptions and language of other professional groups' (p.110). We have no problem with that perspective: it is difficult to critique the advantages of an understanding of the information and evidence provided by those other disciplines which enable law to make decisions which are otherwise beyond its competence (King and Piper, 1995, pp.31-55). Murch has argued that the autopoietic nature of law is not an obstacle to the collaboration envisaged - the problem is rather institutional barriers that could be reduced or removed by learning and training which itself crosses disciplines (Murch, 1995).

But other commentators appear to view inter-disciplinarity as more than 'understanding' each other. Mr Justice Wall, for example, refers to the 'multi-faceted discipline which is family law' (Wall, 1995, p.52) and the research referred to above suggests there is a self-denying ordinance by lawyers not to 'talk law' and unwritten rules which deem as 'good' the solicitor who whole-heartedly operates within a welfare discourse. In relation to divorce, there has been a convergence, not only of the normative framework of lawyers and mediators (Piper, 1996) but also of lawyers and court welfare officers. Bailey-Harris *et al* note their intention to explore further the nature and extent of this convergence (1998, p.33).

This inter-disciplinary 'discipline' is of theoretical interest: its existence in other contexts, for example the youth justice system, is leading to similar discussion of the nature and ethics of such developments.[8] It is also a practical issue: in the area of public law relating to children it has been used as a reason not to impose a common law duty of care on local authorities. Therefore *W v Essex County Council* [1997] 2 FLR 535 distinguished *X (Minors) v Bedfordshire County Council* [1995] 2 AC 633 on the ground, *inter alia*, that the multi-disciplinary tasks had been completed before the placement of the fostered child which formed the basis of the action (see Oliphant, 1998). A similar case in New Zealand, *Attorney General v Prince* [1998] 1 NZLR 262, has distinguished the New Zealand legislation from the English/Welsh Children Act 1989 in relation to the issue of whether multi-disciplinary decision-making is 'mandated' by rules and guidance.[9] These detrimental undercurrents of an unthinking acceptance of the benefits of an ill-defined interdisciplinarity need considerably more attention.

Listening to Children

As several contributors to this book have pointed out, the divorce reform debates and the justifications for particular forms of change have been heavily influenced by a child-saving agenda with particular ideas about the welfare of the child in this situation. Despite this focus on the children and the inclusion of statutory provisions for children's views to be taken into account, their voices are rarely 'heard' in practice. Much reliance is being placed on the opportunities afforded by mediation but, in practice mediators rarely talk to children (Dasgupta and Richards, 1997).[10] Even where professionals do interview children, there may be considerable problems in interpreting what they say and, as Hall argues, the context of the interview may also be problematic:

> Formal interviews are rarely encountered by children in contexts other than disapproval or reprimand. It is easy to imagine therefore that as a majority of children will be likely to experience being interviewed as a somewhat intimidating event and certainly not one in which they will easily feel that their views are genuinely being solicited (1996, p.69).

Hall advocates that it is only within a psychological framework that children's views can be elicited 'sensitively' and that if this does not happen, there is a danger that views are facilitated which do not properly represent the child's own meanings.

There have been a number of cases where the children's wishes and feelings were elicited, but not followed (see, for example, Bell, 1993; Jones, 1992). In these cases, according to Sherwin (1996), the law draws a distinction between what the child wants and what is in the best interests of that child. Where the two coincide, the decision will reflect the child's wishes; where they do not coincide, the judge's view prevails. The Association of Lawyers for Children (ALC) argues that these current procedures and practices do not meet the requirements of Article 12 of the UN Declaration of Human Rights for Children. As a result:

> Many children are often powerless to effect plans and decisions made by their parents in respect of them. However, intervention by the court or an authorised representative is often seen as unhelpful and intrusive as well as being contrary to the philosophy of the Children Act 1989 (ALC, 1998, p.406).

The image of the child, the 'semantic artifact' with which the law operates in these proceedings (King and Piper, 1995), is that of a vulnerable victim to be protected and not an autonomous, reliable participant.[11] During the debate on the FLA Parliament did air the possibility of making the Official Solicitor or a new children's officer available to represent the child's interests but no amendments to this effect became law. Section 64 of the FLA allows for the provision of separate representation for children and the debate on these issues continues (Timms, 1997),[12] but the likelihood of the extra funding being made available is slim.

It will not be an easy task to formulate policy which does ensure that the wishes of the real children involved become part of the decision-making process. Davis has recently remarked, 'One might conceive the Family Law Act 1996 as an attempt by the Lord Chancellor's Department to change a culture' (1998, p.66); the task, therefore, becomes that of creating a counter-culture. The recent formation of NYAS (National Youth Advocacy Service), by the amalgamation of IRCHIN and ASC, has been accomplished with that aim in view. The hope is that its members can help to create a culture where children are listened to, clearly heard, involved and have their views acted upon.[13]

Others have argued that there does not have to be an exclusive focus on mediation or on the judicial/legal arena to secure the implementation of Article 12 of the UN Convention (Eekelaar, 1992, p.234). Douglas, Murch and Perry (1996) argue, for example, that the best site is not the legal system but the mental health system and Kroll (1996) similarly advocates facilities to treat the child as in 'crisis' and needing to be listened to in the interests of ensuring psychological health. The USA has seen the development of 'seminars' especially for children of divorcing parents[14] and, in the UK, the first Child Counselling Services have been established (Pitrusu, 1998). These initiatives may well be necessary and beneficial for some children but should be part of better and wider provision of services for all children 'in need'. To attach them to the process of divorce simply further problematises and pathologises divorce and solidifies constructions of children as 'victims'. Such developments inevitably downgrade the views of the child as important in their own right.

The current policy emphasis on the importance of 'good' parenting[15] is also of concern to us. First, it may further divert attention from the child as a legitimate participant. For example, the Parenting Plans currently being piloted encourage parents to take children's views and feelings into account, but there is a danger that this will be seen as sufficient, therefore perpetuating children as dependent and vulnerable. Secondly, such policy initiatives may be seen as part of a development of the 'therapeutic state' whereby social problems are addressed through individualised psychological techniques.

Conclusions

This book has sought to explore a range of what we have called 'undercurrents of divorce' which, hitherto, have been neglected or ignored in the debates. In this chapter, we have discussed these issues more specifically in relation to the implementation of the FLA and to professional practices, since these undercurrents affect the actual experience of divorcing people and their children via the practices of divorce professionals. There are, however, a range of outstanding issues, relevant to both policy and practice, which have yet to be brought into the public arena. Broader questions, such as those relating to 'race' and ethnicity, have been notable for their absence in both research and policy-making (Day Sclater, 1995; Irving and Benjamin, 1995; Taylor and Wang, 1997): a situation which can only be seen as lamentable. There is some evidence that these issues are being addressed (see, for example, Gale, 1994; Schutz, 1996; Shah-Kazemi, 1996) but this research is surely long overdue.

In the meantime, it is likely that the implementation of the divorce reforms will be predicated on a very particular model of 'the family' which may have little to do with the diversity of ways the majority of folk, including those in minority ethnic groups, organise their domestic lives. Such research as we do have on this issue (see, for example, Dallos and Sapsford, 1995; Gelles, 1995; Hutter, 1991) indicates that family life is characterised by diversity, across a range of cultures, classes and ethnic groups, and that the dominance of the white, middle class 'nuclear' ideal (see Smart, 1997), assumed by so much British social policy, accords with the experience of an ever-decreasing proportion of people. The issue is further complicated by the persistence of racial stereotypes and the neglect of within-group diversities. As Taylor and Wang (1997) argue, in an American context, much early research on processes and patterns in ethnic minority families was guided by an assumption that minority families were 'pathological', or was conducted in the context of intervention and prevention efforts. Thus we know little about the ordinary lives, meanings and values of people who do not readily fit the white, middle class model so valued by our society.

There is, then, a critical lack - which we hope will be addressed as a matter of urgency - of culturally sensitive research in the area of marriage and divorce to inform any sensible social policy in Britain. It is essential, however, that future research should not start with an assumption of a dominant mean from which some families depart or deviate. Separation and divorce, for all people, are replete with a multitude of meanings, which have cultural origins as well as personal significance; a humane and 'fair' social policy would be one which respected those meanings. Family Law in other jurisdictions has gone some way towards making provision for the kinds of diversities we have mentioned here (see, for Australian developments, Bordow and Gibson, 1994; Moloney *et al*, 1996; Love *et al*, 1996; for developments in New Zealand, see, Maxwell, 1989a, 1989b).

The dominance of particular models of family life, both in research and in the divorce debates, also has the effect of marginalising, or even excluding, some people (for example, gay and lesbian families) from consideration altogether, and of downplaying the significance of wider kin and step-relationship networks: a prime example is the question of grandparents. Research at the end of the 1980s (Kaganas and Piper, 1989, 1990)[16] showed that court welfare officers and mediators believed that grandparents were of great help to children in their psychological adjustment to divorce and in their sense of belonging to a family but, nevertheless, felt unable to promote such links if those links were not wanted by the parents. Again, particular dominant ideas about the benefits to children of parental autonomy and co-operation outweigh other benefits and risks. Similarly, the recent research on solicitors found that solicitors would not mention grandparents unless either the client raised the issue or the solicitor felt that a grandparent might be the resource which would solve a contact or even residence problem, or might be a resource to ensure continuity of care by the residential parent. The dominant attitudes to contact and parental responsibility, therefore, make the role of the extended family in the child's welfare at least partially invisible.

Changing Families, Changing Law

We have discussed a range of undercurrents of divorce which family law and policy ignores at its peril. In some cases they are the very stuff of professional practice, in others of family life. The Right Honourable Mrs Justice Hale (1997) has pointed to the futility of any attempt to turn back the clock: families have changed and will continue to do so and laws must be formulated with that fact in mind. As Jones *et al* also argue,

> Only one thing is certain: there is no turning back. The future will contain many kinds of families ... And those families will not be like families of the past. More than at any time in the past, our personal lives will reflect the powers of our imagination and the state's willingness to support variety (1995, p.157).

This process will involve tensions: new ones are likely to arise as old ones are resolved. The contributors to this book have brought to the surface some of the undercurrents which can be taken into account in future debates and in the many decisions still to be made. We have identified the dominant discourses of welfare and harmony, together with an implicit model of family life, as constraining the debates to date in particular ways. It is crucial that we continue to subject these discourses, and the practices which flow from them, to critical scrutiny if family law is to be any other than as a crude mechanism for social control.

Notes

1. But see, Barnett (1998).
2. In the USA 'A unique mediation service using the telephone to help parents resolve conflicts [over contact]' was terminated solely for budgetary reasons and the concerns expressed focused, *inter alia*, on 'the lack of non-verbal cues' rather than whether 'the series of telephone calls to the individuals involved' rightly deserved to be called mediation (Coltri and Hunt, 1998, p.183).
3. Family Law Act 1996 section 27. The Mediation Working Group of the Lord Chancellor's Advisory Committee on Legal Education and Conduct funded a review in 1998 of relevant literature on the education requirements applying to lawyer-mediators and non-lawyer mediators in England and Wales and comparable jurisdictions with a view to deciding on standards to be applied to family law mediation.
4. Whilst it is possible to question what is meant by the notion of professionalisation, this is not relevant here: for whatever reason, mediators want to be considered as professionals. For a brief discussion see Black-Branch (1998).
5. See Chapter 22 of the Guide to the Professional Conduct of Solicitors.
6. For a summary of developments and views up to the publication of this research report see Fisher, 1994.

7. A notable example is the Butler Sloss enquiry into the events in Cleveland (Report of the Enquiry into Child Abuse in Cleveland 1987 (1988)).
8. Note, for example, the the workshop entitled 'The Ethics of Interdisciplinarity' held at Brunel University, 20 November, 1998.
9. I am grateful to Geoff McLay (Victoria University of Wellington) for bringing this to my attention.
10. The same would appear to be true of practice in the Australian family courts: 'Although most family mediators do not seek directly the views of children in the mediation process, some have advocated the limited involvement of children in mediation to ascertain their views and to check that parents arrangements are in accord with the children's wishes' (Pryor and Seymour, 1996, p.240).
11. Even when the child's liberty is at stake, as in an application for secure accommodation under section 25 of the Children Act 1989, the child has no right to attend (see *Re W (minor)(secure accommodation order: attendance at court)* [1994] 2 FLR 1092.
12. See also the debate between Judith Timms and Michael King in the pages of *Family Mediation* (1997), vol 7 (3) and (1998), vol 8(1).
13. See the comment in 'Newsline' (*Family Law*, 1998, p.448).
14. These are a spin off of divorce education programmes for parents: their genesis is in the USA (see Di Bias, 1996).
15. Two examples of this emphasis are the Government's support for the National Family and Parenting Institute and the provision in the Crime and Disorder Act 1998 of a power by which courts can make a Parenting Order.
16. See also, for other research on grandparents in the divorce process, McCarthy and Simpson (1990).

References

Barnet, A. (1998), *Contact and Domestic Violence: The Ideological Divide*, Dissertation submitted for the LL.M. in Child Law and Policy, Brunel University.

Bell, V. (1993), 'Governing Childhood: Neo-Liberalism and the Law', *Economy and Society*, vol 22, pp.390-405.

Black-Branch, J. (1998), 'The Professional Status of Mediators', *Family Law*, pp.39-41.

Booth, Dame Margaret, (1994), 'Mediation as a Profession', *Family Law*, p.661.

Bordow, S. and Gibson, J. (1994), *Evaluation of the Family Court Mediation Service*, Family Court of Australia Research and Evaluation Unit, Office of the Chief Executive.

Coltri, L. and Hunt, E. J. (1998), 'A Model for Telephone Mediation', *Family and Conciliation Courts Review*, vol 36(2), pp.179-194.

Conciliation Project Unit (1989), *Report to the Lord Chancellor on the Costs and Effectiveness of Conciliation in England and Wales*, University of Newcastle.

Dallos, R. and Sapsford, R. (1995), 'Patterns of Diversity and Lived Realities', in J. Muncie, M. Wetherell, R. Dallos and A. Cochrane (eds), *Understanding the Family*, Sage, London.

Dasgupta, C. and Richards, M. (1997), 'Support for Children of Separating Parents: Developing Practice', *Representing Children*, vol 10, pp.106-116.

Davis, G. (1998), 'Monitoring Publicly Funded Mediation', *Family Law*, pp.64-66.

Davis, G. and Bader, K. (1985), 'In-Court Mediation: The Consumer View' Parts I and II, *Family Law*, pp.42-49 and 82-86.

Day Sclater, S. (1995), 'The Limits of Mediation', *Family Law*, pp. 494-497.

Di Bias, T. (1996), 'Some Programmes for Children', *Family and Conciliation Courts Review*, vol 34(1), pp.112-129.

Eekelaar, J. (1992), 'The Importance of Thinking that Children Have Rights', *International Journal of Law and the Family*, vol 6, p.221.

Fisher, T. (1994) 'Family Mediators Go Comprehensive', *Family Law*, pp.697-700.

Fricker, Judge Nigel (1998), 'A Unified Family Court and Family Courts Support Services Part I', *Family Law*, p.462.

Gale, D. (1994), 'The Impact of Culture on the Work of Family Mediators', *Family Mediation*, vol 4(2), p.4.

Gelles, R.J. (1995), *Contemporary Families: A Sociological View*, Sage, London.

Hale, Dame B. (1997), *Private Lives and Public Duties: What is Family Law For?*, 8th ESRC Annual Lecture, October 1997.

Hall, N. (1996), 'Eliciting Children's Views: The Contribution of Psychologists', in R. Davie, G. Upton and V. Varma (eds), *The Voice of the Child: A Handbook for Professionals*, Falmer Press, London, pp.61-77.

Hutter, M. (ed) (1991), *The Family Experience: A Reader in Cultural Diversity*, Macmillan, New York.

Irving, H.H. and Benjamin, M. (1995), *Family Mediation: Contemporary Issues*, Sage, London.

Jones, C.L., Tepperman, L. and Wilson, S.J. (1995), *The Futures of the Family*, Prentice Hall, New Jersey.

Jones, S. (1992), 'The Ascertainable Wishes and Feelings of the Child', *Journal of Child Law*, vol 4, pp.181-185.

Kaganas, F. and Piper, C. (1989), 'Grandparents: Conciliation or Litigation?', *Family Law*, pp.479-484.

Kaganas, F. and Piper, C. (1990), 'Grandparents and the Limits of the Law', *International Journal of Law and the Family*, pp.27-51.

King, M. (1999), '"Being Sensible", Images and Practices of the New Family Lawyer', *Journal of Social Policy*, (forthcoming).

Kruk, E. (1998), 'Practice Issues, Strategies and Models: The Current State of the Art of Family Mediation', *Family and Conciliation Courts Review*, vol 36(2), pp.195-215.

Lord Chancellor's Department (1993), *Looking to the Future, Mediation and the Ground for Divorce*, Cm 2424, HMSO, London.

Lord Chancellor's Department (1995), *Looking to the Future, Mediation and the Ground for Divorce*, Cm 2799, HMSO, London.

Love, A., Moloney, L. and Fisher, T. (1996), *Federally-Funded Family Mediation in Melbourne: Outcomes, Costs and Client Satisfaction*, National Centre for Socio-Legal Studies, La Trobe University.

Maxwell, G.M. (1989a), 'Family Court Counselling Services and the Changing New Zealand Family', *Family Court Counselling Research Report 1*, Policy and Research Division, Department of Justice, New Zealand.

Maxwell, G.M. (1989b), 'A Counsellor's Perspective on the Family Court and its Clients', *Family Court Counselling Research Report 2*, Policy and Research Division, Department of Justice, New Zealand.

McCarthy, P. and Simpson, B. (1990), 'Grandparent and Family Conflict: Another View', *Family Law*, p.484.

Moloney, L., Fisher, T., Love, A. and Ferguson, S. (1996), *Managing Differences: Federally Funded Family Mediation in Sydney*, National Centre for Socio-Legal Studies, La Trobe University.

Murch (1995), 'The Cross-Disciplinary Approach to Family Law', in Bainham, A., Pearl, D. and Pickford, R. (eds), *Frontiers of Family Law*, 2nd ed, Wiley, Chichester.

Murch, M. and Hooper, D. (1992), *The Family Justice System*, Family Law, Bristol.

Oliphant, K. (1998), '*W v Essex County Council*: Local Authority Liability for Acts of Children in Foster Care', *Child and Family Law Quarterly*, vol 10(3), pp.303-310.

Pigott, S. (1996), 'Lawyer Mediators and Supervision - The FMA View', *Family Law*, p.313.

Piper, C. (1996), 'Norms and Negotiation Mediation and Divorce' in *Divorce - Where Next?*, Dartmouth, Aldershot.

Piper, C. (1998), 'How Do you Define a Family Lawyer?', Paper presented to the Family Law Section of the SPTL, 9 September, University of Manchester.

Report of the Enquiry into Child Abuse in Cleveland 1987 (1988), Cm 412, HMSO, London.

Richards, C. (1998), 'Reframing in Mediation - Moving from Stalemate into Conversation', *Family Law*, p.488.

Roberts, M. (1997), *Mediation in Family Disputes* (2nd ed), Arena, Aldershot.

Shah-Kazemi, S. (1996) 'Family Mediation and the Dynamics of Culture', *Family Mediation*, vol 6(3), pp.5-7.

Sherwin, M. (1996), 'The Law in Relation to the Wishes and Feelings of the Child', in R. Davie, G. Upton and V. Varma (eds), *The Voice of the Child: A Handbook for Professionals*, Falmer Press, London.

Schutz, R. (1996), 'Divorce and Ethnic Minorities', in M. Freeman (ed) *Divorce: Where Next?*, Dartmouth, Aldershot.

Smart, C. (1997), 'Wishful Thinking and Harmful Tinkering: Sociological Reflections on Family Policy', *Journal of Social Policy*, vol 26, pp.1-21.

Smart, C. and Neale, B. (1997), 'Arguments Against Virtue - Must Contact the Enforced?', *Family Law*, p.332.

Taylor, R.W. and Wang, M.C. (1977), *Social and Emotional Adjustment and Family Relations in Ethnic Minority Families*, Lawrence Erlbaum, New Jersey.

Wall, Mr Justice (1995), 'The Judicial Role in Interdisciplinary Cooperation', *Representing Children*, vol 8(2).

Walker, J., McCarthy, P. and Timms, N. (1994), *The Making and Re-Making of Co-operative Relationships*, Newcastle University: Relate Centre for Family Studies.

Walsh, E. (1997), Review of *Mediation in Family Disputes* (Roberts, 1997), in *Family Law*, p.762.

Walsh, E. (1998), *Working in the Family Justice System*, Family Law, Bristol.

Index

For Product Safety Concerns and Information please contact our EU representative GPSR@taylorandfrancis.com Taylor & Francis Verlag GmbH, Kaufingerstraße 24, 80331 München, Germany

Batch number: 10725923

Printed by Printforce, the Netherlands